D1557216

# Islam's Jesus

UNIVERSITY PRESS OF FLORIDA

Florida A&M University, Tallahassee
Florida Atlantic University, Boca Raton
Florida Gulf Coast University, Ft. Myers
Florida International University, Miami
Florida State University, Tallahassee
New College of Florida, Sarasota
University of Central Florida, Orlando
University of Florida, Gainesville
University of North Florida, Jacksonville
University of South Florida, Tampa
University of West Florida, Pensacola

# Islam's Jesus

❧ ❧ ❧

Zeki Saritoprak

UNIVERSITY PRESS OF FLORIDA

Gainesville / Tallahassee / Tampa / Boca Raton

Pensacola / Orlando / Miami / Jacksonville / Ft. Myers / Sarasota

Copyright 2014 by Zeki Saritoprak
All rights reserved
Printed in the United States of America on acid-free, recycled paper

This book may be available in an electronic edition.

19  18  17  16  15  14   6  5  4  3  2  1

Library of Congress Cataloging-in-Publication Data
Saritoprak, Zeki.
Islam's Jesus / Zeki Saritoprak.
pages cm
Includes bibliographical references and index.
ISBN 978-0-8130-4940-3 (alk. paper)
1. Jesus Christ—In the Qur'an. 2. Jesus Christ—Islamic interpretations. 3. Qur'an—Relation to
the Bible. 4. Islam—Relations—Christianity. 5. Christianity and other religions—Islam.
I. Title.
BP134.J37S27 2014
297.2'465—dc23    2013044112

The University Press of Florida is the scholarly publishing agency for the State University
System of Florida, comprising Florida A&M University, Florida Atlantic University, Florida
Gulf Coast University, Florida International University, Florida State University, New College
of Florida, University of Central Florida, University of Florida, University of North Florida,
University of South Florida, and University of West Florida.

University Press of Florida
15 Northwest 15th Street
Gainesville, FL 32611-2079
http://www.upf.com

JKM Library
1100 East 55th Street
Chicago, IL 60615

For my wife, Özlem,
for her continuing unremitting support

# Contents

# Note on Transliteration

In this work, I have avoided the specialized language of academia as much as possible. I have limited the use of diacritics, with a few exceptions. The only diacritics used are the 'ayn and the hamza. Underdots and other diacritics have been removed. Instead of having a separate glossary, Arabic words have been italicized and explained within the text.

The name Muhammad is interchangeable with the terms "the Prophet" and "the Prophet of Islam" (capitalized) but should be distinguished from "prophet" or "prophets" (lowercase). The word "Hadith" (sayings of the Prophet) has been used for both plural and singular forms. Hadith is capitalized when the corpus of the Hadith is meant and lowercased when referring to individual hadith. Note citations are given in full when they are first cited, then in short form. Some authors have been cited in the notes and bibliography by their most commonly known names. For example, Abu Dawud al-Sijistani is cited as "Abu Dawud" instead of "al-Sijistani." To make this work friendly for nonspecialists, I have provided English translations of Arabic titles in square brackets; for example: *Al-Isha'a li Ashrat al-Sa'a* [Unveiling the Portents of the Hour]. The translation is omitted for some well-known titles.

Unless otherwise expressed, all Qur'anic verses, sayings of the Prophet, and renderings from Arabic and Turkish sources used herein are my own translations. In translating Qur'anic verses, I have occasionally used the translations of A. J. Arberry, Mohammad Pickthall, and Muhammad Asad for guidance. I have used the New American Standard version for all direct quotations from the Bible. As for the citations of Hadith references, I preferred to use, with slight changes, A. J. Wensinck's method, which he employed in his famous concordance to the Hadith, *Concordance et Indices de la Tradition Musulmane*. Thus, the Hadith collections are cited by the name of the author, followed by the name of the work in italics, followed by the name of the book/chapter in quotes, ending with the number of the section in the chapter.

# Introduction

After September 11, 2001, the world, particularly the Western world, witnessed a tremendous rise in interest in Islamic studies, including works about what Muslims believe and practice. This book explores one of the most important themes of Islamic theology: Jesus and his role in this tradition. Not many people in the West comprehend how Jesus is understood by Muslims generally, nor do they understand the role of Jesus in the Qur'an. After one of my lectures to an audience of about seventy people, I discovered that only one person in the audience knew that a chapter of the Qur'an was named after Mary, the mother of Jesus. A similar experience occurred when I presented a lecture about Jesus in Islam to a different audience. I found that only about 10 percent of the audience knew that Jesus was a prominent messenger of God in Islam, and only 2 percent knew that Muslims believe in Jesus's eschatological descent, or the return of Jesus. The media coverage of Reza Aslan's book *Zealot*, which equates Aslan's Jesus with Islam's Jesus, drives home this point further. The book is about the historical Jesus and has nothing at all to do with the Islam's Jesus, who, as I hope to show in this book is, in reality, not at all dissimilar from Christianity's Jesus.

Even among Muslims, it is not well known that there are diverse interpretations of references to Jesus in the Qur'an and the Hadith, a fact that can provide inspiration for pluralism. The present work aims to illuminate Islam's rich theological engagement with the figure of Jesus; work of this nature can lay the groundwork for Muslim-Christian dialogue. The focus of this book involves many questions for both Muslims and Christians. How does the Qur'an speak of Jesus? What is the place of Jesus in Islamic theology? What do Muslims believe about the coming of Jesus at the end of time? Can beliefs about Jesus provide common ground for Muslims and Christians? What is the Islamic approach to dialogue between Christians and Muslims?

It is important to note that as a scholar, I am trained in classical Islamic theology, which is composed of three major themes: divinity, prophethood, and eschatology. My training, more specifically, is in eschatology. Eschatology is the study of things related to the end times and the afterlife. Among Muslim theologians, there is no doubt that Jesus is an important figure in Islamic eschatology. Almost all manuals of Islamic theology contain a statement that includes the words "and we believe in the descent of Jesus." For me, this is both interesting and challenging. How an individual could descend from heaven to earth is a perplexing theological problem. This book is a result of my attempts to find an answer to this question. My response is from a Turkish Muslim scholar's perspective, one that has also been enriched by contemporary Muslim theologians and by my experience working at American Catholic institutions, more specifically teaching courses on Islam and general religious studies courses at a Jesuit university, and by my significant engagement in interfaith dialogue.

Belief in Jesus is one of the major principles of faith in Islam, as he is considered one of the five elite prophets; the others are Abraham, Moses, Noah, and Muhammad, peace and blessings be upon them all. They are called the *ul al-'azm* prophets, meaning the possessors of steadfastness. Jesus is a messenger of God like his brother Muhammad, peace and blessings be upon him.[1] He is so important in Islam that the highest Muslim in rank after Muhammad still cannot reach the spiritual level of Jesus. Jesus is the messenger of God, but in contrast to the traditional Christian teachings, he is not believed to be a part of God or an incarnation of God. This is also true for all other prophets of God. In the afterlife, Jesus is allowed to intercede and ask God to forgive sinners, but he cannot forgive sinners by himself. This is also true for the Prophet of Islam. It is God who forgives the sins of human beings.

In Islamic theology, the limited power of prophets does not negate the fact that Jesus was among the highest of prophets in the chain of prophethood. Islam gives remarkable spiritual rank to the messengers of God but never allows a monument or statue to be erected in their honor. This is mainly a result of Islamic sensitivity to any possible exaggeration of the statues of highly regarded personalities, which could easily lead to worshipping them as deities. In Islam, one should worship only God. It should be noted that, similar to Muslims, some Christian denominations such as the Anabaptists and followers of Huldrych Zwingli (d. 1531) reject the presence of icons in their places of worship. The Islamic understanding of prophethood should not be confused with the term "prophecy" as is often used in the English-speaking world to connote predictions of the future. Similar to many theologically responsible Christians, followers of Islam do not use the term "prophet" loosely. In Islam there are very strict criteria regarding prophethood, and not everyone who speaks about the future can be called a prophet. A prophet speaks on behalf of God and in some cases meets with the angel Gabriel to receive revelation from God. Therefore, a prophet is an appointee of God on earth, one who declares the message of God to people. Considering Jesus a prophet in Islam is not degrading the level of Jesus; in fact, it puts him among the highest figures in the realm of humanity. Theologically speaking, when Muslims say he is among the five greatest messengers of God, they express their belief that these messengers are the highest throughout human history.

Jesus, as a messenger of God, is an integral part of Islamic theology, literature, culture, and civilization. As I shall discuss in the following chapters, a saying of the Prophet speaks of Jesus's return and of his praying in a mosque with the Muslim community when the Muslim messianic figure, the Mahdi, asks Jesus to lead the prayer. Since the early period of Islam, Muslims have read the sayings of the Prophet, referred to as Hadith, about Jesus and the end-time scenario, finding nothing strange about Jesus's praying in a mosque. Muslims see no incongruity between Jesus and the mosque since the Prophet Muhammad and Jesus are considered spiritual brothers. This clearly indicates that Muslims have honored Jesus as a part of their faith and culture. Perhaps for this reason many adherents of Islamic faith name their children 'Isa, the Qur'anic name for Jesus.

Jesus also has an important role in Islamic eschatology. According to Islamic theology, only Jesus, among all prophets of God mentioned in the Qur'an, will come as a messianic figure with an eschatological role that includes bringing justice and the revival of religion. Islamic theology encourages Muslims to prepare a good environment and participate in the process of end-time restoration. Islam does not accept the idea of waiting for the coming of Jesus without the participation of individuals to make the world a peaceful place. One can argue that Jesus's role in Islamic theology is even greater than the role of Moses or Abraham.

Both the Qur'an and the Prophet of Islam speak extensively of the birth, life, message, and end of Jesus's life on earth as well as his current state. Muslims believe that when Jesus's enemies attempted to crucify him, they could not do it. Instead, God raised Jesus to himself and rescued him from persecution by his enemies. I shall discuss this belief in detail in the following chapters.

His return to earth is not explicitly mentioned in the Qur'an, yet it is highly emphasized in the sayings of the Prophet. His return is among the major portents of the final moment of human history, known in the Qur'an as the Hour or al-Sa'a. This is understood from the body of the sayings of the Prophet as good news for Muslims. While Jesus's return is known in the Christian tradition as the Second Coming of Jesus, it is described in Islamic theology with the Arabic phrase "nuzul 'Isa," which I translate as the descent of Jesus, usually meaning from heaven. This has no connection to the Christian understanding of Jesus's descent into hell. Etymologically speaking, the word *nuzul* is used to describe both physical descent and spiritual arrival from on high. The same word is used for the coming of the mercy of God, the coming of the rain (which indicates that rain comes from the sky and from the mercy of God), and the coming of angels. Throughout this work, I will consider these nuances while interpreting the descent of Jesus from an Islamic theological perspective. The roots of the term *nuzul* lie in the sayings of the Prophet of Islam, the second most important source (after the Qur'an) for Islamic theology. Some classic secondary Islamic sources have used terms such as "emergence" or "coming" instead of "descent." In prescientific cosmology, these terms were understood literally, but they generally are understood allegorically in contemporary Islamic understanding. As I shall discuss, what is common to all sources is that Jesus's return will happen at the end of time as a sign of the Final Hour.

The Prophet's sayings indicate both minor and major signs of the Hour. Jesus's descent is among the major signs, alongside the emergence of the Antichrist and the rise of the sun from the west. These have been commonly understood by Muslims in a literal way, but they can be understood in an allegorical way as well. The image of Jesus's return in the mind of Muslims is related to Jesus coming from heaven; thus, the word "descent" has been used for Jesus's return in both the sayings of the Prophet and later Muslim literature. Theologically speaking, no one can determine the time of Jesus's descent. The only thing that is known for sure is that the Prophet spoke about the descent, and since the Prophet spoke about it, it is believed as truth. But the texts on the return can be understood in both allegorical and literal ways.

It should be noted that the prophetic remarks on the role of Jesus are all related to this world and not to the afterlife. Present existence in Islam has paramount importance. This worldly life is a test. Thus, the descent of Jesus entails a remarkable struggle jointly performed by Jesus and the Muslim messianic figure in Islamic eschatology, the Mahdi. The realm of the afterlife is where struggle no longer exists.

In the Qur'an, Jesus is mainly characterized by his message, which centers on worshipping the one God. However, in sayings of the Prophet, Jesus is characterized as someone who must come at the end of time as a mercy from God. Jesus will come to bring justice to the world. Muslims understand his coming as

the promise of change in the course of history and as the onset of the establishment of justice. Jesus, with his Muslim messianic helper, a symbol of goodness,
will defeat the Antichrist, a symbol of oppression and evil. This Islamic understanding of Jesus's victory over the Antichrist should not be confused with
certain Christian concepts of the coming of the kingdom of God, where no evil
remains. From an Islamic theological perspective, as long as this world exists as
a place where people are tested, it is impossible to fully get rid of evil.

In this work, my perspective is that of a Muslim scholar of Islamic theology
who looks at the text in its context using the methodology of Islamic sciences,
such as the commentary of the Qur'an (Usul al-Tafsir) and the sayings of the
Prophet (Usul al-Hadith). I am inclined to interpret Islamic texts in light of
modern scholarship rather than read them simply on a literal level. For the
sake of a complete investigation of the topic, I will examine those literalist views
and discuss their theological validity. Many Muslims may find my approach
very new because it synthesizes classical and modern sources. While limited
Qur'anic verses are cited as sources for Jesus's eschatological role, more than
100 sayings of the Prophet can be found in the Hadith collections, some of
which are examined in this work. Exploring Jesus as an eschatological figure in
Islam also requires a brief discussion of other figures that appear in the same
scenario and have strong relationships with Jesus. These figures are the Mahdi,
the Islamic messianic figure who is supported by Jesus, and the Antichrist, the
evil persona, who is presented in the sayings of the Prophet as al-Dajjal, the
Liar, and the stern opponent of Jesus. Also, because I argue that Jesus is pivotal
to both Muslims and Christians, the discussion of Jesus's descent necessitates a
discussion of the future of interfaith cooperation, particularly between Christians and Muslims, who together constitute more than half of humanity. I hope
this study will be a valuable contribution to interfaith dialogue and will enhance
understandings in the English-speaking world about Muslims and their faith,
including their belief in Jesus.

•

My goal in this book is to shed light from an Islamic theological perspective on
Jesus as a prominent theme of Islamic eschatology. I am confident that focusing
on Jesus as a major figure in Islamic theology will be of interest to contemporary Christians, Muslims, and all people interested in interfaith endeavors.

The book has nine chapters that lay out major elements of Muslim theology related to Jesus and his decent and their implications for contemporary
Muslim-Christian understanding. Chapter 1 explores the Qur'anic Jesus and

presents a foundational knowledge of Jesus as a messenger of God. More specifically, it asks whether the descent of Jesus has taken place in the Qur'an. It also examines Qur'anic verses on the birth of Jesus, his attributes, the matter of his death and crucifixion, and his ascension to God. Chapter 2 discusses the eschatological role of Jesus from a Qur'anic perspective. Chapter 3 situates knowledge of future events in Islamic theology and the place of Jesus among these eschatological events as one of the signs of the Hour foretold by the Prophet of Islam. Chapter 4 presents concrete examples from the Hadith literature on the eschatological descent of Jesus. The chapter investigates the sayings of the Prophet through a thorough discussion based on the methodology of Hadith criticism. Chapter 5 explores various speculations about the time and place of Jesus's return, all of which indicate in some way the presence of Jesus as a helper, rescuer, and bringer of justice. The Islamic eschatological scenario of an alliance between Jesus and the Mahdi against al-Dajjal is the main subject of discussion in chapter 6. Chapters 7 and 8 examine the differences between the literal and allegorical approaches to Jesus's eschatological role in Islamic theology. These chapters demonstrate the importance of allegorical understandings of certain religious texts. The final chapter argues that Jesus and his descent in Islam can serve as a common ground for Christians and Muslims, a contribution to broader interfaith dialogue between the members of the Abrahamic family—Jews, Christians, and Muslims—and adherents of other religions.

I have enriched the present work with two appendices from prominent Turkish Islamic scholars, Muhammed Hamdi Yazir (d. 1942) and Fethullah Gülen (b. 1941). The translation from Yazir (appendix 2) is my own and the first available in English. Appendix 1 is an original document provided to me by Gülen, to which I have made slight editorial revisions.

While there are a few books written in English on the place of Jesus in Islam, to my knowledge there are almost no books written in English on the eschatological descent of Jesus in Islam. I hope this work will help fill this gap in scholarship and be a resource for those who wish to explore this material in greater depth. It is my hope that *Islam's Jesus* will contribute to an Islamic understanding of Jesus and will advance the dialogue between Muslims, Christians, Jews, and adherents of other faiths.

# ONE

# Jesus as God's Messenger in the Qur'an

One of the most important aspects of the Qur'an is the inclusiveness of its message. It does not limit the story of salvation to the emergence and later development of Islam; instead, it takes the story back to the beginning of humanity, the time of Adam, the first prophet of God in Islam. The chain that started with Adam continued through many prophets and ended with Muhammad, who is the final Prophet and confirms the absolute truthfulness of all prophetic messages. One of the links in this chain is Jesus, a possessor of steadfastness and one of the most important of God's prophets in Islam.

Islamic theological literature uses several terms for those who are appointed by God to convey His message. One of these terms is *al-rasul*, or the messenger. Linguistically speaking, the Arabic term *rasul* means the person who is commended by the sender of the message to either convey a message or to receive a message on behalf of the sender. Theologically speaking, "*al-rasul* is a human being who is sent by God to convey divine laws to the people."[1] Similarly there is another term used for the prophets of God, *al-nabi*. The Arabic term *nabi* "refers to the one who receives revelation through an angel, or for whom an inspiration comes to the heart or through wholesome dreams."[2] In theological terms, a *rasul* is higher than a *nabi* because a *rasul* receives a special revelation from God through the angel Gabriel; that is to say, every *rasul* is also a *nabi*, but not vice versa. Consequently, Jesus in Islam is both a *rasul* and a *nabi*. It is believed that there had been 124,000 prophets, or *nabi*, before the emergence of Islam. Of these only 313 were *rasul*. Among these were five *ul al-'azm*, the Possessors of Steadfastness. These five messengers of God are the most important of all the prophets and hold the highest spiritual rank of all human beings. In chronological order, these five are Noah, Abraham, Moses, Jesus, and Muhammad. Therefore, Jesus is of paramount importance to Muslims not only because he was a prophet confirmed by all Muslims but also because he is the closest in the chain of the prophethood of all divine messengers to Muhammad because of his temporal proximity and the fact that he revealed the good news of the coming of Muhammad.

Both Jesus and Mary are very important Qur'anic figures. Some Muslim theologians have debated whether Mary was one of the prophets since she received a revelation from God when angels (Qur'an 3:42–48) or "Our Spirit," the angel Gabriel, gave her good news about her immaculate pregnancy and the miraculous birth of Jesus. Both Mary and Jesus deserve great attention and discussion, but this chapter will focus on Jesus as seen from the perspective of Islamic theology presented in the Qur'an.[3]

The Qur'an honors Jesus as a messenger of God whom Muslims must affirm as God's messenger. The Qur'an criticizes those who deny the divine messengers and says of them, "Alas for human beings, My servants! Never came there unto them a messenger but they did mock him" (36:30). This verse encompasses the stories of many prophets who came to declare the divine message to their people but were mocked while conveying the message of God. Jesus was not an exception. The conclusion one can draw from this is that the Qur'an considers all historical prophets who brought the message of the belief in one God to be prophets of God whether we know their names or not. Thousands of prophets of God may have walked the earth and we may know nothing about their names and locales.

The story of Jesus is one of the most well-known prophetic stories in the Qur'an. Chapter 3 of the Qur'an, "The Family of 'Imran," discusses the matter of Jesus. As we shall examine, this chapter of the Qur'an speaks of Mary as chosen by God; Zachariah's care for her; Mary's encounter with angels; Jesus's birth; his miracles, which are performed with permission from God; the support of Jesus's disciples; and Jesus's "death" and ascension (3:42–64). Jesus is repeatedly mentioned by name in various chapters of the Qur'an. The Qur'an makes explicit connections between Jesus and the message of Islam. Those who were against Jesus were against the Qur'an as well, theologically speaking. Commanding Muslims to declare their belief in the message of Jesus, the Holy Book states: "Say we believe in God, in what is revealed to us and what is revealed to Abraham, Ishmael, Isaac, Jacob, and the Tribes. We believe in the Torah revealed to Moses, in the Gospel revealed to Jesus and in what is sent to the prophets, of their Lord; we make no division between any of them, and to God we surrender" (2:136).

In the fourth chapter, one of the longest, the Qur'an connects the message of Muhammad to the message of Jesus and other prophets before them. It confirms that what was revealed to the Prophet of Islam was not something unprecedented but that he who was giving the revelation of the Qur'an to Muhammad was the same God who sent the divine message to the prophets before him. Jesus is mentioned as the predecessor of the Prophet of Islam. To indicate the universality of the message of Islam, the Qur'an touches on the history of divine revelation, which includes messengers of God such as Noah, Abraham, Ishmael, Isaac, Jacob, Jesus, Job, Jonah, Aaron, Solomon, and David (4:163). The following chapter further emphasizes the importance of the message of Jesus and its relationship with earlier messages, namely the Torah. Jesus does not reject the divine message sent before him; on the contrary, he accepts and confirms the message of the Torah. He came after all prophets ("We sent Jesus after them" [Qur'an 5:46]), but the closest to him among all prophets is the Prophet of Islam. In the Islamic eschatological scenario, Jesus and the Islamic messianic figure that represents the Prophet of Islam are hand in hand against "the Liar," or the false prophet known as the Antichrist. Both share the final victory over the Antichrist.

In "Mary," chapter 19 of the Qur'an, when Jesus miraculously speaks from his cradle, once again he declares his message to his people that he is the servant of God, that God revealed the Gospel to him, that God appointed him as a prophet, that God blessed him wherever he might be, and that God enjoined him to pray and give charity as long as he lived (19:30–31). The Qur'anic Jesus is a messenger of God to the children of Israel (3:49; 4:157; 5:75). His mission was to proclaim the monotheistic, ethical message of God. The Qur'an also presents him as the one who is supported by the holy spirit (2:87).[4]

Jesus is mentioned in more than ninety verses of the Qur'an. The Qur'anic Jesus is a receiver of divine scripture. God revealed to him a special message, al-Injil, the Islamic name for the Gospel (3:48, 5:46, 19:30, 57:27). The Qur'an refers to the Gospel as a source of guidance, light, and admonition for God-fearing people (5:46). Jesus made certain things that were forbidden to Israelites lawful, such as work on the Sabbath and some dietary items that had been restricted (3:50). Jesus called upon the people to become muslims, with a lowercase "m"—that is, to submit themselves to the will of God (5:116–17). Therefore, Muslims revere the followers and disciples of Jesus for their struggle in the way of God and their support for Jesus. Hence, because of their submission to the will of God, Muslims see them as fellow Muslims.

The Qur'anic Jesus is the Messiah (4:171–72), and his frequently used title, the Son of Mary, is mentioned in thirty-three verses of the Qur'an. In the Qur'an,

Jesus is given at least ten other titles: *al-nabi* (the prophet, 19:30), *al-rasul* (the messenger of God who received a scripture from God, 3:49), *min al-muqarrabin* (of those close to God, 3:45), *mubarak* (the blessed one, 19:31), *qawl al-Haq* (the true word, 19:34), *'abd Allah* (the servant of God, 4:172), *kalimat Allah* (the word of God, 4:171), *kalimat Minh* (a word from Him, 3:45), *ruh Allah* (a spirit from God, 21:91 and 66:12), *wajeeh* (a person of distinction, 3:45), and confirmer of the Torah (3:50). The Qur'anic Jesus speaks as a precursor of Muhammad and consoles his disciples by giving them good news of the coming of Muhammad after him: "Jesus, son of Mary, said: O Children of Israel! Lo! I am the messenger of Allah unto you, confirming what was revealed before me, the Torah, and giving good tidings of a messenger who shall come after me, whose name shall be Ahmad" (61:6). The names Ahmad and Muhammad are derived from the same root, a word connoting "the praised one." According to Muslim theologians, the good news about Muhammad in the Qur'an is paralleled by verses in the Gospel of John, where Jesus speaks of the Paraclete, or comforter (14:16). Historically, Muslim theologians have been nearly unanimous in believing that the Greek word for "comforter" in John's gospel refers to Muhammad. Therefore, Muhammad is considered to be both the seal of the prophets and the fulfillment of Jesus's message.

From a Muslim perspective, theologically speaking, the essence of the message of Muhammad is consistent with the original ethical and pastoral teachings of Jesus. Any difference is due to the different contexts in which the two men lived. According to Islamic teaching, when Jesus came as a messenger of God to convey the divine message, he needed certain social conditions before he could proclaim his message, conditions that would prove its truthfulness. For example, in his time healing was a very important practice in the community; therefore, God supported Jesus with miracles of healing. Jesus was able to raise the dead to life, heal lepers, and give sight to the blind. These were all possible through permission from God, not through Jesus's own power. On the other hand, when Muhammad came to proclaim the same message of God, his society was dominated by the culture of eloquence in Arabic poetry and prose. Therefore, his major miracle was given in the form of an eloquent book, the Qur'an, which invited all composers of Arabic literature to replicate its eloquence.

Muhammad, by bringing his community from idol worship to worship of the one true God, has fulfilled the message that Jesus and all other prophets of God had proclaimed. The Prophet of Islam was able, in twenty-three years, to change the entire Arabian Peninsula and make the divine message dominant not only in the political arena but also in the hearts and minds of the people. What Muhammad achieved in such a short period of time was unprecedented. The Qur'anic message suggests that when Jesus announced the coming of Muhammad, he was giving the good news of the coming of a messenger of God who would bring an end to the suffering of people and would succeed in teaching about belief in one God.

Jesus's place in the Qur'an as one of the great prophets of God is a highly revered position in Islam. Sunni theologians agree that since the time of the Prophet, the highest people in religious rank after Muhammad in the Islamic community are the four caliphs, Abu Bakr, 'Umar, 'Uthman, and 'Ali, of which Abu Bakr comes first. However, even Abu Bakr cannot reach the spiritual rank of Jesus. Jesus is a prophet and a messenger of God who speaks on behalf of God, while Abu Bakr is not a prophet but a companion of the final prophet of God, Muhammad.

Jesus's proper name in the Qur'an is 'Isa, the Arabic equivalent of Jesus. Medieval Muslim theologians and linguists have developed a sizable body of literature on the terms and names used for Jesus in the Qur'an and on the origin of these names and titles.[5] The name 'Isa is mentioned twenty-five times in the Holy Book of Islam.[6]

While the Qur'an teaches that Jesus was a messenger of God who brought a divine message to humanity, it does not contend that he was God or a part of God. The Qur'an warns people about this: "They are unbelievers who say, 'God is the Messiah, Mary's son.' Say, [O Muhammad[7]]: 'Who then shall overrule God in any way if He desires to destroy the Messiah, Mary's son, and his mother, and all those who are on earth?' For to God belongs the kingdom of the heavens and of the earth, and all that is between them. He creates what He wills. God is all powerful" (5:17).

The word "Messiah" in the Qur'an is a title of Jesus and is not used for any other individual in the Holy Book. The term "messiah" is a common term used by Muslims, Jews, and Christians, but they each apply a different meaning to the term. In the Jewish tradition, the messiah is a job description that includes bringing peace, ending injustice, and securing the return of Jews to the land of Israel. The Islamic messianic figure will also bring justice, prosperity, and peace to the world. However, neither Muslims nor Jews consider their messiah to be divine. In this regard, one can argue that there is an alignment between Jews and Muslims in contradistinction to Christianity. However, by using this title for Jesus, the Qur'an does not make any connection between Jesus and the messianic expectations of the Old Testament.

In the Islamic tradition, to go too far is as bad as falling short. This Islamic theological principle is particularly important with regard to the personality of Jesus. Muslims believe that a group of people went astray because they denied Jesus. Another group of people went astray because they exaggerated the status of Jesus. Instead of accepting him as a messenger of God, they raised him to the level of God. The Qur'anic understanding of Jesus is somewhere between these two. Moreover, one of the roles of Muslims as the followers of the "middle way" is to bring harmony and peace between Jews and Christians who have departed from each other in their understanding of the personality of Jesus.[8] A verse warns that there should be no exaggeration about the nature of Jesus, a servant of God.

O People of the Book! Do not exaggerate in your religion. Do not say anything about God except the truth. Surely, the Messiah, Jesus, son of Mary, is God's messenger and God gave His word through Mary and he [Jesus] is a spirit from Him. Therefore believe in God and His messengers and do not say God is "three." Avoiding this is better for you. There is no doubt that God is but One God. He is too exalted to have a son. Whatever is in heaven and on earth belongs to Him and God is All Sufficient as the Trustee Jesus never disdains to be a servant of God. Neither do God's close angels. The one who disdains the worship of God and becomes arrogant, God will gather them all together before Himself." (4:171–72)[9]

In Islamic theology, Muslims must love Jesus as much as they can, perhaps more than their parents and children, but they should not exaggerate or elevate him to the level of God. This Islamic theological principle applies to Muhammad as well. Despite a general rejection of Jesus's message by his own people, the verses do mention that some pious people from his community followed him and accepted the truth. Twelve verses in the chapter of the Family of 'Imran supplement a well-known birth narrative.

According to the Qur'an, Jesus's message was to invite people to worship only one God, not himself. Jesus says, "Surely God [or Allah] is my Lord and your Lord. So worship Him and this is the straight path" (3:51).[10] Therefore, neither Jesus nor Muhammad can be worshipped. Both are among the greatest worshippers of God.

## Jesus's Personal History and His Message

The story of Jesus's birth is mentioned in two chapters of the Qur'an. Both stories have to do with Mary. Chapter 3, the second-longest chapter of the Qur'an, is named after the family of 'Imran, or Al-'Imran, the family of the father of Mary and of the father of Moses; commentators have suggested that one of the chapter's main aims is to show Jesus's family tree. Mary's father and Moses's father share the same name but are two different people. Mary's father is known in the Gospel of Luke as Heli, a short version of Eliachim. While this is the name of Mary's father in Hebrew, 'Imran is the Arabic version of Eliachim. Through the use of her Qur'anic title, Maryam bint 'Imran, or Mary the daughter of 'Imran, the Qur'an leaves no doubt about the identity of her father.

The Holy Book of Islam presents Mary as an example for believers: "And [Allah cites an example for those who believe] Mary, the daughter of 'Imran, who preserved her chastity and into whose womb We breathed Our spirit. And she truly believed in the words of her Lord and in His scriptures. She was among the truly devout" (66:12). The verse from which the chapter takes its name, Al-'Imran, is about how the family of 'Imran is chosen by God: "Surely God [or Allah] has chosen Adam and Noah, Abraham's descendants, and the family of 'Imran above [the peoples of] the worlds" (3:33).

Chapter 19, named after Mary, also contains a similar account of Jesus's birth. However, each chapter presents a unique birth story. I focus on the story as presented in chapter 3. For further elaboration and an alternative Qur'anic narrative of Jesus's birth, the reader is referred to chapter 19 of the Qur'an, verses 16–37.

The Qur'an presents the entire story of Jesus's birth in a concise way that assumes the reader's knowledge of the topic. Many of the details are omitted and, as is common throughout the Qur'an, shows the Qur'an's concern for only the most important aspects of the story: that Jesus was not left alone, that his Lord was with him to protect him, that Jesus was not God, and that he was performing miracles with permission from God.[11] The Qur'an also states that this knowledge about Jesus and Mary was a revelation from God to Muhammad, who did not possess this knowledge before the Qur'anic revelation. According to verses in chapter 3, Jesus's miraculous birth was similar to the creation of Adam, who had neither a father nor a mother. Both Jesus and Adam were great manifestations of divine power. God was able to create two human beings, one without a father and mother and the other without a father. Another verse has a clear reference to the power of God: "Surely, the story of Jesus in the sight of God is similar to the story of Adam. God has created him (Adam) from soil and then said to it 'be' and it has become" (3:59). In his commentary on this verse, Mahmud bin 'Umar al-Zamakhshari (d.

1144), a linguist and well-known commentator on the Qur'an, remarks that the miraculous case of Jesus was similar to that of Adam and suggests that the creation of Adam was even more miraculous since he was created with neither father nor mother. What is common between Adam and Jesus in this regard is that both creations defy natural laws: "That is to say, both are created outside of the current laws of human reproduction. They both are similar in this sense. And creation without a father or mother is more miraculous and in greater defiance of the laws of nature than the creation of a human being without a father. Here a miracle is compared to something more miraculous to strengthen the argument [that Jesus is not God] and silence the opponent."[12] Thus, neither Adam nor Jesus is considered a deity in Islam. If creation without a physical father made Jesus a deity, Adam would have been considered a deity. The Qur'anic logic concludes that there is only one God, the most powerful. Other than Him, no one can claim to be a deity.

Because of the Qur'an's reference to Jesus's birth without a human father, the tradition records that the second caliph, 'Umar, was angry at a man who had a son named 'Isa and called himself Abu 'Isa, or the father of Jesus. Muslims often name their children after prophets mentioned in the Qur'an, particularly Jesus. Abu Dawud, one of the collectors of the sayings of the Prophet, narrates that 'Umar rebuked the man and said: "Is it not enough for you to name yourself Abu 'Abdillah, the father of the servant of God?"[13] 'Umar does not mention a reason for his rebuke, but it is evident from the reference to "the servant" that 'Umar was sensitive to the possible denigration of Jesus, who had no human father.

Prior to revealing the birth of Jesus, the Qur'an speaks of Mary and how she was chosen among all the women of the world and purified: "And remember when angels said to Mary: surely Allah has chosen you, purified you and elevated you over all women of the world. O Mary, worship your Lord, prostrate, and bow down with those who bow down before God in their worship." The verse goes on: "This is the news from the realm of the unseen that We reveal it to you, O Muhammad. You were not with them when they were casting lots on who would be the guardian of Mary, and you were not with them when they were quarrelling" (3:42–45). According to the Qur'an narrative of the story of Mary, many people wanted to be her guardian. The prophet Zachariah, who was a prominent messenger of God according to Islam, was the most pious of those who wanted to take care of Mary. He and the others cast lots by throwing arrows into the Jordan River. The arrows of the others fell into the water and went down with current, but God made Zachariah's arrow stand up. This was a sign that Zachariah won the contest and that it was God's will. Zachariah embraced Mary, and she embraced Zachariah.

After emphasizing that this information comes to the Prophet Muhammad from the divine, the Qur'an goes on to speak of the birth of Jesus through a conversation between the angels and Mary:

> And remember when angels said, "O Mary, surely God gives you good news with a word from Him, his name is the Messiah, Jesus, Son of Mary. He is illustrious in this world and in the hereafter and he is among those who are close to God. He will speak to people from his cradle, and in his manhood, and he is among the righteous." Mary said, "My God, how can I bear a child when no human being has touched me?" The angels replied, "That is God's command. Allah creates what He wants. When He decrees a thing, He just says to it 'be,' and it happens. God will teach Jesus in book [scriptures, writing], the wisdom, the Torah, and the Gospel." (3:44–48)

In his commentary on Qur'anic verses about the birth of Jesus, Sayyid Qutb, the contemporary Egyptian commentator on the Qur'an who is more well known in the West for his ideas on political Islam, refers to Mary as a "female heroine." He finds her story the most unusual event in human history: "Surely the event of the birth of Jesus is the strangest event that humanity throughout its history has ever witnessed. It is an event like none that has ever happened, either before Jesus or after him." Qutb contends, "Jesus was a mercy to the Israelites in particular, and to all humanity in general. The event of Jesus's miraculous birth leads them to the knowledge of God, to worshipping God, and to seeking God's blessing."[14] It is not unusual to consider a prophet of God as a mercy from God. Like Jesus, Muhammad also is presented in the Qur'an as a mercy to all worlds: "We have sent you not, but as a mercy to all worlds" (21:107). Mary gave birth to such a divine mercy, Jesus.

In the conversation between Mary and the angels, Jesus is clearly presented as a word from God. The term "word" has resulted in two major points of interpretation by Muslim commentators on the Qur'an: the first is the angels' verbal promise to Mary and the second is Allah's intervention in the birth of Jesus by creating him through His word "Be!" The story goes on to present how Jesus will become a messenger of God to the Israelites and how his miracles will prove that he is truly a messenger from God. The Qur'anic Jesus is not illiterate; he is learned and full of wisdom: "And God will teach him the book, the wisdom, the Torah and the Gospel" (3:48). In the following verses, one can also see the core of the divine message to Jesus:

God will make him a messenger to the children of Israel. Jesus will say: "I have brought to you a sign [miracle] from your Lord that I make for you from clay, a sign in the likeness of a bird, and I breathe into it and it becomes a bird by God's permission. I shall heal the blind, the leper, and raise the dead to life. I shall foretell to you [as a miracle] what you eat and what you store up in your houses. Surely in this there is a sign for you if you are true believers. I come to confirm the Torah, which preceded me, and to make lawful for you some things that have been forbidden to you. I have come to you with a sign from your Lord, therefore, be fearful of God and obey me. Allah is my Lord and your Lord. Worship Him. That is a straight path."(Qur'an 3:49–51)

To indicate what Jesus felt at his people's refusal of his message, the Qur'an narrates Jesus's request for help in God's cause: "Who will be my helpers in God's cause?" (3:52). A group of people known as "the white-garbed ones" or the "white-garment makers," who would later be his disciples, said that they would be his helpers in God's cause. They believed in God and asked Jesus to witness their submission to God. Interestingly enough, the term used for them is "*muslimun*," which means "muslims," or those who submit themselves to God's will. The Qur'an presents an example of their prayer, which has been repeated by Muslims since the revelation of the Qur'an until the present day: "Our Lord, we believed in what You have revealed [the Gospel] and we follow Your messenger [Jesus]. Inscribe us among the witnesses [to your truth]" (3:53). This prayer of Jesus's disciples has become a model of supplication in Muslim piety. Muslims repeat this in their regular prayers as well as in their daily prescribed prayers when they read passages from the Qur'an. The next verse begins a new phase of the story, in which Jesus's opponents have gone beyond simply rejecting his message and are plotting to kill him. However, God is aware of their scheme: "And the disbelievers plotted, and God plotted against them. And God is the best of plotters" (Qur'an 3:54). The Qur'an then explains how God rescued Jesus from the plot of his enemies.

## The Concept of Prophethood in Islamic Theology

To understand the place of Jesus in Islam, one should understand the concept of prophethood in Islamic theology. Prophethood constitutes one of the three major themes of Islamic theology, alongside divinity and the afterlife. Approximately one-fourth of the Qur'an discusses the concept of prophethood. Prophets are chosen by God to convey God's message. It is believed that God sends prophets to humanity to help them with both their worldly life and their afterlife. Perhaps because of this Qur'anic emphasis, Muslim theologians, both contemporary and classical, have engaged the Islamic eschatological imagination and have heavily discussed the concept of prophethood.

It is a principle in Islamic thought that revelation and reason do not contradict but complete each other. Reason, in the Islamic perspective, is a gift from God and must be used for the betterment of individual and communal life. However, reason by itself cannot determine what is false and what is true. For this, reason needs the guidance of revelation. Reason is a key to understanding revelation but cannot replace it. Revelation comes through prophets, and through revelation prophets have contributed to the social and spiritual life of people throughout history. Prophets receive revelations from God through an angel or receive inspiration or even visions. On one occasion the Prophet was asked about the number of prophets that had come to humanity until his time. He said, "They have been one hundred and twenty-four thousand, three hundred and thirteen of which are *rasul*, a big group."[15]

In Islamic theology, the first of these messengers of God is Adam and the last is the Prophet of Islam, Muhammad. God supports prophets with miracles that sometimes defy laws of nature. Some of these prophets and divine messengers are mentioned in the Qur'an by name, including Noah, Lot, Abraham, Moses, David, Zachariah, John the Baptist, and Jesus. However, the Qur'an explicitly states that some of the prophets are not mentioned. On this matter the Qur'anic verse says: "Surely We sent messengers before you [Muhammad], among them those of whom We have told you, and some of whom We have not told you; and it was not given to any messenger that he should bring a portent save by Allah's permission. When God's command comes, justly the issue shall be judged; then the followers of falsehood will be lost" (40:78).

Not everyone can be a prophet or a messenger. Muslim theologians have developed five attributes that a prophet of God must possess: trustworthiness, truthfulness, innocence, the ability to convey God's message, and intellect. Anyone who lacks one of these principles cannot be accepted as a prophet or a messenger of God. Therefore, based on this principle of Islamic theology, Muslims do not accept some biblical stories such as the story of David and Bathsheba (2 Sam. 11:1–4), Noah's drunkenness (Gen. 9:20–27), and Lot's sexual relations with his daughters (Gen. 19:30–35). Such acts, if they were true, would disqualify David, Noah, and Lot as prophets of God. Since the Holy Book of Islam speaks of them as great messengers of God, Muslims consider those stories to be untrue. The stories may refer to other historical figures, but not to the prophets.

Furthermore, if David was not trustworthy, he would not have received the divine revelation of the Torah. The David of the Qur'an recites the Torah in such a beautiful way that even birds listened and mountains echoed his recitation (Qur'an 34:10).

Despite the high position of prophets in the sight of God, none of them are considered worthy of worship. In fact, the Islamic understanding of oneness of God, or *tawhid*, strictly requires that nothing and no one can be worshipped but God. Prophets and saints, theologically speaking, are shining suns of the realm of humanity but not at the level of God or a part of God. They are higher than angels, but they are human beings and worshippers of God. Therefore, when Muslims speak of Jesus or Muhammad as messengers of God, they mean the highest religious rank in the realm of creation.[16]

Beyond just being messengers of God, one important aspect of the prophets' personalities is their mutual friendship. The close friendship between Jesus and Muhammad is emphasized even more. This emphasis leads al-Qurtubi (d. 1274), the Cordovan Muslim theologian and renowned commentator of the Qur'an, to quote the well-known saying of the Prophet: "I am the closest to Jesus in this life and the afterlife." The companions of the Prophet asked him "How?" and the Prophet replied, "The prophets are brothers even though their mothers are different. Their religion is one and there is no prophet between me and Jesus."[17] As evidence of the strong relationship between Jesus and Muhammad, reference is made to the Qur'anic verse that refers to Jesus as the one who gives good news of Muhammad's coming after him (61:6). From an Islamic theological perspective, the Prophet of Islam's real spiritual level is beyond comprehension. His meeting with Jesus during his night journey and his leading of all prophets in prayer in Jerusalem before his ascension to divine presence occurred in a different dimension. In order to understand the personality of Muhammad accurately, one has to remember both his spiritual life and his worldly life together. Thinking of him only as a historical figure is misleading. The following analogy helps us to better understand the two aspects of the Prophet. Think of the egg of the peacock and the peacock itself. One can hardly imagine how such a beautiful array of feathers could initially come from such an ugly egg. That is to say, if we did not see with our naked eyes that the source of such a peacock is such an egg, we might not believe in this fact. Thus, in order to appreciate the beauty of the peacock one has to consider the egg and the peacock at the same time. Focusing only on the egg from which the peacock comes and ignoring the amazing beauty of the peacock is misleading. The human life of the Prophet is like the egg, and his spiritual life is more like the beauty of the peacock. Without understanding the Prophet's spiritual dimension, it is difficult to understand his spiritual life and close relationship to Jesus and other prophets.[18]

## Foundations of Muslims' Belief in Jesus

The following verses of the Qur'an constitute the foundation of Muslims' belief in Jesus and thousands of pages of Qur'anic commentaries have been written on these verses: "O you believers, say, 'We believe in Allah and that which is revealed unto us and that which was revealed unto Abraham, and Ishmael, and Isaac, and Jacob, and the Tribes, and that which Moses and Jesus received, and that which the prophets received from their Lord.' We make no distinction between any of them, and unto Him we have surrendered" (Qur'an 2:136; for similar sentiments, see also 3:84 and 4:163). As a theological principle in Islam and a part of faith, Muslims must believe in all prophets.

Islam is the continuation of the religion of the prophets mentioned earlier, including Noah, Abraham, Moses, and Jesus (Qur'an 42:12). Its role is to confirm, complete, or, in some cases, correct pre-Islamic understandings. For example, the Qur'an is very clear about addressing the Christian understanding of the nature of Jesus (4:171–72). One can see that the Qur'anic verses referring to the sayings of Jesus are similar to biblical verses, such as Jesus's statement "I ascend . . . to my God and your God" (John 20:17). While many Christian theologians have seen in this text a reference to the divinity of Jesus, Muslim theologians have understood this text as a reference to Christ as a servant of God. "And the Messiah said: Children of Israel, worship God, my Lord and your Lord" (Qur'an 5:72).[19] The Qur'an reminds its readers that some People of the Book, meaning Christians, have exaggerated the nature of Jesus. The Qur'an aims to present a balanced view of Jesus. In the Qur'an, although he is not a deity, he is more than just a religious teacher. He is a great messenger of God whose birth is a divine miracle, and he is appointed by God to convey His message (4:171–72).

The Qur'anic Jesus is the receiver of unique, divine gifts. The Qur'an recounts the divine favors and bounties given to Jesus, but God also interrogates him. God's questions appear in an eloquent verse style that refers to future events in the past tense to assert the certainty of the future event. In one verse, God asks Jesus if he instructed people to worship him, and Jesus responds to God that he did not have the right to do that. Jesus then converses with the Divine and asks His mercy for his people by referring to God's wisdom and majesty. The verse says:

Remember when God said: "O Jesus, son of Mary! Did you say to people 'Take me and my mother as two gods beside Allah?'" Jesus said: "Glory be to You! I cannot say what I do not have the right to say. If I had said it, You would know it. You know what is in me and I do not know what is in You. Surely You are the Knower of all unseen. I did not tell them anything but what You have commanded me to say: 'Worship Allah, my Lord and your Lord.' And I was witness upon them as long as I lived among them. When You caused me to die You remained watchful over them and You are Witness over everything. If You punish them surely they are Your servants. If You forgive them, You are the Mighty and the Wise." (5:116–18)

Sources of Islamic history show some debates between Muhammad and some Meccan polytheists who attacked Jesus. It seems that the Prophet defended Jesus against their accusations. Commentaries on the Qur'an record a debate between Muhammad and 'Abdullah bin al-Zaba'r (d. 636), a poet and one of the unmoved polytheists of Mecca before his conversion to Islam. The debate occurred after the revelation of one of the Qur'anic verses addressing polytheists. The verse says, "You and what you worship are the fuel of hell. Surely you will enter it" (21:98). In response to this verse, using juvenile logic, Ibn al-Zaba'r says, "Muhammad, do not Christians worship Jesus? And you say that he was a messenger of God and a pious servant of God. If he is in hell we are pleased that we and our gods will be with him there."[20] With this, the group of polytheists of Mecca laughed and mocked the Prophet in raised voices. The Qur'an responds that Jesus will not be put in hell, and that instead Jesus is the sign of the Final Hour:

When Jesus, the son of Mary, was given as an example [of an object of idol worshipping by Ibn al-Zaba'r], your people cried out and said, "Are our gods best or is he?" They did not give him as an example but for the sake of argument. They are a contentious people. Jesus was no more than a servant upon whom we have bestowed our bounties and we made him an example for the children of Israel. If we will it to be so we can destroy you and replace you with angels on earth. Surely he is a sign for the Hour. Do not have any doubt about it. And follow Me on this right path. Do not allow Satan to hinder you. Surely, he is an open enemy to you. (43:57–62)

In the following two chapters I will discuss this verse and examine how Jesus is considered a sign of the Hour. Here I will note that as part of the Qur'anic mission to correct pre-Islamic traditions, the Holy Book holds that Jesus was the continuation of the chain of prophethood of Noah and Abraham and their offspring and that God gave Jesus the gospel as divine revelation. It also states that followers of Jesus invented monasticism to receive the favor of God and that this was something God never prescribed. The Qur'an does not imply that monasticism is a bad thing but indicates that living a monastic life is extremely difficult and goes against the nature of human beings. The Qur'an criticizes Christians who prescribe a celibate life and eventually failed to fulfill it themselves. The verse says:

> And We sent Noah, and Abraham, and We appointed the Prophecy and the Book to be among their seed. Some of them are guided, but many of them are ungodly. Then We sent, following in their footsteps, Our messengers; and then We sent Jesus, son of Mary, and gave unto him the Gospel. And We set in the hearts of those who followed him tenderness and mercy. But they invented monasticism—We did not prescribe it for them—only seeking the good pleasure of God; but they observed it not with right observance. So We give those of them who believe their reward; but many of them are sinful. (57:26-27)

This verse praises the followers of Jesus, for in their hearts they have tenderness and mercy, but another verse criticizes Christians for worshipping Jesus and saying that Jesus is the son of God: "That is what they say with their own mouths. They imitate the sayings of disbelievers of old . . . and they were not commanded to worship anyone but God. There is no deity save Him. God is above their claims that idols are partner to Him" (9:30–31).

The Qur'an speaks of Jesus and events that happened in the time of Jesus. The Holy Book of Islam and its commentaries have interesting accounts of events such as his "death," crucifixion, and ascension. It is very important for the Qur'an to speak of these events. This elaboration on Jesus in the Qur'an suggests that he is a part of the Islamic faith and that the followers of the Qur'an should believe in him. In fact, the statement of faith "I testify that there is no deity but God, and I testify that Muhammad is God's Messenger" includes the belief in Jesus and in all pre-Islamic prophets whose message was essentially the same as the message of the Prophet of Islam. This is evidenced when Muslim mystics repeatedly say in their invocations, "There is no deity but God and Muhammad is His messenger." They also say, "There is no deity but God and Moses is His messenger. There is no deity but God and Jesus is His messenger," and so on.[21] The invocation continues with the naming of other prophets. Accordingly, a belief in Jesus is an essential part of a Muslim's faith. In other words, in order to be a Muslim, one has to believe in Jesus and his miracles as mentioned in the Qur'an. The stories relating to the life of Jesus are an important part of the Qur'anic narrative.

## The Crucifixion and Resurrection of Jesus

Jesus is among the righteous. As a messenger of God and an eschatological figure presented in Islam he is among the leading figures who will inherit the earth: "Surely we have written in the Psalms after the Torah that my righteous people will inherit the earth" (Qur'an 21:105). But despite his opponents' attempts and contrary to Christian belief, the Qur'anic Jesus was not crucified. The following verses indicate that Jesus merely appeared to be crucified while in reality he was not.

> And [We, God, punish them] because of their grave calumny against Mary, and because of their claim, "Definitely we killed the Messiah, Jesus, son of Mary, the messenger of God." They did not kill him, nor did they crucify him, but it appeared to them so. Those who are in disagreement about him are in doubt of it. They have no certain knowledge about it, they are following their own assumption. They did not kill him for sure. On the contrary, God raised him to Himself. God is Majestic and Wise." (Qur'an 4:156–58)

In the Qur'an, which contains more than 6,000 verses, Jesus is mentioned more than 100 times with his various titles. It is very interesting that this is the only place where the crucifixion of Jesus is mentioned. As Todd Lawson rightly claims, "The sacred book thus de-emphasizes what is generally considered to be the single most important event in Christian salvation history."[22] The verse indicates that there was a crucifixion but that those who thought that they had crucified Jesus were confused. The difficult part of the verse is the Arabic "wa lakin shubbiha lahum," or, roughly, "but it appeared so to them." That is to say, they thought they crucified Jesus, but in fact they had not. An examination of a few English translations of this part of verse 157 in chapter 4 might be helpful for understanding the overall approach of the translators of the Qur'an.

Mohammad Marmaduke Pickthall's translation is "but it appeared so unto them," while Dr. Mohsin Khan's translation is "but the resemblance of 'Isa (Jesus) was put over another man (and they killed that man)." Similarly, Abdullah Yusuf Ali's translation is "but so it was made to appear to them," while A. J. Arberry's translation is "only a likeness of that was shown to them." Muhammad Habib Shakir's translation is "but it appeared to them so (like 'Isa)." And finally,

Muhammad Asad's translation is "but so it was made to appear to them." Considering the grammatical structure of the Arabic phrase, Muhammad Asad's translation seems to be the most compatible with the Arabic original, but this does not mean the others are wrong. I translate this part of the verse as "but it appeared to them so."

Since the Qur'an clearly states that "they did not kill him, nor did they crucify him," Muslims believe that Jesus was not crucified, that he was raised by God to heaven, and that he is still alive there and will return when God wants to send him. The verse constitutes one of the primary sources for Muslims' belief in the descent of Jesus and his eschatological role. Later the prophetic sayings revealed the ambiguous aspects of the verse, particularly with regard to Jesus's eschatological descent. The next part of the same verse emphasizes the lack of certainty regarding Jesus's crucifixion. Because of this ambiguity, the crucifixion of Jesus has been a matter of debate between Muslim and Christian theologians since the early period of Islam. John of Damascus, an eighth-century father of the Syrian church, responded to the Qur'anic verses on Jesus in some of his apologetic writings. He considers the Islamic tradition a heresy and names the followers of Islam as "Ishmaelites," a reference to Ishmael, the son of Abraham, who is the ancestor of the Prophet. However, it is believed that John of Damascus's knowledge of the Qur'an was considerably limited since he mistakenly mixed the verses of the Qur'an and the interpretations of the commentators on these verses.[23]

Although many Qur'anic exegetes see these verses as leaving room for interpretation, it should be noted that interpretations are not a part of the Qur'an itself. In other words, commentators of the Qur'an are not infallible; they can misunderstand the Qur'an and present some verses in ways that show their limited understanding. In the commentaries, one can find both contradictory views and occasional consensus on certain topics. Differences of opinion are a mercy for the community of Islam, as the Prophet says, and are an integral part of Islamic theology.[24] As for commentary on this particular verse, despite various disagreements on the current state of Jesus, the consensus of the majority of Muslim theologians is that Jesus did not die on the cross.[25] Most Muslims believe that Jesus appeared to die or that the authorities who attempted to kill him were confused and failed to kill him, that God in fact raised him to heaven. A reference from a prominent medieval Muslim theologian, Abu Mansur al-Maturidi (d. 944), serves as a good example of a classical Islamic theological approach to the subject. In his interpretation of the verse on the death of Jesus, al-Maturidi says: "With regard to the part of the verse 'We have killed the Messiah, Jesus the son of Mary, the messenger of God,' for some people there are two explanations. One about the possibility of confusion and their being mistaken in what they witnessed. The second is that even if news is *mutawatir* [that is, transmitted recurrently by reporters], the spread of false news is possible."[26] He goes on to speak of the story commonly narrated among people about the crucifixion of Jesus. "The story of Jesus's death became widely spread but it was a lie; this shows that even a recurrent transmission of a report, a *mutawatir*, can turn out to be a lie and a mistake."[27]

Once again al-Maturidi makes a theological argument. Theologically speaking, a report transmitted recurrently is considered reliable and one can build a belief upon it. If it is argued that the crucifixion of Jesus was transmitted recurrently and therefore the Christian belief in the crucifixion of Jesus is valid, al-Maturidi would argue that this principle of Islamic theology is applied when there is no counteraccount from a higher source, the Qur'an. Because in this case there is a counterargument from the Qur'an, which is the highest authority, this means that there was confusion about the crucifixion of Jesus and that those claiming that Jesus was crucified were not sure, so reports of the crucifixion are invalidated.[28]

Many may wonder about the theological foundations for this Qur'anic approach and the spread of such a belief among Muslims. This belief comes from an Islamic theological principle that God does not allow his elite prophets to be humiliated and tortured by their opponents. This Qur'anic principle proclaims that good is always victorious over evil: "Surely, God protects those who believe. God does not love the treacherous and the thankless" (22:38). This is thought to be the way of God in dealing with his beloved messengers. Accordingly, the killing of Jesus on the cross by his enemies would be incompatible with the overall divine principle of victory for the righteous. Even though God's messengers may be defeated temporarily, according to the Islamic tradition, they will be victorious at the end of the day. This is evident in the stories of Noah, Abraham, Moses, and Muhammad, who struggled and eventually received victory from God against their oppressors. The Qur'an keeps the same logic and standard by adding Jesus to the category of prophets who were victorious against their enemies.[29] While there might be some examples in Islamic tradition of prophets who were murdered, these prophets would not be among the elite. Even further, the Qur'an strongly suggests that the final victory is for the righteous (11:49). If it is not in this world, it will be in the afterlife.

Despite different views on whether or not Jesus escaped death, there is a near-consensus among commentators on the Qur'an that the phrase "I will raise you to Myself" (3:55) is a reference to the ascension of Jesus, both physically and spiritually. In Islamic theology, three main figures are known for their ascensions: the first is Enoch (or Idris), "We [God] raised him to a lofty place" (19:57); the second is Jesus; and the third is the Prophet Muhammad, whose ascension is partially narrated in the Qur'an: "Exalted be God who made His servant [Muhammad] go by night from the Sacred Mosque [Mecca] to the Farthest Mosque [Jerusalem] whose surroundings We have blessed" (17:1). It is believed that from Jerusalem the Prophet ascended to heaven to see God. This ascension, which is called the Mi'raj, takes up a great part of Islamic mystical literature. Since Muslims believe that Jesus is alive in the third level of heaven with other prophets, according to some narratives that take place in the Hadith literature, the Prophet Muhammad is believed to have met with Jesus and other prophets during the Prophet's ascension. Muslims believe that when the time comes, God will send Jesus again to this world. Interestingly, some early Christians have similar narratives of the crucifixion of Jesus. According to some records (for example, Irenaeus's *Adversus Haereses* [*Against Heresies*]), Basilides, a second-century Gnostic of Egypt, believed that Jesus was not crucified but was replaced by Simon of Cyrene, who is mentioned as Jesus's substitute in some Qur'anic commentaries as well. Gnostic ideas of substitution are also provided in Nag Hammadi documents.[30]

Islamic sources draw our attention to a theory that eventually gained prominence among Muslims. According to this theory, one of the disciples of Jesus voluntarily accepted death in place of his master. This story was related by one of the Qur'anic exegetes on the authority of Qatada, a well-known companion of the Prophet of Islam: "It has been related to us that Jesus son of Mary, the prophet of God, said to his companions, 'Who among you would accept to have my likeness cast upon him, and be killed?' One of them answered, 'I, O messenger of God.' Thus that man was killed and God prevented Jesus from being crucified and 'took him up to Himself.'"[31] Stories of sacrificing oneself for the other, or more specifically a disciple sacrificing himself for the master, are typical in the Islamic tradition of piety. Many disciples of prominent mystics would ask God to give the rest of their life for their master so that the master would live longer and serve more.

With this we come to the questions of Jesus's ascension. Did he ascend? Where is he now according to Muslim theology? How can he survive without eating and drinking if he is alive?

## Jesus's Ascension

The nature of the divine protection of Jesus and his ascension has long been a matter of discussion among Muslim scholars and theologians. Two Qur'anic verses are presented as textual references for the ascension of Jesus.

> And remember when God said "O Jesus, I will cause you to die [*inni mutawaffika*, or take you away from earthly life] and raise [ascend] you to Myself, and distance you from those who disbelieve, and make those who follow you superior until the day of Judgment over those who disbelieve. Then your return is to me. I will make the final judgment on the matters that you have been in disagreement." (3:55)

> And [We, God, punish them] because of their grave calumny against Mary, and because of their claim, "Definitely we killed the Messiah, Jesus, son of Mary, the messenger of God." They did not kill him, nor did they crucify him, but it appeared to them so. Those who are in disagreement about him are in doubt of it. They have no certain knowledge about it, they are following their own assumption. They did not kill him for sure. On the contrary, God raised him to Himself. God is Majestic and Wise. (4:156–58)

It is evident that the literal meaning of these verses about the ascension of Jesus leaves no space for doubt about the divine protection of Jesus. The position of the Qur'an is clear: Jesus was not killed but ascended to God.[32] But to where did Jesus ascend? It is believed that Jesus ascended to the realm of angels in heaven, or *sama'*, the Arabic word for heaven. *Sama'* in classical Islamic theology is understood as the location in the physical realm to which Jesus ascended. However, it can be understood as a part of the unseen world, as indicated in the story of the Prophet's ascension, the Mi'raj. The majority of Qur'anic commentators believe that Jesus ascended bodily and spiritually and that the body of Jesus had an angelic quality. If this is the case, the dimension in which Jesus lives is different than the dimension in which human beings live. Therefore, he does not need food or drink to survive, similar to angels, who are, according to Islamic theology, creatures of God made of light and do not need to eat and drink; praising God is their sustenance.

To elaborate further on the location to which Jesus was ascended, one can argue that the diverse nature of the physical world strengthens the argument that diverse heavens exist as well. For example, even in the physical world one can see many different realms. Fish cannot live in the air, nor can birds live underwater. The theological argument follows that it is possible that an unseen or metaphysical world that is not comprehensible to our normal human senses exists just beyond this material world. One Muslim theologian describes this material world as an "ornamented curtain" over the world of the unseen. It can be understood from the overall Qur'anic presentation of the idea that since God states that He raised Jesus to Himself, one must not understand Jesus as living in a material or physical world but as instead residing in a realm of the unseen. Because Jesus was a spirit from God, despite his physical existence, his body could be like those of angels. It should be noted that in Islamic teaching, angels are real creatures who are obedient to God and are able to appear and communicate in the form of human beings. For example, the Qur'an states in several places that the angel Gabriel visited Muhammad and other prophets on various occasions. It also mentions that angels appeared to Mary, Abraham, and Lot in the form of human beings.

Here we are challenged by another question: Is this ascension of Jesus a kind of death? The answer depends upon one's understanding of death. If one accepts different levels of death or understands death as a cutoff from eating and drinking, the answer would be "yes." The Qur'anic understanding of life and death is different from the common understanding. For example, according to the Qur'an, martyrs are not dead; they are alive and receive sustenance from their Lord (2:154). In this understanding, Jesus has likewise been freed of the conditions of worldly life by his ascension and thus is alive. In commentating on the same line, Sa'id Hawwa', a contemporary Syrian Qur'anic scholar, suggests that Jesus is alive now. The verse that speaks of the "death" of Jesus may also be understood as referring to "sleep," as the root of the word used for death in this verse is used for sleep elsewhere in the Qur'an (6:60). Although he expresses certain doubts about its veracity, at the end of his comments, Hawwa' narrates a story from the Gospel of Barnabas in which Jesus says, "O mother truly, I am telling you the truth, I have never died. God has protected me until the nearness of the end of the world."[33]

Many commentaries on the verses in question are in line with the prophetic sayings about Jesus's eschatological descent. According to Islamic theology as understood from the Qur'an and the sayings of the Prophet, Jesus is alive and will descend to earth. Debates over the nature of his descent, whether it is symbolic or literal, have dominated Muslim intellectual life. I shall discuss these debates in the following chapters.

# TWO

# A Qur'anic Perspective
# on the Eschatological Role of Jesus

Before delving into the details of the Qur'anic verses that deal with Jesus's messianic role, it is appropriate to briefly introduce the terminology used in Islamic theology when discussing Jesus's eschatological role. The most commonly used Islamic term for Jesus's return (or the Second Coming, as it is known in the Christian tradition) is "nuzul 'Isa," which can be translated as "the descent of Jesus." This refers to Jesus's descent from heaven to earth to fulfill his mission.

There are several other instances when the Qur'an uses a form of *nuzul* to indicate a descent. Using the verb form of the word, the Qur'an says, "We [God] have sent down [*anzalna*] iron for you" (57:25), which metaphorically indicates, along with many possible meanings, that the presence of iron on earth is a gift from the mercy of God. In another verse the Qur'an speaks of the descent of cattle, probably not because they have descended from heaven literally but because they are gifts from the mercy of God to human beings (39:6). These examples make it clear that the Islamic term *nuzul* need not be understood literally but can be taken as a metaphor. The Holy Book also speaks in various verses of the descent of angels, the descent of the Qur'an, and the descent of the spirit on the Night of Power, Laylat al-Qadr, which is believed to be in the month of Ramadan. The use of the same word by the Prophet of Islam for Jesus's return indicates that his descent is a gift of divine mercy. This particular term in relationship to Jesus's descent is not found in the Qur'an, but is found in the various sayings of the Prophet, such as in the collections of Muhammad al-Bukhari (d. 870) and Muslim bin al-Hajjaj (d. 875), collections both known as *al-Sahih*, which means "the sound" or "the reliable." Indeed, in the Qur'anic verse that recounts a conversation between Mary and the angel Gabriel, when she asks how she could be pregnant without being touched by any human being, Jesus is presented as a mercy from God. "And We will make of him a sign for people and a mercy from Us" (19:21).

Because the life and message of Jesus are major themes of the Qur'an and because he is presented among the five elite prophets in the Muslim tradition, Muslim theologians and commentators have disagreed about whether or not the Qur'an addresses his eschatological role as a messianic figure. Scholars of Islamic theology have attempted to find references in the Qur'an to support the Hadith references that clearly speak of the descent of Jesus. In Islamic theology, the slightest hint in the Qur'an is important and has great merit. Some argue that the Qur'an elucidates Jesus's eschatological descent, but since his eschatological role is not explicitly stated in the Qur'an, the descent of Jesus is not considered one of the major themes of Islamic theology. In the following passages, I will elaborate on Jesus's role as a sign of the Hour. The first thing to consider is the question of how Jesus is considered a sign of the Hour. Does his being a sign relate to his eschatological role or to his creation by God outside of natural laws? It is believed that at least four different passages in the Qur'an refer to the eschatological descent of Jesus. This chapter elaborates on these verses and cites some interpretations by Muslim theologians on the subject.

## Speaking in Manhood

> He [Jesus] will speak to humanity from his cradle and in manhood, and he is of the righteous. (Qur'an 3:46)

The key point in this verse is the use of future tense: "Jesus *will* speak to humanity." Some commentators report that this verse contains a reference to the return of Jesus. They argue that the future tense used in the verse implies the unfinished nature of Jesus's mission. If he is to speak to people, it will be after his descent.[1] In fact, the message of Islam and of the Prophet Muhammad's emergence was to continue to bring the divine message that had been taught by Noah, Abraham, Moses, Jesus, and other earlier divine messengers. The Prophet of Islam is clear about this. On one occasion when one of his companions asks sincerely, "O messenger of God, what is the beginning of your message?" Muhammad replies, "I am the fulfillment of the prayer of my father Abraham, I am the good news of Jesus, and my mother saw in her dream that a light comes from her to enlighten the palaces of Damascus."[2]

The verse about Jesus's speaking in manhood may suggest that in the beginning of his mission Jesus spoke to his clansmen and a limited number of people.

Some accepted his message while many rejected it. It is possible that the reason the Qur'an uses the future tense is to indicate that Jesus will address people after his descent. The second part of the verse indicates a more universal mission of Jesus. Arguably, his mission (which is also the mission of Muhammad, according to the Islamic theological teaching) will no longer be limited to his own people but will include all human beings. Fulfillment of such a message is the "good news" that the Prophet of Islam gave to his community—that Jesus will descend. Muslim theologians do not see Jesus's message as contradicting the universal message of Islam.

The chapter named after Mary also includes a reference to the miraculous speech of Jesus from his cradle. The verse in chapter 3 focuses only on Jesus's speech as a baby and as an adult; the verses in this chapter emphasize the mission of Jesus, which includes his gospel, his prophethood, his prayer, and his charity. According to the story, soon after Jesus's birth Mary brought him from seclusion and presented him to her people: "Carrying the child she came to her people. They said: 'This is indeed an unbelievable thing! Sister of Aaron, your father was not a whoremonger, nor was your mother adulterous'" (Qur'an 19:28). The Qur'an narrates that they addressed Mary here as the sister of Aaron, who was known as a pious person. Mary resembled him in her chastity, so her pregnancy was very strange.[3]

Frustrated by their accusation of her, Mary pointed to the baby Jesus, indicating that they should question the baby and not her. They said, "How can we speak to a child who is in the cradle?" (Qur'an 19:29). Jesus responded: "I am indeed the servant of God. He has given me the Book and made me a prophet. He made me blessed wherever I am and advised me of prayer and charity as long as I live. He made me kind to my mother and never made me [an] arrogant, disobedient [person to my Lord]" (Qur'an 19:29–32). The Qur'an uses past tense when Jesus speaks. According to the rule of Qur'anic eloquence, when past tense is used for future events, it is to indicate certainty that those events will take place. Fakhr al-Din al-Razi (d. 1209), a giant of Islamic theology in his own time and a well-known commentator on the Qur'an, using logic rooted in his twelfth-century context and making commentaries on the relevant verses in chapter 19, explicates Jesus's statement "I am the servant of God" and draws a conclusion based on four theological points that explain why Jesus is a servant of God and why he is not God.

First, al-Razi contends that because "Jesus's words at that time have confused some Christians, he [Jesus] clarified emphatically that he was not God, but a servant of God." Second, "when Jesus confessed his servanthood to God, if he was a true person, which he was, his goal was achieved by uttering this statement. If he was not a true person, again his power would not be a divine one; in both cases, the claims of his divinity are nullified." Third, "the most important thing at that moment was to deny the accusation of adultery against Mary. Jesus, by emphasizing his servanthood even before defending his mother, indicates that to refute accusations against God was more important than to refute accusations against his mother. That is why he, first, spoke of his servanthood to God." Fourth, the "refutation of such an accusation against God was also a refutation of accusation against his mother. God almighty would not assign an adulterous woman to be the mother of a personality of such a high level and majestic status."[4]

In his voluminous commentary on the Qur'an, al-Razi speaks of a conversation he had with some Christian theologians that sheds light on some medieval debates between Muslim and Christian theologians. In all his arguments, al-Razi seeks to prove through logic and dialectic theology the standpoint of Islamic thought: Jesus was a messenger of God, not God. He argues first that Muslims and Christians agree that God's word became Jesus and not God's essence. This was a common understanding among Eastern Christians in the twelfth century. Muslims believe that Jesus is the word of God, but not the essence of God. Al-Razi makes a second argument that if God's word became Jesus, why did it not become another individual? Third, using Aristotelian logic, al-Razi argues that because Jesus consistently showed that he was an ardent worshipper of God, the evidence of his being a worshipper of God is much stronger than the evidence of his divinity. Fourth, Jesus is either eternal or created; we cannot say he is eternal because we know that he was born.[5] Fifth, the son should share the characteristics of the father. If the son and the father are not distinguished from each other at all, they are one and the same; that is to say, the son is the father and the father is the son. This would require that the essence of God be composed of many things, compromising the oneness of the Almighty. Everything that is composed is contingent; that is, its existence is equal to its nonexistence. Accordingly, the Necessary Being (God) would have to become contingent, and this is impossible.[6] For many Christian believers, this constitutes a major challenge: to make certain that their Trinitarian claims do not negate the oneness and integrity of the Divine.

The argument that Jesus's speaking in his adulthood is a reference to his descent, as al-Razi and many other commentators of the Qur'an assert, is convincing only if the commentators interpret the verse in a way that indicates that Jesus's mission was not completed in his lifetime but will be finished when he descends. Commentators have tried to come up with additional support from the Qur'an for this subject in the Hadith. However, it is still possible to interpret the verse in many ways. Each Qur'anic verse is thought to have multiple meanings.

## The People of the Book's Belief in Him before Death

> And there shall be no one of the People of the Book left not believing
> in him before his death . . . (Qur'an 4:159)

This second verse from which classical commentators infer the descent of Jesus may convey at least two meanings. First, the People of the Book—Christians and Jews—will be unified in believing in Jesus before Jesus's death. This interpretation is valid if the Arabic pronoun *hu* (he) in the word *mawtihi* (his death) refers to Jesus. The second interpretation—each individual Christian and Jew is to believe in Jesus before his or her own death—is valid if this pronoun refers to individuals. Grammatically speaking, both interpretations are possible. It should be noted that this verse about Jesus relates to the future and that in Islam, the future is known only by God. God speaks in the Qur'an about the People of the Book's belief in Jesus. Muslim theologians have speculated about the possible meanings of the verse. Since the verse is ambiguous and Arabic words often have multiple possible meanings, especially in the Qur'an, no one can claim to have a full understanding of the verse.[7]

Medieval and contemporary commentators have found a variety of interpretations in this passage. First, who are the People of the Book? There is a consensus that when the Qur'an speaks of the People of the Book, Christians and Jews are the only people designated. However, the term may include some people of other faiths. The second and more challenging question is when and how these People of the Book will "believe in him [Jesus]." Will this belief in Jesus come before the death of every individual of the People of the Book, or will it come at the end of time when Jesus will descend? If the latter, then the verse means all People of the Book will believe in Jesus before Jesus dies. Commentators and theologians have spoken of this Qur'anic verse and responded to some of these questions. Among these is al-Maturidi, who presents an interesting method of interpretation of the verse in question. He refers to several possible viewpoints. First, the People of the Book will believe in Jesus when he descends from heaven. Second, when God sends Jesus at the time of the emergence of the Antichrist or al-Dajjal, Jesus will kill al-Dajjal, and then the remaining People

of the Book will believe in him. Under the leadership of Jesus, al-Maturidi contends, "There will be no Christians or Jews who do not become muslims [i.e.,
people who submit themselves to the will of God]."[8]

Both interpretations refer to the eschatological return of Jesus. Based on the
first interpretation, it is believed that when Jesus returns, he will stay on earth
for a while; then Christians and Jews who did not believe in him before his
descent will believe in him. This approach seems to be supported by narratives
from the time of the Prophet on how he and his companions understood the
verse. Two of the companions of the Prophet, Abu Huraira (d. 679) and Ibn 'Abbas (d. 688), presented this verse as a reference to the descent of Jesus when they
narrated the hadith in which the Prophet foretells the descent of Jesus. Many
Muslim theologians and the majority of Qur'an commentators argue that this
verse serves as a textual reference that alludes to the return of Jesus and thus
contradicts those who claim that the Qur'an does not make any mention of the
eschatological descent of Jesus.[9]

Questioning the reliability of the prophetic narrative in the previous approach, another comment seems even more interesting; it relates to a human
state of great importance to the Muslim understanding of "death agony." According to the Muslim tradition, when people are experiencing the agony of
death, they see everything in its real form: truth as truth and falsehood as falsehood. In fact, they even see their place in the afterlife, either in paradise or
in hell. Drawing upon this Islamic principle, commentators have developed a
second interpretation of the verse that contends that all Peoples of the Book
will recognize and understand the reality of the truthfulness of Jesus's message
during the final moments of their lives. Thus, the verse does not speak of the
eschatological return of Jesus; rather, it speaks of the truthfulness of Jesus's message, which Christians are believed to have greatly changed from its original
form. The verse indicates that Christians, before they die, will each recognize
the true message of Jesus.

## Jesus Is a Sign of the Hour

And surely, he [Jesus] is a sign for the Hour, so have no doubt about it
and follow me. This is the straight path. (Qur'an 43:61)

In order to understand the context in which this third Qur'anic reference to
Jesus's descent was revealed, we need to examine the occasion of this revelation.
Several narratives are informative here. One involves the discussion between

the Prophet and his people when the following verse was revealed: "Surely the story of Jesus is similar to the story of Adam" (Qur'an 3:59). That is to say, just as Adam was created without a human father or mother, Jesus was created by God and lacks a human father. After the revelation of this verse, the people of Mecca claimed: "Muhammad wants us to worship Jesus as Christians do." Then they said, "Our gods are better than Jesus." Since some of them were worshippers of angels, they claimed that angels were better than Jesus. Then the Qur'anic verse revealed that Jesus is a sign of the Final Hour. According to many Muslim theologians, this verse is a reference to Jesus's descent because the Arabic pronoun *hu*, or in English "he," refers to Jesus, who is mentioned in the story preceding the verse. The entire story presented in the Qur'an is as follows:

> When Jesus, the son of Mary, was given as an example [of an object of idol worshipping], your [Muhammad's] people cried out and said, "Are our gods best or is he?" They did not give him as an example but for the sake of argument. They are a contentious people. Jesus was no more than a servant upon whom We have bestowed our bounties and We made him an example for the children of Israel. If We will it to be so we can destroy you and replace you with angels on earth. Surely he is a sign for the Hour. Do not have any doubt about it. And [say] follow me [Muhammad]. This is the right path. Do not allow Satan to hinder you. Certainly, he is an open enemy to you. (43:57–62)

This Qur'anic story indicates that a heated debate was going on between Muhammad and the pagans of Mecca. One can see how the Prophet of Islam defended Jesus against the idol worshippers. This passage also speaks of Jesus's descent. Both early Muslims and later Muslim scholars understood this verse as a reference to the eschatological role of Jesus in Islam. For example, Ibn Jarir al-Tabari (d. 923), after mentioning that scholars have differed on the meaning of the verse, says, "And some said the pronoun 'he' refers to Jesus. Therefore, the verse means that the emergence of Jesus is one of the signs by which the coming of the Hour is known. That is because Jesus's emergence is one of its signs. His descent on earth is evidence of the transient nature of the world and the coming of the afterlife." Al-Tabari reports that eleven different companions of the Prophet understood the verse as a reference to the descent of Jesus.[10] Since the term "emergence," or the Arabic *khuruj*, replaces the term "descent," or *nuzul*, in this narrative, it can be argued that early Muslims were not thinking of the descent of Jesus in a literal way; that is, they did not believe Jesus's body would descend from the sky.

The term "emergence" as it occurs in some early Islamic sources has a broader connotation. The use of the term in such an early period of Islam strengthens the argument of those who claim that Jesus's descent is allegorical and not the literal descent of an individual from the sky. It is noteworthy that in this verse the phrase that refers to Jesus as a sign has been recited in three variations. The first, *la 'ilmun*, refers to the fact that he is the knowledge of the Final Hour; that is, by Jesus the knowledge of the Hour is acquired. In other words, it is believed that when Jesus comes, people will know that it is time for the Hour. The second, *la 'alamun*, points to his being a sign of the Hour, and the third, *la dhikrun*, means that he is a reminder of the Hour.[11] In three recitations, the meaning essentially remains the same with regard to Jesus's connection to the Final Hour.

This particular verse is one of the most direct references to the eschatological descent of Jesus in the Qur'an because the Final Hour and Jesus are connected in the verse. Many Muslim theologians and commentators on the Qur'an have offered this verse as a textual reference to the descent of Jesus.[12] It should be noted that according to the rules of Arabic grammar, the pronoun *hu* can refer to both human beings and inanimate objects. Interpreting the Qur'anic verse in this way is not violence to the text. Thus, there is no obstacle to considering Jesus as the point of reference for the pronoun in question. Many companions of the Prophet understood the verse in this way. In the same context, al-Qurtubi, another prominent commentator, refers to a narration from 'Abdullah bin 'Abbas, one of the most knowledgeable companions of the Prophet (known as "the ocean of knowledge" in the Islamic community), in which he reports the Prophet's meeting with Jesus during his night journey, the Mi'raj:

> During his night journey, or his ascension to heaven, the Prophet met with Abraham, Moses, and Jesus. They discussed among themselves the matter of the Hour. They asked Abraham about the Hour and Abraham had no knowledge of it. Then they asked Moses; Moses also had no knowledge of it. Then the conversation came to Jesus, the son of Mary, and Jesus said, "I have been given some duties prior to its happening, but as for the exact time of the Hour, no one knows except God." Then he mentioned the emergence of the Antichrist. He said, "I will return and kill him."[13]

Muslim theologians such as al-Zamakhshari (d. 1144) and al-Razi (d. 1209), two leading commentators of the Qur'an, and al-Suyuti (d.1505), a prolific Egyptian Muslim scholar, have presented verse 43:61 from the Qur'an as textual proof of the eschatological descent of Jesus. In their commentaries on the verse, all three authors refer the descent of Jesus as a sign for the coming of the Hour. Although individual instances of Islamic scholars questioning the soundness of these apocalyptic prophecies can be found, their accuracy was generally accepted until the twentieth century, when critical reflection on theological themes and their sources began in earnest among Islamic scholars. This trend, which was not limited to the Islamic world, is the natural result of a growing dependence on reason rather than a blind acceptance of religious principles. The case of the descent of Jesus is no exception. Muslim scholars want to find some logical explanation for this Islamic theological theme.

In parts of the Islamic world, such as Egypt and Turkey, the debate over Qur'anic references to Jesus's descent is still quite heated. Many scholars of contemporary Islamic theology have become involved in these ongoing debates. Giving space to all the current debates on Jesus's descent is beyond the scope of this work. As an example of the nature of the debates among Muslim theologians, here I will refer only to three of them: the influential Egyptian jurist and theologian Rashid Rida (d. 1935); the Ottoman scholar, theologian, and a deputy director of the Bab-i Meşihat, the highest religious institution of the Ottoman Empire, Muhammad Zahid al-Kawthari (d.1951); and the famous grand mufti Mahmud Shaltout (d. 1963). Later in this chapter I will elaborate on the views of some other scholars and theologians, such as Bediüzzaman Said Nursi (d. 1960), an Islamic scholar and thinker from Turkey, and Mustafa al-Maraghi (d. 1945), a commentator of the Qur'an from Egypt.

Neither Rida nor Shaltout accept the verses discussed in this section as textual references to either Jesus's ascension or his descent. Rida summarizes his view as follows: "The summary of the story is that there is no clear dogma in the Qur'an with regard to the ascension of Jesus. . . . And there is no clear dogma stating that Jesus will descend from heaven."[14] With this, Rida issues a fatwa, a religious decree, supporting the view that negates the Qur'anic source for the descent of Jesus. He refers to the influence of Christianity in this regard. This does not mean that both scholars deny the descent of Jesus in Islamic theology. As we shall discuss, they incline toward an alternative approach. They are clear that the Qur'an does not speak of the descent of Jesus, although many sayings of the prophet have been narrated in this regard. Shaltout is more precise in his claim.

Examining the fiery debate between two prominent scholars of Islamic theology in Egypt, al-Kawthari and Shaltout is useful. The debate about the passage from verse 43:61 ("And surely, he [Jesus] is a sign for the Hour, so have no doubt about it and follow me. This is the straight path") is a good example of intra-Muslim discussion on Jesus's eschatological role. Shaltout speaks of three possible interpretations of this verse and then he gives his own preference. His preferred interpretation is that Jesus's miraculous birth is a sign indicating the power of God to bring the hereafter. While this is a possible interpretation, when one looks at the flow of the Qur'anic narrative, there is almost no mention of the hereafter and the resurrection of human beings at the Final Hour. Instead, it is all about the debate between the Prophet of Islam and the idol worshippers of Mecca concerning Jesus. Therefore, although it is accurate to say that Jesus's miraculous birth provides evidence of the bringing of the hereafter, that is not what is primarily understood from the verse. Shaltout was most likely led to this approach by the literalist view of many of his contemporaries that would go against the use of reason. For him, instead of accepting such an irrational view of the descent of Jesus, it would be more reasonable to interpret this type of Qur'anic verse in a different way.

According to Shaltout, "Surely the fact that the verse contains these three possible meanings . . . is enough to show that the verse is not a 'certain dogma' on the descent of Jesus. As for us, we prefer the view that Jesus's creation without a father is a proof of the coming of the hour."[15] Shaltout supports his view with various arguments. He believes that the birth of Jesus from a virgin mother is a sign of the Final Hour rather than a sign of Jesus's descent. Shaltout contends that this verse addresses those who deny the hereafter and find it strange, namely the people of Mecca. Accordingly, by mentioning Jesus as a sign of the Hour, the Qur'an indicates that the miraculous birth of Jesus shows the power of God and should convince the unbelievers that such a divine power is able to bring about the hereafter. Jesus is proof of God's power to bring about the afterlife.[16] This approach would fit well if the debate between the Prophet and a group of the people of Mecca centered on the possibility of resurrection. However, according to the sources on the occasion of the revelation of this verse, the debate was about Jesus, not the hereafter.

Shaltout is insistent. He states, "There is no doubt that a sincere and balanced reader . . . will be of the opinion that there is nothing in the literal meaning of the Qur'an that attests to the descent of Jesus or his ascension, either at the level of certainty that informs the creed, the deniers of which are unbelievers, or even at the level of a strong assumption (*ghalabat al-zann*), as some claim."[17]

The reader may wonder why Muslim theologians are so concerned about whether the theme of Jesus's descent—or any other theme, for that matter—is present in the Qur'an or not. The Qur'an is the main source of Islamic theology. Anything that takes place in the Qur'an becomes a part of faith and all

Muslims must believe it. Intentionally denying anything in the Qur'an drives an individual outside the pale of Islam. If something is ambiguous, it needs interpretation, but one cannot reject it or deny it. Hence, if the descent of Jesus is clearly mentioned in the Qur'an, then the deniers of the return of Jesus will be considered outside the pale of Islam. Therefore, given its grave theological consequence, it is an important point of debate among Muslim theologians.

In an article written in English and published in *Al-Azhar Magazine*, the main journal of Al-Azhar University, Shaltout speaks of the situation of Muslims who deny the ascension and the descent of Jesus from a theological point of view and of whether such rejection puts one outside the pale of Islam. Here Shaltout concludes, "It is obvious, therefore, that Jesus was exalted in God's presence, and because the Arabic word *rafaʿ* is mentioned in the verse in question after the word death, it means the spiritual exaltation of Jesus, not the elevation of his body to heaven."[18]

Furthermore, if the descent of Jesus is accepted as part of clear Qur'anic verses, it becomes an essential principle of Islamic theology. No one can argue about the fact that the persona of Jesus is as an essential part of Islamic theology, given the many direct references to him and his message in the Qur'an. However, when it comes to his descent, the case is different. Is the belief in the descent of Jesus at the end of time a principle of Islamic theology or a secondary belief in Islam? For Shaltout and the scholars who follow his line of thought, it is a secondary issue of Islamic faith and is not one of the principles of Islamic theology. Thus, another question arises: what is the state of Muslims who deny it?

Shaltout and other theologians have spoken of the situation of those Muslims who reject Jesus's ascension to heaven and deny his return at the end of time. Shaltout does not see a theological problem with such a denial and considers those people to still be Muslims because such a rejection does not entail the rejection of a clear verse of the Qur'an. "The denial of the notion that Jesus was raised to heaven bodily where he is alive now and wherefrom he will fly to earth when the world comes near its end does not place a Muslim outside of the pale of Islam or faith. Such a denial does not justify the verdict of apostasy passed against those who question the dogma. . . . The rejection of this notion does not imply a rejection of any fundamental principle of Islam."[19]

Al-Kawthari, on the other hand, accuses Shaltout of lacking knowledge of the Qur'an, and he diametrically opposes him. Following earlier theologians, he opines that the verse in question (43:61) refers to the descent of Jesus as a sign of the Hour and maintains that the verse is clear enough. According to al-Kawthari, the majority of the commentators on the Qur'an find a reference to

Jesus in this verse. Al-Kawthari's approach seems more linguistic, etymological, and contextual. According to him, the grammatical context indicates that the Arabic pronoun *hu* refers to Jesus, whose story precedes the verse. In Arabic grammar, when a pronoun comes after several names, it refers to the closest name in the sentence. There is no doubt that in this particular verse the closest name is Jesus since the entire story is about him. This is why the majority of Qur'anic commentators have understood that the pronoun in question refers to Jesus and that "Jesus is the sign of the Hour" (43:61).

The issue has occupied the minds of other people as well. For instance, the question was posed to Rashid Rida: "Did Jesus rise to heaven only spiritually, or bodily and spiritually? And is Jesus's descent at the end of time and his ruling according to Islamic law referenced in the Qur'an and the reliable sayings of the Prophet? Inform us, may God benefit us with your knowledge." Rida was asked to give a fatwa on the subject. In response to this question, Rida says, "As for the rise [*su'ud*] of Jesus to heaven, there has been no mention of such a term, but instead the term 'ascension' [*rafa'*] is mentioned in the Qur'an. 'They did not kill him for sure, but God ascended him to Himself' (Qur'an 4:158)." Rida mentions another Qur'anic verse related to the ascension of another prophet, Enoch, or Idris. The verse says: "And We ascended him [Enoch] to a lofty place" (19:57). According to Rida, this verse does not necessitate a bodily ascension.

Despite all these debates, generally speaking, both Sunnis and Shi'ites, based on a consensus of theologians, particular sayings of the Prophet, and indications in the Qur'an, believe that Jesus did not die on the cross but was raised to heaven and is still alive. The consensus is that his enemies mistook someone else for him. Most Muslims believe that Jesus will eventually die a normal death after his descent or Second Coming because no one can have eternal life on earth. The Qur'an states that "every soul will taste death," and Jesus is not an exception (3:185, 21:35, 29:57). Like all other prophets of God, he will then be resurrected and live in paradise eternally.

## Muhammad Does Not Speak Out of His Own Fancy

He [Muhammad] does not speak out of his own fancy. It is nothing
but an inspired revelation. (Qur'an 53:4–5)

In addition to the three verses directly related to Jesus, this fourth passage is believed to refer to Jesus's messianic role, given Muhammad's truthfulness. There are a number of these indirect verses including 61:9 on the dominance of "true religion"; however, I will limit myself to this one. The literal meaning is that Muhammad does not speak in vain. Whatever he speaks is a direct revelation from God (that is, the Qur'an) or an indirect revelation (that is, the divinely inspired sayings of the Prophet, the Hadith).

Theologically speaking, there is a difference between revelation and inspiration. Revelation comes only to the Prophet from God through the angel Gabriel. Inspiration, however, comes from God to the hearts of prophets, saints, and pious people. The verse clearly states that if a statement related to the Prophet of Islam has a reliable chain of narration, that statement is true. Therefore, if the hadith that will be discussed in the following chapters are proven to be reliable and sound as far as their relationship to the Prophet is concerned, that means the Prophet has spoken the truth about the coming of Jesus.

## Reconciling Different Approaches to Jesus's Descent

Scholars have debated whether indirect references are valid for the descent of Jesus. Those who consider these indirect references to be valid argue, as we shall discuss in the following chapter, that the Prophet of Islam on different occasions emphatically spoke of Jesus and his eschatological role, including his descent. Muhammad's companions have retold his various sayings. The Prophet, some scholars contend, would not mention the descent of Jesus without receiving either revelation or inspiration from God: the Qur'an clearly states, "He does not speak in vain" (53:4).

The verses discussed in this chapter have served as textual references for the view of the majority of the Qur'an's commentators who share the view of mainstream theologians. However, some modern scholars and theologians opine that all the proofs mentioned earlier regarding the descent of Jesus are contradicted by the literal meaning of the verses. These scholars and theologians argue that the earlier commentators were motivated to find such a meaning in the verses out of a desire to make sure that there is no conflict between Qur'anic verses and the sayings of the Prophet pertaining to the descent of Jesus. Therefore, Shaltout contends that there is no evidence from either the Qur'an or the sayings of the Prophet on the descent of Jesus.[20]

One can, however, reconcile these two approaches. In fact, one can see why some contemporary Muslim scholars and theologians deny the descent of Jesus in Islam, in spite of allusions in the Qur'an and clear references in many Hadith sources. It seems that many contemporary scholars view the interpretation of the majority of Muslims, which is generally inclined toward a literal understanding of Jesus's descent, as unreasonable and therefore against general Islamic principles. If a theme becomes the object of faith, it has to be verified by reason and, at the least, reason should not find it impossible. If we take the descent of Jesus literally, as some scholars do, this entails something that is rationally impossible. There is no record of a person who came from the sky in front of the eyes of everyone. Unless we open the door for allegorical interpretation, this impossibility will continue. Therefore, many modern scholars rightly criticize the account of Jesus's descent for describing the coming of a physical person from heaven, which seems to be illogical. Furthermore, the images conceived of by the literalists do not seem compatible, in principle, with the teachings of the Qur'an. The literalists ground their view in the omnipotence of God. That is to say, they believe that because God is all powerful, He can bring the body of an individual, namely Jesus, down from heaven. The problem with the literalist approach is that it neglects the wisdom of God that deals with matters in this world. Yes, all Muslims accept this Qur'anic verse about the power of God: "The possession of heaven and earth belongs to God. He is the Giver of life and death. He is able to do all things" (57:2). However, despite the general acceptance of the unlimited power of God, theologically speaking, God does not exercise His power to compel people to believe because this would deny human free choice. Free will is an essential principle of accountability. To compel people to believe is to negate free will, which is incompatible with the principle of Islamic theology.

Many theologians who agree on the descent of Jesus differ as to the form of his descent. The question becomes one about the form in which Jesus will descend. Will the descent of Jesus from heaven be physical *and* in spirit or only in spirit? The Arabic word *nuzul* (descent) does not necessarily refer to material descent. In Qur'anic language, the word *nuzul*, or "sending down," has various meanings and can refer to the distribution of God's bounty, as in "God sent down for you eight cattle in pairs" (39:6). Here the phrase "sent down" means God sent His mercy. Accepting the literal meaning would be to believe that animals descend from heaven. This is a misunderstanding of the verse; at least according to the current science. Therefore, this verse should be understood in a figurative way. The word *nuzul* should be understood metaphorically. Moreover, in some sayings of the Prophet we see the same word related to God: "God descends every night to the lowest heaven when the last one-third of the night is left and says: 'Whosoever supplicates to Me, I will respond to him. Whosoever asks Me, I will answer him. Whosoever asks for forgiveness, I will forgive him.'"[21] Theologians agree that the divine descent here is not material.

Therefore, it can be argued that the descent of Jesus as narrated by the Prophet can be understood as a spiritual descent and not necessarily a physical one. Accordingly, Jesus's descent from the heavens can imply that God will send him out of mercy. Such a descent will strengthen the spiritual lives of people.

This idea informs another line of thought. According to this interpretation, the descent leads to the purifying of Christianity and its return to the original message of Jesus. The spiritual leaders of Christianity, who are close to Jesus in a spiritual sense, will lead this purification. Although this approach does not reject the possibility of Jesus's physical return, Jesus, because of his spiritual strength and angelic nature, can come down from heaven and go back without being noticed, in the same way the angels do.

The important point is Jesus's spirituality will be seen as in sync with Islamic spirituality. Then the true religion that comes from the convergence of Islam and Christianity will be powerful. Accordingly, the materialistic philosophies will be too weak to fight the true religion. This view is presented by the famous Islamic scholar Bediüzzaman Said Nursi and to a certain extent by Siddiq Hasan Khan (d. 1890) and modern Egyptian scholars and reformers such as Muhammad Abduh (d. 1905) and Mustafa al-Maraghi. For example, al-Maraghi, who is also a contemporary commentator on the Qur'an, refers to the descent of Jesus in a more spiritual way. He says that the descent of Jesus is "the domination of his spirit and the mystery of his message over humanity in order that men may live by the inner meaning of the law [shari'a] without being bound by its outer shell."[22] Like many figures of Islamic spirituality, al-Maraghi also thinks that too much attachment to the legalistic aspect of religion goes against the teachings of Islam. When Muslims become too legalistic and abandon the spiritual dimension of religion, there will be a great need for the renewal of religion. Therefore, the Prophet gives good news that the descent of Jesus will contribute to the strength of spirituality, not only among Muslims but worldwide.

Islamic scholars such as Said Nursi and al-Maraghi respond to the need of members of the Islamic community who are perplexed by prophetic statements on Jesus's descent and other end-time events. Some Muslims believe that denying those sayings of the Prophet will negatively impact their faith, while accepting them will go against their reason. Nursi responds to this group of Muslims. His goal is to respond to the spoken and unspoken questions of these perplexed Muslims and to prove that sayings of the prophet on Jesus's descent are absolutely rational. He is confident that the descent of Jesus is both logical and even necessary.

Said Nursi, who expressed his view much earlier than Mustafa al-Maraghi did, emphasizes cooperation between Muslims and Christians. He refers to a spiritual group of devout Christians known in Turkish as Isevi Müslümanlar, or followers of Jesus who are Muslims. They are known as Christians, but in reality they are Muslims in the sight of God. This interpretive approach is as an important step to Muslim-Christian dialogue in our time. The interpretations of the descent of Jesus can be seen as a powerful occasion for a dialogue between members of Abraham's family in general and between Muslims and Christians in particular.

A historical event cited in the Qur'an sheds light on an early alliance between Christians and Muslims. One understands from the chapter of Romans in the Qur'an (30:1–5) that Muslims hoped for a Christian victory against the pagan Persians in the struggle between the Byzantine and Persian Empires. The Qur'an very clearly states that the Muslims of Mecca who were supporters of the Christians against the Persians would rejoice in that victory because Muslims consider Christians and Jews to be the People of the Book. The Qur'an gives them certain privileges in comparison with the adherents of other religions. According to the Qur'anic teaching about war between a country of the People of the Book and a country that denies God, for example, the Qur'anic way of thinking must be to support the People of the Book against the deniers of God. Therefore, Muslims have supported Christians and Jews against idol worshippers or communist regimes.

Jesus and his descent as an important element of Islamic theological discourse can be a powerful factor in engaging dialogue between Muslims and Christians. With more than one and a half billion adherents, Islam is the second-largest religion in the world, exceeded only by Christianity. This shows the importance and urgency of dialogue between Muslims and Christians, a relationship essential for a peaceful world.[23] As well-known Turkish commentator Muhammed Hamdi Yazir (d. 1942) suggests, peace can be restored by the spirits of Jesus and Muhammad, hand in hand.

Considering the references from the Holy Book of Islam discussed in this chapter, one can argue that the Qur'anic verses about Jesus's death and descent are not very clear, but the possibility of an allusion to the descent of Jesus in the Qur'an cannot easily be denied. Many verses at least hint at the eschatological role of Jesus. It is clear that Jesus's "death" in the Qur'an is unique, because it states that his opponents could not kill him or crucify him. Instead, God caused Jesus to die and raised him to Himself. Jesus's death (3:55 and 4:159) was different from a regular human death. Such an emphasis on God's direct involvement in Jesus's death sets it apart.

# THREE

# Islamic Eschatology
# and Jesus as a Sign of the Hour

Jesus is an important figure in Islam's apocalyptic eschatology. This chapter situates the knowledge of future events in Islamic theology and the place of Jesus among these eschatological events as one of the signs of the Final Hour of human history foretold by the Prophet of Islam. It is important to examine the eschatological scenarios in which Jesus figures so prominently in order to understand the "eschatological Jesus" within Islam.

## The Final Hour

From an Islamic theological perspective, there will eventually be an end to this worldly life. The Qur'an does not give a specific time for this end and is always clear that the knowledge of it belongs only to God: "The knowledge of the Hour is with Him" (31:34). But throughout the history of Islam, Muslims have been curious about the signs of the end, which include the signs of the day of resurrection when all people will face judgment. Humankind's curiosity about the future has contributed to a proliferation of Islamic literature about the coming of the Final Hour and things related to it. According to the Hadith, the signs are numerous. Geological, moral, social, and cosmic signs are thought to mark the end. Hadith sources speak of the erosion of the earth, the spread of immorality, the loss of trust among people, and the administration of unjust rulers as some signs of the Hour. There are references to the emergence of the Antichrist and the rising of the sun from the west, the final sign.

Collections of the sayings of the Prophet of Islam have dedicated chapters to these signs. The signs are categorized as "minor" and "major." Minor signs include the loss of truthfulness and trust, the spread of adultery, and the emergence of many false messiahs or liars. The emergence of the Antichrist, the descent of Jesus, and the rising of the sun in the west are among the major signs that indicate the imminence of the Final Hour. According to the Islamic escha-tological scenario, after the occurrence of the final sign, the rising of the sun in the west, the archangel Israfil, or Seraphiel, will sound the great trumpet. Israfil is one of the four archangels in Islam, alongside Jabra'il (Gabriel), 'Azra'il (the angel of death), and Micha'il. At the trumpet's sound, according to the Qur'anic description, God will bring the order of this world to an end through a mighty earthquake.[1] The celestial bodies will crash into one another, the earth will be replaced with a different plane, and every living creature will die. God's final gift to believers will be a natural death that will spare them from witnessing this last horrible moment.

According to the Islamic eschatological literature, for unbelievers, living and witnessing this last horrific moment will be their painful experience before death. After the destruction of earth, according to the divine plan and under the control of the divine, the archangel Seraphiel will sound the second blow. According to Islamic theology, in that moment all people, "good" and "bad," will be resurrected both in body and spirit (Qur'an 18:99, 36:51). In Islamic cosmology, since God does everything through Divine fiat, the resurrection of all human beings is as easy as one individual's resurrection: "Your creation and your resurrection are like a single soul," (Qur'an 31:28). This verse refers to the great power demonstrated by God in this moment of resurrection

Although the Qur'an and Hadith explicitly mention the afterlife and human-ity's ultimate fates are known, the sequence of related events and the manner of their occurrences are ambiguous. However, both classical and contempo-rary Muslim theologians have deduced various visions of the end of time from verses of the Qur'an and the sayings of the Prophet. Many verses of the Qur'an note the imminence of the Final Hour, and the Qur'an uses a variety of expres-sions to refer to it.

From both the Qur'an and Hadith, it is clear that the Prophet of Islam was often asked to reveal the exact time of the Final Hour.[2] The question was posed sometimes out of simple curiosity and sometimes as a challenge. The Prophet had a variety of responses to this question. On one occasion when a questioner asked about the time of the Final Hour, instead of mentioning the exact time, the Prophet said, "When honesty is lost, then wait for the Hour." His questioner rejoined, "And how will it be lost?" The Prophet answered, "When power comes into the hands of the unfit, then wait for the Hour."[3]

On another occasion a man asked the Prophet, "When is the Hour?" The Prophet did not mention the signs but instead answered him, "What have you done to prepare for it?" The man said, "I haven't prepared for it with many prayers, or fasting, or charity. But I love God and God's messenger." The Prophet said in response, "You will be with those you love."[4]

On another occasion some Bedouins came to the Prophet and asked him to reveal the exact time of the Final Hour. The Prophet, pointing to the youngest in the group, said, "Perhaps many of you will see your final hour before this young man dies."[5] A conversation occurred between the Prophet and some of his companions a month before his death. The Prophet said, "You are asking me about the Hour. The knowledge of it belongs to God, the Almighty. By my God, no soul that breathes today will live more than a hundred years."[6] Here again the Prophet speaks of *individual* eschatology. Consistently, though his companions were anxious about the end, thinking they would see the end of the world in their lifetime, the Prophet was ambiguous. He never mentioned the time of the Hour; he would only tell them about some of its signs.

The Prophet's most common response to this question was that the knowledge of the Final Hour is only with God, that the eschaton (the end time) is among the matters related to *al-ghayb*, or the realm of the unseen (Qur'an 33:63–68). This is similar to what Jesus said in the Gospel of Matthew, where he states that no one except God knows about that day, not even the angels, not even himself (Matt. 24:36). The Qur'an says, "To God belongs the keys of the unseen [*al-ghayb*]; no one knows except God" (6:59). The prophets and saints learn divine secrets only when they receive a special revelation or inspiration. Therefore, in Islamic theology, if God does not tell Muhammad, even he will not know the exact time of the Final Hour. In a well-known hadith, Gabriel visits the Prophet and asks him a series of questions, including one about the time of the Final Hour. He answers all but the eschatological question. "In regard to that," he is said to have answered, "the questioned [the Prophet] has no more knowledge than the questioner [the angel Gabriel]."[7]

In Islamic theology, five things are known only to God. Our understanding of these five unknowns, the *mughayyabat khamsa*, originates in the following verse: "With God is the knowledge of the Hour; God sends down the rain; God knows what is in the wombs; no soul knows what will happen to it tomorrow; and no soul knows in what land it will die. God is the most knowing and the most aware" (Qur'an 31:34). Since the exact time of the Final Hour cannot be known, Islamic sources contain only certain portents to indicate its imminence.

It is important to remember that the imminence of the Final Hour is relative. In Islamic cosmology, our planet is considered a living creature, appointed by God to serve humans and other creatures for a certain period of time. Eventually it will die, as does every other living being. If modern science were able to prove that the sun will continue to burn for several billion years until it exhausts its fuel supply, Muslim theologians would support these findings. Such findings would simply be scientific evidence for the Muslim belief that God has declared a particular time for the death of the earth. This particular time may be measured in seconds, minutes, hours, days, weeks, months, years, centuries, millennia, or even light years. These finite units of time indicate only that there is an end that will eventually come. We measure what is finite. From an Islamic theological perspective, there is no disagreement between science and Qur'anic eschatology.

For there to be a Qur'anic confirmation of scientific discoveries and theories, the science must have moved past hypothesis. Islam presents the realm of nature and the Qur'an as two divine books: the book of the universe is the created book of God and the Qur'an is the revealed book of God. The two books are believed to confirm each other. If one finds apparent conflict between the two, it is because of a lack of understanding or information on the part of scholars or theologians. Therefore, the Qur'anic verse "perhaps the Hour is near" (42:17) should be interpreted from the perspective of what we know through scientific discoveries about the age of the earth. One also has to understand the relativity of the word "near." What is near to a fly is not near to a human. Likewise, what is near to a human is not near for the universe. Hence, even if the Hour is "near," the time of its coming is still not known.

## Islamic Theology of Jesus as a Sign of the Hour

Based on some Qur'anic verses and some sayings of the Prophet, Muslim theologians have developed a theology of the portents of the Final Hour. This has become an important genre in Islamic eschatological literature. Eschatology constitutes one of the three most important themes of Islamic theology, alongside divinity and prophethood. The place of Jesus in Islam is developed in two of these. As one of the great messengers of God, he is a part of the Islamic theology of prophethood, and as one of the signs of the Final Hour whose descent is foretold by Muhammad, he is part of Islamic eschatology. Jesus is a sign and a reminder of the Day of Judgment. While certain eschatological themes, such as judgment day, paradise, and hell are thoroughly described, signs of the Final Hour are mentioned in the Qur'an only briefly.[8]

The Qur'an does speak of the occurrence of a doomsday. It describes the fall of the stars and the darkened sun, physical events that will occur on the final day, but unlike Hadith literature and other classic apocalyptic texts that reveal the signs of the eschaton in the form of a prophetic vision, the Qur'an is concise when it speaks of the signs of the Final Hour. In fact, there is only one instance in the Qur'an of the word *ashrat*, which can be translated as signs or portents (of the Final Hour). That verse says that the signs of the Hour have already come: "They are awaiting nothing but the sudden coming of the [Final] Hour. In fact its signs have already come" (47:18). One possible meaning of "its signs have already come" is the coming of the Prophet of Islam himself. Muhammad, who is considered the "seal of the prophets," (Qur'an 33:40) regards his presence as a sign of the Hour. "The Hour and I are like these two," he says, displaying two fingers on his hand and the closeness between them.[9] Because of these types of statements and the emphasis on eschatology in Islam, some authors have suggested that Islam originated as an apocalyptic movement.[10] It seems that such a suggestion is related directly to the finality of the Prophet of Islam as the last prophet. Theologically speaking, there will be no prophet after Muhammad and no revelation after the Qur'an. Besides this verse and one to be discussed later which presents Jesus as the sign of the Hour (43:61), any references in the Qur'an to signs of the Hour are ambiguous.

In contrast, many hadith contain references to the signs of the Final Hour. The Prophet, warning his companions about the imminence of the Final Hour, speaks of certain social and cosmic events that will indicate the nearness of its coming. The Islamic understanding of the signs of the Hour is generally based on references in the Qur'an and the Hadith, which do not take the form of classic apocalyptic literature as represented by the Book of Daniel or the Book of Revelation. Although these two books are among the major sources of their eschatological ideas, one should note that there is more than one eschatological framework in both the Jewish and Christian traditions.[11]

Hadith literature gives detailed accounts of the signs of the end of time. However, the time when the events are to occur, the places where they will occur, and the ways in which they will occur often conflict. In many cases the community of Islam was perplexed by the mystery of the eschatology detailed in the body of the Hadith. For example, the famous Muslim apocalyptic author Nu'aym bin Hammad (d. 843) dedicates the entirety of his book *Kitab al-Fitan* (*The Book of Trials*) to the trials that will happen before the Final Hour and how believers might be protected from them. Interpreting some political changes in the history of Islam among the signs of the Hour, he starts with the end of the Umayyad dynasty, then continues with the beginning of the Abbasid dynasty, the emergence of al-Sufyani (a figure of evil like the Antichrist but less powerful), and al-Sufyani's conflict with the Mahdi (the Islamic messianic figure). Ibn Hammad then tells of the emergence of the Antichrist and the descent of Jesus, who will come down from heaven to struggle against the Antichrist and defeat him. It is noteworthy that in this early book the themes related to end-time events are explored in such a detailed way.

Some eschatological narratives came from Jewish and Christian converts to early Islam, including the Yemenite rabbi Kaʻb al-Ahbar (d. 652), who converted to Islam after the death of the Prophet, and Wahb bin Munabbih (d. 732), the famous historian known as the narrator of the legends of early nations. The detailed segments of these narratives cast doubt on their reliability, as they show evidence of being influenced by Jewish and Christian sources, and it is hard to imagine that the Prophet would have spoken in so much detail about future events.[12] The essence of Ibn Hammad's narrative can be found in other more reliable Hadith sources, but many of Ibn Hammad's details are not present.

Because of ambiguity, confusion, and conflicting stories, some Muslim theologians and scholars have denied the reliability of the Hadith on the matter of the signs of the Hour. Others have accepted these narratives as containing literal truth and have attempted to solve these puzzles of Islamic apocalyptic literature.

One of the prominent companions of the Prophet said that the Prophet told his companions all the things that would happen until the end of time, but they forgot most of them. They would remember the events that the Prophet foretold only when they encountered them in their lives. These kinds of prophetic sayings in regard to end-time events are not apocalyptic in the classical sense, but from an Islamic theological perspective they are considered to be the Prophet's accurate visions of certain future events, and thus these visions are among the miracles of the Prophet, showing the truthfulness of his prophethood. Some of these events may have been shown to the Prophet in a veiled way and seem not to have come to pass. If he is not told by God, even the Prophet does not know the future. However, God on occasion shows His messenger some future events and the Prophet informs his community. Some events that the Prophet foretold have come to pass, such as his foretelling that his grandson Hasan bin ʻAli (d. 669) would be a peacemaker between two large rival groups, the establishment of the Abbasid Caliphate, and the conquest of Constantinople. Many contend that the fulfillment of his prophecies evidence his prophethood.[13]

Some of the Prophet's companions also had visions of the events preceding the eschaton, although their visions were not necessarily as accurate as the Prophet's. The visions of his companions are to be understood as the visions of saints or other spiritual personages, not as divine revelation. Tamim al-Dari (d.

660), an enigmatic companion of the Prophet and a convert from Christianity to Islam, told the Prophet of a vision he had. The Prophet considered it to be important, and he recounted it from the pulpit. The vision is a considerably detailed account of the Antichrist, his informant animal, known as Jassasa, and other signs of the Final Hour. Despite the fact that this vision is found in reliable Hadith sources, some Muslim scholars find details of it and conflicting aspects of the narration problematic. This vision and all other references to the signs of the Hour are contained in the various collections of the sayings of the Prophet generally within the following sections: *Alamat al-Sa'a* [The Signs of the Hour], *Alamat al-Qiyama* [The Signs of the Day of Resurrection], and *Al-Fitan* [The Trials].

The events that the Prophet of Islam foretold and that precede the Final Hour can be roughly divided into three categories, according to when they will occur:

1. The events that occurred immediately after the time of the Prophet, such as the civil war between Muslims. The Prophet even praised his grandson Hasan bin 'Ali because he would make peace between the two groups. In fact, Hasan did make peace between the two groups by stepping down from his position as the caliph.[14]

2. The events that occurred after a considerable period of time. The Mongol invasion of the Islamic world in the thirteenth century was one such event. The Prophet said, "It is from the signs of the Hour that you will fight a nation that wear sandals of hair. Again, it is from the signs of the Hour that you will fight a nation with large faces like shining shields."[15] It is believed that with this description the Prophet was referring to the Mongols, who invaded the Islamic world and destroyed many institutions, particularly libraries, greatly damaging the Islamic heritage.

3. The events that will occur immediately before the Final Hour. These include the descent of Jesus, the emergence of the Antichrist, and the rising of the sun in the west. The Prophet directly says, "The Hour will not come until the Sun rises from the west."[16] Muslims understand this as the so-called cosmic eschatology. Like many branches of Christianity, Islam also envisions both an individual eschatology and a cosmic eschatology, an end for the life of every individual and an end for our planet and other celestial bodies. In the Islamic eschatological scenario, Jesus returns before the cosmic eschaton.

In their discussions of the eschaton, Muslim theologians have been primarily concerned with the major signs of the Final Hour. One portent of this final moment is expressed in the Qur'anic verse "The Hour is near, and the moon is split" (54:1). This verse has been interpreted to mean that the splitting of the moon is a sign of the nearness of the Final Hour.[17] According to the Islamic vision of eschatology, when the moon splits and the stars fall, the earth will be changed and the Day of Judgment will have arrived.

The signs of the Hour can also be categorized according to their magnitude. There are two groups of events, the *'alamat al-sughra* (minor signs) and the *'alamat al-kubra* (major signs). The minor signs relate to the decrease of spirituality and the spread of corruption on the earth. The Hadith speak, for instance, of the decrease of knowledge, the spread of adultery, fornication in common places, famine, wars, fires, small earthquakes, the emergence of liars or pseudo-messiahs, and an increase in the number of murders.[18]

The major signs are cosmic in nature. There are ten, according to the hadith of Hudhayfa bin Aseed, a prominent companion of the Prophet. They are as follows:

1. Smoke covering the land
2. The emergence of the Antichrist
3. The emergence of al-Dabba, the Beast
4. The rising of the sun in the west
5. The descent of Jesus
6. The emergence of Gog and Magog
7. The disappearance of land in the east
8. The disappearance of land in the west
9. The disappearance of land in the Arabian peninsula
10. The emergence of fire from the south to bring the people into the final gathering place[19]

This hadith of Hudhayfa bin Aseed is a major reference in Islamic theology for the signs of the Final Hour. It should be noted that this list does not imply that these signs will occur consecutively or literally. Muslims believe that five of these signs will signal that the time of the Hour is imminent: the emergence of the Antichrist; the descent of Jesus; the emergence of the Beast; the emergence of Gog and Magog; and finally the rising of the sun in the west. It is understood from the overall tone of the hadith that the Prophet spoke of Jesus's descent as good news and as fulfillment of hope for Muslims against the horrific actions of the Antichrist.

Should these prophetic predictions be taken literally? Muslims have no consensus about how to understand these sayings of the Prophet. Some have taken all of these signs literally, including the descent of Jesus, while others have either denied the reliability of these sources or interpreted them allegorically. The literalist approach has given no attention to the allegorical nature of the prophetic statements. Wahabbism generally takes the Hadith literature literally, and eschatology is no exception. They oppose any kind of interpretation. However, some major schools of thought in Islam are open to interpretation. It should be noted that the Prophet often spoke in allegorical and metaphorical language when explaining future events. Metaphorical language is part of the art of eloquence of Arabic. In the art of metaphor, it is possible to describe human beings with certain nonhuman characteristics. Thus, some events of the signs of the Hour that are mentioned in the body of the Hadith should not necessarily be taken literally, although many Muslim scholars and theologians have done so.

Are these apocalyptic narratives fabricated and wrongly attributed to the Prophet? There are two ways to evaluate these kinds of hadith. One way is to deny that the Prophet said them because the Prophet would not say something so nonsensical. Some modern Muslim philosophers have preferred this method. The other way is to accept them with interpretation and through the perspective of Hadith criticism. Using the methodology of Hadith criticism, if the attribution of these sayings to the Prophet is reliable, there should be a way to evaluate them. Interpreting the Hadith as metaphors or allegory can be preferable to denying the relationships of these sayings to the Prophet. This is the approach I have favored in this work. For example, describing the extraordinary height of an individual may indicate the authoritative power of the individual or even the collective power of an ideology rather than an actual measurement of height of a human being. This is similar to many elements of recent popular communications media, for instance cartoons. Some detailed descriptions of Jesus such as his cleanliness, the color of his clothes, and the manner of his descent can be understood in the same allegorical way. There is no doubt that eloquence, both in prose and poetry, allows for a more powerful expression of some truths, beyond the surface of literal appearances.

The Prophet also spoke about certain nations, ethnicities, and civil wars among Muslims. Because of the allegorical nature of these types of sayings of the Prophet and their ambiguous meanings, it is difficult to determine his exact intentions in mentioning such events. It is theologically acceptable in Islam to present future events that are not directly related to the essence of faith using metaphorical and allegorical language. Given the ambiguity of the language, members of the Muslim community can offer multiple meanings and interpretations of such events and still all be Muslims. In Islamic theology, the five pillars of Islam are much more important; believing in God and in Muhammad as His messenger, giving compulsory charity, fasting in the month of Ramadan, performing the five daily prescribed prayers, and making pilgrimage to Mecca are all based on the firm, unambiguous statements of the Qur'an and the Prophet, statements in which there is no space for metaphorical language.

## Three Major Approaches

To clarify my methodology of evaluating these texts about the descent of Jesus, it is useful to mention three major approaches to the sayings of the Prophet on the portents of the Hour and on Jesus's return.

Muslim theologians have developed a variety of approaches to interpreting the signs of the Final Hour as they are presented in the sayings of the Prophet and hinted at in the Qur'an. Here an example will be given using the descent of Jesus. The first approach denies all signs because they are believed to be improperly attributed to Muhammad. Some modern Muslim thinkers believe that prophetic traditions on the subject are far from being reliable.

The second approach, which can be called literalist, stands in opposition to the ideas of such thinkers as well as the interpretive approach (detailed below) to the texts. Contemporary literalists have developed a literature that refutes modernist ideas. This group believes that all signs of the Final Hour listed in the body of the Hadith should be taken literally, including the descent of Jesus. They reference a common idea in the Qur'an, "Truly, God is powerful over everything" (2:20), arguing that since God has power over everything, the literal occurrence of these signs is possible and will happen.

The third approach is a more balanced interpretation of the hadith on the subject. This approach accepts the authenticity of the sayings of the Prophet in this regard as long as their reliability is supported by well-founded Hadith criticism. There is no doubt that some hadith dealing with this subject, especially later ones, are apocryphal. If authenticity is established, for instance by an unbroken chain of narration or by a knowledge of the truthfulness of the narrators, the principle of understanding the Prophet's sayings metaphorically can be employed. When the Prophet speaks of the descent of Jesus, one should not understand this literally. To expect the person of Jesus to come physically from the sky in front of the eyes of the people is incompatible with the overall teachings of Islam.

Some principles of Islamic theology necessitate this interpretative approach.

When we refer to the sayings of the Prophet regarding the descent of Jesus and related themes, it is important that we use the accepted methodology of interpreting the holy texts of Islam about Jesus or other future events. A general theological principle of the Islamic tradition is that Muslims are to make peace instead of war. War is allowed only in some circumstances, but it is not a principle. The Qur'an says, "Peace is better" (4:128). If the Prophet speaks of a future war among Muslims or between Muslims and other nations, it is because God has shown him the future and he explains it based on his vision of the future. This is not meant to encourage war—in fact the Prophet praises those who prevent war as in the case of his grandson Hasan—but instead is a warning that conflicts may happen if precautions are not taken to prevent them. Further, in keeping with the general metaphorical language of the Hadith, the war that the Prophet predicts might well be a spiritual one and not a physical one. The sayings of the Prophet in this regard are intended as general warnings for Muslims to maintain spiritual vigilance and piety for the sake of their eternal lives.

The Sunni tradition of Islam does not encourage the idea of making the world a place of conflict to hasten the descent of Jesus or in order to bring about the Final Hour that would fulfill the message of the Prophet. On the contrary, it encourages Muslims to make the world a more peaceful place and therefore prevent the Final Hour from arriving prematurely. Muslims are described as those who live in peace, make peace, and greet each other with peace. This Sunni approach is considerably different from that of people who feel that they are called to bring about Armageddon as soon as possible. For some fundamentalist Christians, particularly those who follow extreme dispensationalist ideas, this manifests itself as a desire to bring about Jesus's Second Coming.[20] Some Shi'ite Muslims, particularly the small group of the Shi'ites known as Hujjatiyya, hope that they may see the coming of the Mahdi.

Many instances of the belief in the descent of Jesus can be found in the popular culture of the Muslim world. The popular literature in the Islamic world is saturated with the eschatological themes, and many believe eschatological works contain literal truth. Historical and contemporary events have provided the impetus for these works. For example, many people believed that Napoleon Bonaparte's (d. 1821) occupation of Egypt was the sign of the Final Hour. Today the Egyptian public library has many texts from that era related to the signs of the Hour, some of which are referred to in this work.

References to these signs are also found in the Holy Texts. Some chapters of the Qur'an are named to suggest the images of the day or the Hour and its apocalyptic nature.[21] It is believed that after the descent of Jesus and his fulfillment of justice for a certain period of time, there will be another short era of irreligiosity before the Final Hour. Inspired by the Qur'an's illustration of the horrific nature of doomsday, a contemporary Muslim theologian eloquently expounds on the apocalyptic scene:

> If you want to imagine the agonies of the death of the earth as the Qur'anic verses point them out, look at how the parts of this universe are bound to one another with a subtle exalted order. They are held with such a hidden, delicate, subtle bond within an order wherein if a single one of the lofty bodies receive the command: "Be!" or, "Leave your orbit!" the world will begin the agony of its death. The stars will collide, the heavenly bodies will fly over each other, a great devastating sound will start in infinite space as a result of millions of cannonballs, and great guns the size of globes will collide. Clashing and colliding with one another, sending out showers of sparks, the mountains taking flight, the seas burning, the face of the earth will be flattened. Thus, through this death and those agonies God the All-powerful will shake up the universe. God will purify the universe, and Hell and the matters of Hell will draw to one side, while Paradise and the matters appropriate for Paradise draw to the other, and the world of the Hereafter will become manifest.[22]

This serves as a good interpretation of the Qur'anic verse: "The day when the earth will change into a different earth" (14:48). In this interpretation of eschatological verses, a time is certain to come "when this world, which is the shell and form of the mighty reality of the universe, will break up, with the permission of the Creator. Then it will be renewed in a better form."[23] This will be a time when each individual will sharply see pure as pure and ugly as ugly, good as good and evil as evil. There will be no confusion. Jesus will be seen clearly as the personification of goodness while his opponent, the Antichrist, will be seen as the personification of evil. Therefore, as described in many manuals of Islamic theology, Jesus comes to end human suffering and injustice.

## Mystical Eschatology and the Signs of the Hour

In the mystical tradition of Islam, remembering the prophetic statements about the signs of the Hour, the final moment of an individual's life, and the existence of the afterlife as well as being aware of the coming of the Final Hour have always been parts of spiritual development.[24] It is believed that such contemplation prepares the mystic for the realm of eternity and helps with detachment from worldly desires. Both Jesus's return and his personality are great examples for Muslim mystics, especially his ascetic lifestyle and his warnings about the imminence of the Final Hour: "Repent, for the kingdom of heaven is at hand" (Matt. 4:17). Generally speaking, when people think of death, they think of it as a faraway issue; yet for Muslim mystics death is immanent, since no one can escape from it and it is a universal reality. Through contemplation they imagine the coming of death and the end of their lives—their individual and cosmic eschatology—routinely in their daily spiritual practices. The Prophet of Islam asks his community to remember death, a practice that destroys the desire for indulgence. For mystics, practicing *muraqaba*, a Sufi principle related to the spiritual journey, or imagining the sequence of the events that will occur in the afterlife as though they were occurring now is a part of spiritual life. By doing this and hence emphasizing the afterlife while weakening their ties to this worldly life, Muslim mystics follow the way of Jesus and Muhammad. The practice of imagining death and the afterlife is performed periodically. Mystics follow the Prophet's instruction "die before you die" to emphasize the importance of preparing for the afterlife. The following conversation between the Prophet and Haritha, one of his companions, elucidates the mystical experience of the afterlife:

> When the Prophet asked Haritha, "What is the reality of your faith?" Haritha replied: "I have inclined my soul away from this world, have fasted by day and kept vigil by night, and it is as if I behold the throne of my Lord openly, and it is as if I behold the people of Paradise visiting each other, and as if I see the people of Hell at enmity with each other." In response to this, the Prophet said, "The one who wants to see a servant, whose heart has been enlightened by God, let him look at Haritha."[25]

Since the spiritual enlightenment of the heart occurs through actions and achievements of human beings on earth, this worldly life is worthy and is a place for both justice and oppression. According to Islamic theology, Jesus's descent will transform this worldly life from ugliness to beauty and from oppression to justice. By following the pattern of Islam, which contains the essence of the message of Jesus, people are transforming their limited life on earth into the unlimited life of the hereafter. The descent of Jesus helps this transformation.

Transforming this worldly life into an eternal one is possible. Speaking of this possibility, a contemporary Muslim theologian and mystic says, "O Human Beings, do you want to turn your ephemeral, short, useless life into an eternal, long, beneficial and fruitful one? Since such a desire is present in the nature of every human being, spend your life in the way of the real Eternal One [God]. Everything that faces towards the Eternal eventually becomes a reflection of the eternity."[26]

## Jesus: Savior or Intercessor?

Before delving into the details of Jesus's eschatological descent in the following chapters, it is appropriate to discuss briefly Jesus's role in the salvation of human beings. Who, according to Islamic theological principles of salvation, *al-naja*, will be saved and receive the divine rewards in the afterlife?

The Qur'an does not deny the role of prophets as heralds to and of the path of God so that people will receive salvation in the realm of eternity. However, the language used is carefully chosen to indicate that it is God who gives guidance and salvation; prophets, including Muhammad and Jesus, are the conveyers of the message and not the final decision makers. Although Jesus is one of the five most prominent messengers of God (along with Muhammad, Moses, Abraham, and Noah), he still has no authority to give salvation without the permission of God. However, in the afterlife, Jesus and other prophets are allowed to intercede and ask God to save some people from the punishment of hell.[27]

Some Qur'anic verses are quite instructive about this matter. The Qur'an describes "the saved" as those who believe in God and the afterlife and who do good deeds (2:62). The belief in the afterlife is concomitant with the belief in God and His messengers. Historically, Islamic theology has taught that the primary prerequisite for salvation is the acceptance of the Islamic statement of faith, the *shahada*, "There is no deity but God, and Muhammad is God's messenger," from the depth of one's heart. Because belief in Muhammad's prophethood requires belief in all previous prophets, when Muslims state the testimony of faith, "I believe there is only one God and Muhammad is God's messenger," they simultaneously acknowledge that Jesus is God's messenger, Moses is God's messenger, and so forth. Their belief in the prophethood of Muhammad will be invalid if they deny other prophets. In other words, to believe in Muhammad's prophethood without believing in Jesus's prophethood is considered to be a rejection of the prophethood of Muhammad. In the Islamic conception of the afterlife, those who believe in the *shahada* will be spared the fires of hell.[28] That is to say, they will be saved in the afterlife and be among the people of paradise. This statement of faith is the primary component of the six articles of faith, alongside belief in angels, in God's scriptures, in God's messengers and prophets, in the afterlife, and in predestination, or the divine plan. It is also the first of the five pillars of Islam, along with praying five times a day; giving *zakat*, or charity; fasting in the month of Ramadan; and completing the pilgrimage to Mecca. The faith of those who believe in God but deny the existence of life after death will be considered incomplete and not enough for salvation. Once a person has properly received the teachings of the Prophet, that person's salvation is bound up with these beliefs and practices as they are set forth in the Qur'an.

The Qur'anic approach to the question of salvation is inclusive. For example, the Qur'an says, "Those who believe [Muslims] and those who are Jews and Christians and Sabians, whoever believes in God and in the Last Day and does good deeds, surely their reward is with their Lord. And no fear shall come upon them; neither do they grieve" (2:62). Another Qur'anic verse also issues an invitation to the People of the Book (i.e., Jews and Christians) to join with Muslims in the statement common to all three: "There is only one God" (3:64).

One hadith tells of a Bedouin who asks the Prophet, "What shall I do in order to go to Paradise?" The Prophet simply replied, "Say there is no deity but God and you will be saved."[29] Muslim theologians interpret this to mean that faith in one God is the essence and foundation of religious belief; without it there is no salvation. But faith is not merely lip service. It is much more than that. Muslim theologians suggest that if one believes in God, one must also believe in the prophethood of Muhammad, since the belief in the oneness of God comes from the message of the Prophet.

Despite theological arguments about this issue, according to Islamic theology, with the exception of people whose fate is revealed in the Qur'an, for example Pharaoh, no one is able to make a precise judgment about a particular individual's final destination in the afterlife because it is known only to God. One can make a general judgment, for instance that "the deniers of the existence of God will go to hell" or "the believers will go to paradise," but to make a judgment about an individual person would require knowledge that only God can know. Both Jesus and Muhammad are able to make such judgment of salvation with permission from God. God may inform His messengers about the final destination of some of their disciples, and based on this revelation they may declare the salvation of some of their people. This was true for Jesus during his first coming and will obtain during his return as well. He is the Messiah and a messenger of God, but the final decision about the salvation of individuals belongs to God alone. God can put anyone He wants into paradise, whoever that person may be. There is no limitation to God's power or God's mercy. One example of this is the mercy shown to those who have not received the divine message conveyed by the Prophet. In the Qur'an God says: "We do not punish unless We send a messenger [who explains to people their obligations]" (17:15). This verse has become an important principle in the Islamic theology of salvation. Schools of Islamic thought, such as al-Ash'ariyya and al-Maturidiyya, have developed varying concepts of the people of the *ahl al-fatra,* those who lived in a period that did not have any prophet to convey God's message to them. These people will receive salvation. The term is commonly used to refer to the era between Jesus and Muhammad, when there was no prophet. Those who did not receive the teachings of Jesus or the teachings of Muhammad, since his message had not yet been declared, are excused and will be among the people of paradise; they are the people of the *fatra.* Some contemporary scholars apply the concept of the *fatra* to certain modern-day people as well. Even those who have been exposed to the message of the Prophet but have received improper instructions or have been bombarded by negative information are considered to be among the people of the *fatra* and will attain salvation *if* their denial of the Prophet's message is due to an excused ignorance or the lack of access to the proper information. Some people who lack the opportunity to search out and discover the true message of the Prophet are considered to be among the saved. This is true for the messages of both Jesus and Muhammad.

## The Abode of Jesus and the Antichrist

After humanity's resurrection and gathering in Maydan al-Hashr, the place of gathering, Islamic theology speaks of a "book" given to every individual that contains both their good and bad deeds on earth. The Qur'an says of this "book": "And the Book is placed, and you see the guilty fearful of that which is therein, and they say: What kind of a book is this that leaves neither a small thing nor a great thing but has counted it! And they find all that they did confronting them and your Lord wrongs no one" (18:49). Receiving the book through the right hand indicates that the final destination of the individual is paradise. Eventually, the people of paradise are taken there and the people of hell are led away.

The Islamic eschatological vision ends with descriptions of the final destinations for all people. Those who are saved will be in paradise forever, and *generally speaking* those who are disbelievers will be in hell. In this eschatological scenario, one finds a sharp distinction between Jesus and his opponent, the Antichrist. The people of Jesus are the people of Islam who will be the people in paradise. The people of the Antichrist are disbelievers who will be in hell.

Paradise is a place where pleasures beyond imagination can be found. Because of the limits of human imagination, it is not possible to thoroughly describe the beauty of paradise and its pleasures. Muslims believe that all that is known of paradise comes from the Qur'an. According to the Qur'anic descriptions, there will be gardens under which rivers flow and all spiritual and bodily desires will be fulfilled. One of the Qur'an's verses on paradise says, "And give good news to those who believe and do good deeds that they will have gardens under which rivers flow. When they are given a fruit as sustenance they will say 'This is what we were given before.' They will be given what is similar to them in this world. In Paradise they will have pure spouses and they will stay there forever" (2:25). The highest pleasure in paradise is to see God (ru'yat Allah). Describing the life of paradise in a comparative way, Bediüzzaman Said Nursi, a twentieth-century Muslim scholar and theologian, states that a thousand years of happiness in this worldly life cannot be compared to an hour of life in paradise. Similarly, Nursi contends that a thousand years of life in paradise cannot be compared to an hour of seeing the beauty of God. The Qur'an says the people in hell will be without hope when they see the finality of God's judgment upon their actions in the world. They will desire to return to the world to improve their situation by good works. A verse illustrates this dilemma: "When death comes unto one of them, he says, 'My Lord, send me back, that I might do right in that which I have left behind,' but God says, 'Never,' and his wishes are in vain" (23:99–100). Another verse describes the fate of those who deny the existence of God, or worse, actively resist God: "As for those who disbelieve: 'Lo, if everything on earth were theirs twice over, to be used to ransom them from their doom on the day of resurrection, it would not be accepted from them. Theirs will be a painful tribulation: they will wish to come forth from the fire, but they will not escape from it; theirs will be a lasting punishment" (5:36).

Having introduced the signs of the Hour and the final eschatological stages of human beings after the descent of Jesus, now it is appropriate to examine the place of Jesus and his eschatological descent in the body of Hadith.

# FOUR

# The Hadith and Jesus's Eschatological Descent

The Qur'an does not directly refer to Jesus's eschatological descent per se, but there are verses that hint at it; in the preceding chapter I cited at least four of them. The Hadith, or the sayings of the Prophet, give detailed accounts of the descent of Jesus and shape Muslims' belief about Jesus's eschatological descent. Many Muslim historians and biographers who were well versed in the Islamic science of Hadith spoke of Jesus. Some prominent Muslim historians even give details of the story of the life of Jesus and commentary on the Qur'anic verses and sayings of the Prophet about Jesus; these include Abu 'Abdillah Muhammad bin 'Umar al-Waqidi (d. 823), in his book *Futuh al-Sham* [Conquests of Greater Syria]; Ahmad bin Ishaq bin Ja'far al-Ya'qubi (d. 897), a Muslim historian and geographer who wrote the famous *al-Tarikh*; and Abu al-Quasim 'Ali bin Hasan Ibn 'Asakir (d. 1176), who was arguably the most knowledgeable scholar of Islam in his time in both history and Hadith literature, in his famous book *Tarikh Madinat Damashq* [The History of the City of Damascus]. Ibn 'Asakir in particular expected the imminent coming of Jesus to help Muslims against the oppression of crusaders.[1] What was the relationship between Jesus and Damascus that prompted al-Waqidi and Ibn 'Asakir to dedicate sections to Jesus in their books on Damascus? It seems that the Prophet's sayings that the eschatological descent of Jesus was to occur in Damascus drew the interest of both authors. According to some hadith narratives, at the end of time Jesus will descend to the top of the white minaret that is part of the renowned Umayyad Mosque in Damascus. Working with just such an eschatological scenario in mind, Ibn 'Asakir gives many titles to Jesus, calling him a just ruler, a leader, and even the rightly guided Islamic messianic figure, the Mahdi.[2]

## The Hadith and Its Significance in Islamic Theology

Before delving into the details of the descent of Jesus as presented in the body of the Hadith, it is important to elaborate on the concept of the Hadith and its significance in Islamic theology. First, the differences between the Qur'an and the Hadith should be made clear. Muslims believe that the Qur'an is the direct word of God, revealed to Muhammad through the angel Gabriel. It is considered a direct revelation from God rather than an inspiration. The source of a revelation is always divine with an angel, generally Gabriel, as a mediator. According to Islamic theology, Gabriel's major duty is to bring revelation to the prophets of God. Revelation is absolute while inspiration is limited and can be ambiguous. Although inspiration is a spiritual intuition that comes from God, it is below the level of revelation and is not necessarily mediated by an angel. An inspiration that comes to prophets is greater and clearer than the inspiration that comes to saints. Inspiration also comes to the hearts of individuals, be they saints or regular people, which they express in their own words; for that reason inspiration is not as clear as revelation. In fact, in some cases inspiration might even cause some confusion on the part of the person receiving it, similar to when one sees an object through a blurred eyeglass.

Keeping this theological difference in mind, we can look at the Hadith as the divine inspiration of the Prophet. Although the Qur'an calls the Prophet's words a revelation, the term is not used in its precise theological sense (53:4). The Prophet of Islam is the center of the religion and the most important figure for Muslims in the era of the commencement of Islam and even today. Every aspect of his life, including his words, his actions, and his reactions to certain events, were and still are essential for Muslims. The Qur'an presents him as an exemplary personality to be emulated. "Surely for you, O believers, who have hope in God and the Day of Judgment, there is a beautiful example in the Messenger of God" (33:21). The Qur'an explicitly connects the love of God to following the practice of the Prophet. "Say, [O Muhammad, to your people,] if you really love God, follow me so that God will love you" (3:31). Despite the Qur'an's emphasis on the Prophet, we do not have the details of his life in the Qur'an. A chapter of the Qur'an is named after the mother of Jesus, but we do not find a mention of Muhammad's mother in the Holy Book. The Qur'anic verses about Muhammad mostly relate to his message, his great ethics, his compassion for his community, and his being a mercy from God to all mankind and to the entire universe.

After the revelation of the Qur'an was complete, Muhammad's companions began to record his words and actions in a conscientious way. They would narrate his words carefully. If they were uncertain about whether he used a particular word, they would express this uncertainty in their narration. His companions were honest by nature. It is believed that lying was anathema to the Prophet's male and female companions. Such truthfulness is thought to contribute to the authenticity of their accounts of the Prophet.

The narratives about the sayings, actions, and tacit approvals of the Prophet are called the Hadith. Muslims learn almost everything about their social, religious, and family life from the Prophet's life, which is fully recorded in the body of Hadith literature. The term "Sunnah" is also used to refer to the words and practices of the Prophet. These narratives were all put together in a highly sophisticated way by ninth-century scholars who dedicated their entire lives to collecting and authenticating the various sayings of the Prophet. Some of the prominent scholars of the Hadith in the ninth and tenth centuries were Muhammad al-Bukhari (d. 870), Muslim bin al-Hajjaj (d. 875), Abu Dawud (d. 888), Ibn Majah (d. 886), al-Tirmidhi (d. 892), and al-Nasa'i (d. 916). The collections of these six scholars are known as the most reliable references of the Hadith, or the Sunnah of the Prophet. For each saying of the Prophet a way of verification has been developed. Each is evaluated through a method by which the biographical stories of the narrators, including their behaviors, the weakness and strength of their memories, and their doctrinal inclinations are questioned. Because each hadith has been passed on through several narrators, it is necessary to examine the reliability and trustworthiness of those narrators. Decisions were made about whether each hadith should be considered weak or sound. Al-Bukhari used this method in his famous collection, *al-Sahih*, which means "The Sound" or "The Authentic" and contains about 7,000 sayings of the Prophet. Al-Bukhari's collection is considered highly reliable. It is well known among Muslims that if one finds a hadith recorded in al-Bukhari's *al-Sahih*, it is as if one hears it directly from the mouth of the Prophet.

As an Islamic source, the Hadith is secondary to the Qur'an. When Hadith experts accept that the Prophet truly said certain things about a matter related to the faith, future events, or worldly affairs, these become very important for Muslims because the Qur'an says, "Whatever the Messenger gives you, take; whatever he forbids you, avoid" (59:7). Despite the fact that the Prophet of Islam was frugal with his words and did not speak in vain, many people with both good and bad intentions have attempted to imitate his sayings and present their own words and statements as the Prophet's. In order to distinguish what truly came from the Prophet of Islam from what was fabricated, the tradition of scrutinizing the Hadith, or Hadith criticism, developed as one of the major disciplines of the Islamic sciences.

## Hadith Regarding Jesus's Descent

Many hadith refer to Jesus's descent, including some that are known to be fabricated. In this study I have made efforts to avoid the fabricated hadith and include only those commonly accepted as sound. The references mentioned in this chapter are sayings of the Prophet narrated by his companions and recorded by the later hadith collectors mentioned earlier. Two things about the sayings of the Prophet are important and should be kept in mind while reading this section. First, there are many sayings of the Prophet about Jesus's eschatological descent and his role. Some would say that over 100 hadith refer to Jesus's eschatological role. These sayings, if their authenticity is proven, may have come from the Prophet, but they were not recorded verbatim. Second, narrators sometimes impose their own meanings on the words of the Prophet. After his death, his companions and later Hadith narrators transmitted his words orally. That is to say, some companions of the Prophet heard him give these teachings during his lifetime and then narrated orally in their own words what was eventually written. This is likely the way many hadith narratives were transmitted. Many narrators may have added their own understandings of the Prophet's words. This is why there are some contradictions in certain hadith on the subject of the descent of Jesus.

Certain narratives include contradictory information about the location of Jesus's descent. One hadith says Jesus will descend in Damascus, another says Jerusalem, while still others say "A place in Iraq" or "A place in the west." It is very possible that when the Prophet spoke about Jesus and his future role regarding the community of Muslims, some narrators applied his words to their particular locations, presumably with good intentions. This trend caused confusion by creating ambiguity about the topic of Jesus's eschatological descent, yet it did not change Muslims' overall understanding of Jesus's return because almost all narrators share the Prophet's emphasis on the descent of Jesus. The Prophet uses words such as "certainly" or the phrase "by the One my soul is in His hand" to emphasize the importance of the event.

Therefore, one can argue that the inner spirituality of the narrators and their understandings, based on their own circumstances, contributed to the later detailed development of the eschatological scenario. For experts on the Hadith today, the well-founded methodology of Hadith criticism is available to scrutinize any hadith narrative. Using this methodological approach, one finds at least some of the hadith about the descent of Jesus to be reliable and authentic. They belong to the Prophet or are at least consistent with the Prophet's intended meaning if they were not recorded verbatim.

Now a question comes to mind: Why would the Prophet of Islam mention this and similar future events? To answer this question one should understand the Prophet's relationship with his community even after his death. A Qur'anic verse clearly indicates his concern for his community: "Now there has come to you a Messenger [Muhammad], one of yourselves; your suffering is grievous for him, for the believers he is tender and full of compassion" (9:128). There is no doubt that the Prophet was greatly concerned about his community. He was responding to questions from his own companions about events that were to occur in the future. In response he gave some hints about certain events but did not offer clarification. Theologically speaking, the Prophet does not know the future without being informed by God; therefore, either he was not informed by God about certain details of events or he intentionally did not give more information. One hadith contends that the future has been shown to Muhammad by God, that a time will come when his community will have a great era of serenity in which justice and equality are fully practiced. The Prophet shared such good news with his community but also spoke of future conflicts between members of his community and asked them to stay home or be inactive to prevent bloodshed at such a time.

With his extraordinary spiritual strength, Muhammad was given the gift of seeing the realm of the unseen. From an Islamic perspective, Muhammad is a human being who was able to witness the throne of God while he was on earth and could see paradise and hell at the same time. The Prophet of Islam shared with his companions both what he had seen and his feelings and revelations in a way that would give them hope but would also warn them to act properly. For example, he foresaw and warned his community against possible future violence, conflicts often called the *fitna* (trials within Islamic society) that in fact happened in the form of a civil war. The Prophet was very much concerned about bloodshed. A companion of his asked: "What should I do in the times of such great trials?" The Prophet responded, "Control your tongue and strongly keep to your house." Sa'd bin Abi Waqqas (d. 664), another distinguished companion of the Prophet, asked, "What if he [an intruder] broke into my house and stretched out his hand to kill me?" The Prophet replied, "Be like one of the two sons of Adam." This hadith refers to the Qur'anic story of the "two sons of Adam," Abel and Cain, or Habil and Qabil, as they are known in Islamic literature. The Qur'an says: "And recite to them the story of the two sons of Adam truthfully, when they offered a sacrifice and it was accepted from one of them, and not accepted from the other. 'I will surely kill you,' said one. 'God accepts only the God-fearing,' said the other. 'Yet if you stretch out your hand against me, to kill me, I will not stretch out my hand against you, to kill you; I fear God, the Lord of all Being" (5:27–28). Because of warnings from the Prophet about a time of civil unrest in the early period of Islam, the majority of the Prophet's companions avoided the *fitna* and social anarchy. As a result, bloodshed and human catastrophe were prevented.

As the Qur'an states, the Prophet never spoke in vain (53:3). On the contrary, he spoke of divine revelation and through divine inspiration about future events that would concern his community. One of these future events is Jesus's eschatological descent. The Prophet of Islam foresaw and spoke about the descent in the language of his people, which includes all types of eloquence and allegorical styles. It is commonly known that in most cases, the Prophet's speech was brief; perhaps in the case of Jesus's descent, he was brief because the exact knowledge of future belongs only to God. The Prophet and the pious can give information about the future only when God informs them. If they do not receive such knowledge from God, they cannot inform people about future events. Therefore, when the Prophet spoke about certain coming events, such as the descent of Jesus at the end of time, he would have wanted to ensure that the revelations relating to the future would not be seen and understood as certain. Each future event that the Prophet spoke of may have emerged or may have been realized in a different way, since the Prophet did not mention the ways events would unfold.

By leaving the issue of future events ambiguous, the Prophet of Islam made greater room for the exercise of human free will. It is a tenet of Islamic theology that one should not be compelled to faith. A believer looking at the Prophet's sayings about Jesus might say, "Even though the Prophet said this, I still have the duty to use my free will to make our world a more livable place, and not wait for Jesus, or the Mahdi, the Islamic Messianic figure, to do so." The open-ended sayings of the Prophet do not allow the Muslim community to rely on future events and abandon their more immediate duties. Thus, Islamic eschatology in this regard can be understood as a *realized eschatology*, an eschatology that is realized in this world and at the present time, not the one postponed to the afterlife.

The Prophet's emphasis on eschatology was so great that some of his companions expected to see and meet with Jesus in their lifetimes. The Prophet would say, "Whosoever from amongst you lives long enough to see Jesus, son of Mary, let him convey my greetings to him."[3] Muslims believe that with God's permission the Prophet knew that his companions would not see Jesus, but there was a great need to keep believers' motivation alive, to impel them to fulfill their current duties and not wait for the apocalypse. This in part leads to the ambiguity of the prophecies of the eschatological descent of Jesus and the emergence of the Antichrist, which allow for various interpretations. In turn this has led to an ongoing dynamic in Islamic society where charlatans claim that they are Jesus and others are accused of being the Antichrist.

## Understanding the Hadith

The hadith cited in this chapter are for the most part reliable and sound. However, some of these sayings are considered to be weak. This does not mean that the Prophet did not say them but indicates that they have not been authenticated. The chain of transmitters and other aspects of certain hadith on the subject of the descent of Jesus do not meet the criteria that have been put forth by prominent hadith collectors such as al-Bukhari and Muslim bin al-Hajjaj. Although most of the narrations I chose to explicate Jesus's descent have been authenticated by hadith experts, one has to keep in mind that authentication is one thing and understanding what the Prophet meant is something else. For example, if the Prophet speaks of his dream and the narrator reports it, the words used by the Prophet should not be understood in a literal way. A reliable hadith in al-Bukhari's *al-Sahih* states that the Prophet saw both Jesus and the Antichrist in his dream while he was circumambulating the Ka'ba, the holy shrine of Islam in Mecca. He saw Jesus as very clean, with combed hair, and he saw the Antichrist as enormously ugly. The Prophet's descriptions of Jesus and the Antichrist should not necessarily be understood in a literal way. Since this was a dream of the Prophet, the descriptions mentioned can be related to the spiritual characteristics of Jesus and the Antichrist rather than to their physical features. In the same dream the Prophet saw Jesus in a yellow garment. To understand the word of the Prophet accurately one should consider the allegorical meaning of the color yellow in the Arabic language of the time. Does it indicate "spiritual support" or "help for the oppressed" or something else? All of these are possible meanings. Without such an investigation, even if the authentication is established, these meanings will not be understood correctly. In other words, to understand the Prophet of Islam correctly, the meaning of the ambiguous sayings of the Prophet should be acknowledged and clarified.

When the Prophet says Jesus will come or that Jesus will descend from heaven to rescue the oppressed, there is no doubt in the mind of the believer about the truthfulness of the Prophet as long as the authenticity of the hadith is proven. If uncertainty persists, the problem is not with the hadith but with the readers of that hadith. Do they understand the Prophet correctly? One should keep these criteria in mind when looking at the sayings of the Prophet in this chapter. Muslims generally believe that the hadith we are encountering here are not imaginative fantasies. They are reliable and come from the Prophet, whose spiritual experience goes far beyond our imagination. When he was talking about Jesus, he was able to meet with Jesus in the realm of spirituality. His words, like those of other prophets, are correct, but because of their allegorical nature, people differ in their understandings of them. Some understand his words in a literal way and some are inclined more toward a figurative language that is used in these narratives. I prefer the second approach. One should consider the figurative language that the Prophet used and should understand his language about the future figuratively. Literal interpretations are misleading, although they are widespread among Muslims.

Furthermore, theologically speaking, future events are less important than the principles of faith. The Prophet purposefully used allegorical language for certain future occurrences. It can be argued that in the case of Jesus's descent, the bodily coming of a person from the sky understood in the traditional literalist view of the Hadith does not seem to be compatible with the overall principles of Islamic theology. The sayings of the Prophet in this regard should be understood figuratively rather than literally. This world is the realm of cause and effect, which is known in Islam as the law of God. Divine actions in this realm are within the frame of causality. Causes are attributed to God, and God is "the Cause of causes." When God is at work in the realm of nature through causes, this is commonly called natural law. However, from an Islamic theological perspective, natural law is divine law in the realm of nature. Thus, the events mentioned in the body of the Hadith, including the descent of Jesus at the end of time, are all to be fulfilled within the realm of cause and effect and not in the form of miracles, as many Muslims and Christians believe.

## The Significance of the Return of Jesus

Much attention has been devoted to the return of Jesus in the major Hadith sources, both in the *Kutub al-Sitta* (the most reliable six books containing collections of hadith) and in more minor collections, most notably *Kitab al-Fitan* [The Book of Trials] by Nu'aym bin Hammad (d. 844). This source records twenty-two separate sayings of the Prophet relating to the descent of Jesus. In addition to sayings of the Prophet that directly address the question of Jesus's eschatological descent, a group of hadith collections do mention the return of Jesus, but these focus on the Antichrist. Medieval Hadith commentators and contemporary Hadith compilers have collected all available sayings of the Prophet both directly and indirectly on Jesus's descent and in doing so have created a genre in Hadith literature.

One of the important functions of this genre of Hadith literature has been to refute the claims of pseudo-messiahs. In a long introduction to his book on the descent of Jesus, Anwar Shah al-Kashmiri (d. 1933), an Indian Muslim scholar, denies the claims of Mirza Ghulam Ahmad, the founder of the Ahmadiyya movement, who claimed that he was the promised Messiah and the incarnation of Jesus. Al-Kashmiri cites 101 sayings of the Prophet about Jesus, his ascension, his descent, and his fight against the Antichrist.[4] Al-Kashmiri wanted to prove that Ghulam Ahmad was not the promised Messiah and that Jesus would return in the way the Prophet clearly stated. Muhammad Zahid al-Kawthari (d. 1951) likewise supported the certainty of Jesus's return through a number of hadith.[5] Similarly, 'Abdullah al-Ghumari (d. 1993), a Moroccan scholar, again in response to the spread of the Ahmadiyya movement among Muslims, recorded sixty-one hadith on the subject to prove that Jesus will come and that Ghulam Ahmad was not the Messiah whose descent is promised by the Prophet of Islam.[6] He concludes: "These sixty-one hadith have been narrated by the Prophet's companions and by subsequent generations of Muslims in such a way as to leave no doubt about the descent of Jesus in the Islamic creed."[7]

In all these narratives, we know the names of the companions of the Prophet who put forth these hadith on the eschatological role of Jesus. Among those who directly narrated the subject from the Prophet are fifteen well-known companions.[8] It is believed that this first generation transmitted the sayings of the Prophet with the utmost care and accountability to the second generation, and the second generation to the third, and so on. The chain of narration is verified by Hadith scholars for each of these sayings of the Prophet. The following four hadith will be presented as examples of this genre.

## Example of a Sound and Reliable Hadith I

Abu Huraira (d. 680), one of the renowned companions of the Prophet, narrates that Muhammad said: "By God almighty, in Whose hand my soul is, Jesus, the son of Mary, will soon descend among you [Muslims] as a just ruler. He will break the cross, kill the swine, and abolish the jizya [a tax levied by the state on the non-Muslim minority]. He will distribute wealth and there shall be so much wealth that no one will accept it anymore."[9] In another version of the hadith, the following addition is found: "One *sajda* [a prostration before God] will be better than anything in the world."[10] Abu Huraira continues: "If you wish, recite the Qur'anic verse: 'And there shall be no one of the People of the Book left not believing in him before his death'" (4:159). The same hadith, as recorded by Ibn Majah (d. 887), begins with the statement that the Final Hour will not occur before the descent of Jesus.[11] According to the methodology of hadith authentication, this hadith is sound and reliable. The breaking of the cross and the killing of the swine will be discussed in chapter 8, where I discuss the interpretive approach.

Example of a Hadith Whose Authenticity Is Doubted

Following is one example of a hadith whose authenticity many scholars have doubted. It is believed that the narrators of this hadith borrowed some of its elements from the Hebrew Bible. The hadith is one of eleven narrated under a section titled "The Section of the Trials of the Antichrist, the Emergence of Jesus, the Son of Mary, and the Emergence of Gog and Magog." The descent of Jesus and his fight against the Antichrist is narrated in a detailed way. It starts with a dramatic narrative about the Antichrist before it goes into the descent of Jesus. The hadith dramatizes the fight between Jesus and the Antichrist. The Antichrist cannot stand up against Jesus and runs away. In the end he is captured and slain. After Jesus slays the Antichrist the era of peace and comfort starts. The hadith mentions many such details. The full text of the hadith would run through many pages, but an abridged version is presented here to serve as an example of a detailed hadith on the subject from the genre. The hadith can be translated as follows:

> Abu Umama al-Bahili [d. 700], one of the companions of the Prophet, narrates: The Messenger of God, peace and blessings be upon him, gave us a speech. The majority of his speech was about what he told and warned us of al-Dajjal, [the Antichrist]. In part of his speech he said, "Surely there is no trial on earth since God has created Adam that is greater than the trial of the Antichrist. Every prophet sent by God warned his community about the Antichrist. I am the final prophet and you are the final community and there is no doubt he will emerge among you. If he emerges while I am among you I will be an authority for every Muslim against him. If he emerges after me, every individual will be an authority for himself. Instead of me, God will watch over every Muslim. The Antichrist will emerge from a place between the area of Damascus and Iraq. He will spread right and left. [Warning people in his speech, the Prophet says,] O servants of God! Be steadfast! I will describe him for you as no prophet before me has described him. The Antichrist starts by saying, 'I am a prophet.' But there is no prophet after me. Then he says, 'I am your Lord.' You will not see your Lord until you die. He is blind and your Lord is not blind. There

are the letters 'K-F-R' on his forehead, which say that he is a 'disbeliever.' These letters are between his two eyes, and every believer, literate or illiterate, can read them. One of his trials is that he has his own paradise and his hell. In fact, his hell is paradise and his paradise is hell. Anyone who is tested by his hell, let him take refuge in God and read the first verses of the chapter [chapter 18] 'The Cave' from the Qur'an so that his fire will be cool and peaceful as the fire became cool and peaceful on Abraham. Among his trials is to say to one of the Bedouins, 'What do you say if I resurrect for you your father and mother? Will you testify that I am your Lord?' The Bedouin says yes. Two Satans come in the form of his father and mother and say, 'Our son, follow him. He is your Lord.' One of Antichrist's trials is to attack an individual believer and kill him and cut him in half. And then he says, 'Look at this servant of mine. Now I will resurrect him. But he claims now there is another god other than me for him.' God resurrects this individual and the Antichrist says to the man, 'Who is your Lord?' He responds, 'My Lord is Allah and you are the enemy of God, the Antichrist. I swear by God that now I know you even better.'"

Continuing this hadith, Abu Sa'id narrates: "The Prophet said that this man is the highest in [spiritual] rank in my community in paradise. . . . We were thinking of that man as 'Umar bin al-Khattab." The hadith goes on to mention the Antichrist's trials:

Among his trials he commands the sky to rain and it does. He commands earth to grow grass and it does. Also among his trials he passes by a village and because they deny him, nothing is left undestroyed by him. Among his trials he passes by a village, and because they accept him, he commands the sky to rain and it does and he commands the earth to grow grass and it does for them to the extent that their livestock become fat and full of milk. No place on earth remains without being stepped on by him except Mecca and Medina. Whenever he wants to enter these two cities, an angel with swords prevents him. He arrives in a place called Red Zuraib and the city of Medina quakes three times. All male and female hypocrites go out to follow him. The city [Medina] removes its ugliness as the bellows clean iron. That day is called the day of salvation. Ummu Sharik, the daughter of Abu al-'Akr, asks: "O Messenger of God, where are the Arabs on that day?" The Prophet says, "They are very few on that day. The best of them would be in Jerusalem and their leader is a pious man. While their leader proceeds to lead the Morning Prayer, Jesus the son of Mary descends from heaven. The leader of the Muslims goes backwards in order to make a space for Jesus to lead people in prayer. Jesus puts his hands on the leader's shoulders and tells him, 'Go forward and lead the prayer.'"

The hadith goes on to speak of the activities of Jesus and the pious Muslim leader in question. Together they fight the Antichrist and finally kill him in a specific place called the "the door of Ludd," Arabic for Lod, a city nine miles southeast of present-day Tel Aviv, where Arabs and Jews live together today. Then the narration speaks of how the world becomes a peaceful place where wolves and lambs live together. But it also speaks of famine and suggests that in such a time, praising God will become a substitute for food. 'Abd al-Rahman al-Muharibi, one of the narrators of the hadith, recommends that the hadith be taught to children.[12]

The hadith is not found in the two major anthologies of the Hadith, *Sahih al-Bukhari* and *Sahih Muslim*, the two most reliable sources of hadith. When examined using the principles of hadith authentication methodology, this hadith, as narrated by Ibn Majah, shows questionable authenticity to the extent that there is confusion regarding the narrators and the sequence of events is uncertain. Methodologically speaking, the hadith is considered weak for three reasons. First, there is a weakness in the chain of transmitters. The narrator of the hadith, 'Abd al-Rahman al-Muharibi, is known among biographers of hadith narrators as a notorious *mudallis*, one who hides or mixes other words with the words of the Prophet or one who falsely claims to have heard the narrator of the hadith firsthand. Ahmad bin 'Ali bin Hajar al-'Asqalani (d. 1448), al-Bukhari's famous interpreter and the author of a prominent biographical dictionary, considers al-Muharibi to be a third-generation narrator (hence, he could not have heard the first generation) and a *mudallis*.[13] Yahya bin Abu 'Amr is also a third-generation narrator.[14] When a hadith has been transmitted by a third-generation narrator, there is a break in the chain of transmitters of the hadith. Isma'il bin Rafi' al-Ansari, another transmitter of the hadith in the chain of narrators, is also considered weak. Al-'Asqalani says that al-Ansari "later came to Basra and has a weak memory."[15] Al-Kashmiri suggests a similar reason for confusion in the hadith.[16]

It is noteworthy that information found in this hadith also appears in the book of Isaiah. Richard Bell makes a connection between this hadith and the text of the eleventh chapter of the book of Isaiah.[17] Despite the fact that the hadith is found in one of the six most reliable sources of hadith, experts do not treat this particular hadith as reliable. It is very possible the narrators have added to this hadith from their knowledge of earlier scriptures. Thus, any judgment about Islamic eschatology cannot be based on this hadith, although knowledge of the hadith is widespread among Muslims. There is no doubt that the hadith belongs to the Islamic milieu, but this does not mean that it is a reliable Islamic source.

Example of a Sound and Reliable Hadith II

Another hadith is narrated by Nawwas bin Sam'an (d. 678), who settled in Damascus after the death of the Prophet. The hadith is similar to the previous one but is found in the *Sahih Muslim* and not in the *Sahih al-Bukhari*. Based on the methodology of hadith authentication, scholars judge that the hadith is sound and reliable. This notable and detailed hadith makes use of allegorical language, saying that Jesus shall appear on earth after the Antichrist fights against Muslims and kills a young believer. The hadith goes as follows:

The Messenger of God [Muhammad] mentioned the Antichrist one morning and spoke at length about him, [emphasizing his emergence, so] we thought that he was among the palm trees of Medina. When we went to the Prophet, he realized our fear. "Why are you afraid?" he asked. We said, "O Messenger of God, you mentioned the Antichrist and so much emphasized him that we thought that he was in our palm trees." The Prophet said, "For you, I am afraid of something different than the Antichrist." Then the Prophet added: "If he emerges while I am among you, I will defend you against him. If he emerges and I am not among you, every soul should defend himself. God is my successor for every Muslim. He is a young man with curly hair. One of his eyes is like a smashed grape. I almost liken this to 'Abd al-'Uzza bin Qatan's eyes.[18] Those of you who live until the time of his emergence should read the first verses of the chapter 'The Cave' [chapter 18 of the Qur'an] against his trial. He is emerging from a place between Damascus and Iraq. He travels towards right and left." [Against his trial, the Prophet said,] "O servants of God! Be steadfast." We said, "O Messenger of God. How long will his stay on earth be?" He said: "Forty days. One day is like a year, one day is like a month, one day is like a week, and his other days are like your days." We said, "O messenger of God on the day which is like one year is it enough for us to perform the prayer of one regular day?" The Prophet said: "No, measure that day according to your days." We said, "O messenger of God, how fast is he [his spread] on the earth?" The Prophet said: "Like rain backed by wind. He comes to a nation and they believe in him and accept [his message]. He commands the sky to rain and it rains, and the earth to grow grass and it grows. He provides them with plenty of wealth. He comes to another nation and they reject his message. He turns away from them and they become poor with nothing in their hands. He passes a remnant of an ancient city and tells her, 'Take out your treasures.' Her treasures follow him like bees, and then he calls a man full of youth and strikes him with his sword, cutting him in two. Then he calls him and the youth stands up laughing with shining face. At that moment God sends Jesus, the son of Mary, from heaven. He descends on the top of the white minaret at the east of Damascus, putting his hands on the wings of two angels. [He is so handsome that] when he bows his head, it is as if water drops, and when he lifts his head his hair shines like pearls. Any nonbeliever who receives his breath will die; his breath reaches as far as his sight. He pursues the Antichrist and finds him at the gate of Lod; then he kills him. Then certain people who were saved in the trial of the Antichrist come to Jesus. He touches their faces [to remove dust] and tells them about their place in paradise. At that time God reveals to Jesus: 'I have made some of my creatures [Gog and Magog] emerge and no one can defeat them. Take My servants to the mountain of Tour'" (the mountain that is believed to be the place where Moses received God's message.)[19]

One might wonder how the minaret mentioned in this hadith, which could not have been present at the time of the Prophet (maybe it was there as a church tower), came to be a part of the Prophet's saying. Despite methodological authentication of the hadith, it is clear that there are some terms in the hadith that the Prophet never used. It is even more interesting that the scholars of the Hadith did not question this case. For example, Yahya bin Sharaf al-Nawawi (d. 1278), one of the best-known commentators on *Sahih Muslim* and a well-known scholar of Islamic law, gives some linguistic background on the word "minaret" in his commentary on this hadith, saying, "This minaret exists today [in the thirteenth century] in the eastern neighborhood of Damascus."[20] Later we see more commentaries on these types of hadith in which narrators perhaps have added the names of locations where they thought the events that the Prophet foretold would take place. Such additions to the original text of this hadith have caused conflicting and confusing ideas. The same hadith has been recorded by some other prominent Hadith scholars, such as al-Tirmidhi, Ibn Majah, and al-Nisaburi (d. 1014). Al-Tirmidhi, interestingly, points out a confusion of the two hadith transmitted by Walid bin Muslim and 'Abd al-Rahman bin Yazid. According to al-Nisaburi, the hadith meets the criteria for the two authoritative collections of hadith (those of al-Bukhari and Muslim).[21] It is therefore considered a sound and reliable hadith. The same hadith has been recorded by Ibn Majah in his *Sunan*. He uses the word *khuruj 'Isa* (the emergence of Jesus) instead of the phrase "nuzul 'Isa" (the descent of Jesus).[22]

## Example of a Hadith about a Dream of the Prophet

Some hadith are about a dream of the Prophet of Islam. Theologically speaking, the Prophet's dreams are always true, unlike the dreams of ordinary people. Because the prophets are chosen by God, their dreams are part of divine inspiration or revelation. In the beginning of his mission as a prophet, before the start of revelation, Muhammad would have dreams that immediately and clearly came true. For example, things that he would see at night would be realized during the day in such a clear and evident way that the prophet described them as "the break of the dawn."

The dream that is narrated in this hadith occurred in a later period of Muhammad's prophetic life. Muhammad sees Jesus and the Antichrist in his dream. In his dream the Prophet sees a very good-looking man with straight hair. Muhammad inquires about this individual's identity. The people around the Prophet say, "This is Jesus, the son of Mary." The language used in this hadith seems to be very symbolic. Jesus's garments are yellow. The image of "water" dripping from Jesus's head may also symbolize cleanliness, which has to do with his high spiritual level. In this case Jesus seems to be at the highest spiritual level, symbolizing angelic qualities, while the Antichrist seems to be at the lowest level, symbolizing satanic qualities. Jesus and the Antichrist have totally opposite qualities. 'Abdullah bin 'Umar, the narrator of this hadith, was a prominent companion of the Prophet who converted to Islam before puberty and migrated to Medina with other companions of the Prophet in 622 CE. He passed away in 692 CE, sixty years after the death of the Prophet. He narrates the words of the Prophet as follows:

It has been shown to me while I was sleeping. In my dream while I was circumambulating the Ka'ba, I saw a man of brown color, the best one can see among brown-colored human beings. His hair was so long that it fell between his shoulders, among the best hairs one can see. He had combed his hair and it was as if water was dripping from his head, and he was on the shoulders of two men circumambulating the Ka'ba. I asked, "Who is this?" They replied, "This is Jesus, the son of Mary." Then suddenly I saw another man who had very curly hair, his right eye was blind like an exploded piece of grape. I asked, "Who is this?" They replied, "This is al-Dajjal [the Antichrist], the Pseudo-Messiah."[23]

This hadith is found in *Sahih Muslim* and is considered reliable. The hadith clearly describes the Antichrist's deformed appearance by drawing attention to his eyes. Some Muslim commentators take this in an allegorical way and contend that the Prophet meant to say that the Antichrist would have only one world, that he sees only this worldly life, that his second eye is not only blind to the afterlife, it is totally deformed. In this hadith, it is clear that the Prophet related his dream to his companions. The picture of Jesus symbolically shows his purity and should not necessarily be taken literally.

A similar hadith by Jabir bin 'Abdillah, another prominent companion of the Prophet, makes a connection between Jesus and a community of believers making jihad against evil: "A group among my people shall continue till the Day of Judgment. Jesus, the son of Mary, will descend, and their leader will say to him, 'Lead us in prayer.' Jesus will answer: 'No, some of you are leaders to others. This leadership is a gift of God to this ummah [the community of Muslims].'"[24]

These four hadith give a picture of the various ways that Jesus has been described and presented in the broader Hadith literature. In general, shorter hadith are considered more reliable because one can often find evidence of authorial interpretation and additions in longer hadith. Although there might be some hadith that are weak as far as the methodology of hadith is concerned, their meaning still might be true. Thus, a weak hadith doesn't necessarily mean a wrong hadith. Some weak hadith are found in the one of the six reliable sources of Hadith and as such have a place within the Islamic tradition.

# FIVE

# Speculations about Jesus's Return

The examples from the Hadith genre of Jesus's eschatological descent presented in the previous chapter now lead us to an examination of the details Muslim scholars and theologians have elaborated on. These elaborations have brought out important and common themes in the Hadith that have played important roles in shaping the Muslim understanding of Jesus and his place in Islam. Themes include the time and place of Jesus's return, his physical appearance, his prayer behind the Muslim leader, his relation to Islamic law, his followers, and his death. All references to Jesus in the body of the Hadith, be they sound or weak, are indicative of the importance of Jesus for Muslims as a helper, a rescuer, and a bringer of justice. How and when Jesus returns is left to the interpretation of Muslim commentators, although the primary purpose of the sayings of the Prophet about Jesus was to create awareness so that people would do their best in this life to prepare for the afterlife.

The exact time of Jesus's return has occupied the minds of Muslims since the beginning of Islam. Theologically speaking, the most important thing for individuals is not the time of the return of Jesus, which signals the nearness of the Final Hour, but what they do to prepare for the afterlife. The Prophet Muhammad responds to someone who asks "When is the Hour?" by saying "What did you prepare for it?" The Prophet suggests that the most essential question is how to prepare for the afterlife, the coming of which is certain. Muslims believe that without the coming of the afterlife—the place of eternal bliss—this worldly life is incomplete. The analogy compares this world to a farm and the afterlife to the harvest. Without an afterlife, this world would be like a farm with no harvest. The certainty of the coming afterlife is a major principle in Islam. The theological argument is that if we know when Jesus returns, we can then anticipate the coming of the afterlife, the greatest event in human history. Yet the exact knowledge of this transformation belongs only to God.

The Prophet's mission was to both warn people and to give good news. Jesus's return is a sign of the afterlife, the good news for the Islamic community. In other words, the Prophetic promise of Jesus's return is a reminder that the Islamic community will never be abandoned by God. In the time of the most difficult calamities when they are almost hopeless, a messenger of God such as Jesus will come to their aid. This hope has played a vital role throughout history.

## The Time

Predicting the time of Jesus's return is of importance to Muslims because Jesus's descent is one of the most significant events in Islamic eschatological literature, despite the opposition of some Muslim intellectuals who doubt the reliability of the textual references of the descent of Jesus.[1] Knowledge of the future belongs only to God. Even prophets of God cannot know the exact contours of the future. Prophets and saints who have spoken about the future were referring to revelations or inspirations that were given to them by God. Anyone who claims to know the specific time for the descent of Jesus is considered a charlatan, because this is a future event that only God knows.

Considering the rich body of Hadith sources, the event of Jesus's return is a very important occurrence. The Prophet emphasizes Jesus's coming and some sources indicate that it might be near. In the geologic history of the earth, however, "near" is a relative term.

The Prophet wanted to make sure that his companions knew about the descent of Jesus, and he seems to expect Jesus's descent in his own lifetime. He says: "I hope I may live long enough to meet Jesus, the son of Mary. But if I have a short life any of those among you who meets him should convey my greetings of peace."[2] One can see a parallel between this saying of the Prophet and a well-known verse in the book of Acts: "This Jesus, who has been taken up from you into heaven, will come in just the same way as you have watched Him go into heaven" (Acts 1:11). Other hadith make a connection between the emergence of al-Dajjal, the Antichrist, and the descent of Jesus, suggesting that Jesus will emerge shortly after the Antichrist, yet they do not mention when the Antichrist will emerge. It is possible that in making a connection between Jesus and the Antichrist, the Prophet did not intend to give a certain period of time for the apocalypse but wanted to give good news that when there is someone who spreads animosity, such as the Antichrist, there will be someone who performs justice and good deeds, such as Jesus. Therefore, there is no reason for hopelessness.

A hadith narrated by Hudhayfa bin al-Yaman recounts,

Everyone used to ask the Prophet about good, but I asked him about evil. I was afraid that the evil would catch me. I said, "O Messenger of God, we were in ignorance and evil, then God brought for us this good [the message of Islam]. Will there be an evil after this good?" The Prophet said, "Yes." Then I said, "And will there be good after that evil?" The prophet again said, "Yes." . . . then I said, "O messenger of God, what do you command me to do if this time catches me?" The Prophet said, "Stick to the community of Muslims and their leader."[3]

The hadith suggests that the companions of the Prophet were worried about possible future events and their evil consequences and asked Muhammad for guidance.

Another long hadith, narrated by Jabir bin 'Abdillah, a well-known companion of the Prophet, relates how Muslims will be oppressed and tortured by the Antichrist and Jesus will descend to rescue them. This hadith contains important symbolic and allegorical statements and presents Jesus as a redeemer for Muslims. According to this hadith, Jesus will appear at a time when Muslims are surrounded by the forces of the Antichrist. While the Antichrist spreads his tribulation and mischief (fitna) among Muslims, a group of Muslims will escape and take refuge in a mountain, said to be near Damascus, called Dukhan, or Smoke. At this mountain they will be surrounded by the forces of the Antichrist. Jesus will appear at this time of despair for Muslims. A call for prayers will be performed. Muslims will ask Jesus to lead them in the prayer, but he will decline and ask the Muslims' leader (imam) to lead them in the prayer (and therefore pray behind the leader).[4] After performing the morning prayer together, Jesus and the Muslims will move against the Antichrist and he will melt like salt in water.[5] Either to emphasize the importance of prayer or for some other reason, prayer and the call for prayer take place in almost all narratives describing similar events. Most probably since these are symbols of Islam, they occur continuously in the time of the descent of Jesus.

Although the desperate situation of a group of Muslims and the imminence of Jesus's return are emphasized in Hadith literature, this is far from a desire for chaos promoted by the end-times scenarios of certain radical groups. In fact, contrary to this, it can be argued that Islamic eschatological literature suggests that there is a need for a peaceful environment for Jesus to come. The Hadith indicates that it is the duty of Muslims to prepare a peaceful world for the descent of Jesus and not to cause chaos to force him to come. Mainstream Muslim theologians would consider it against the teachings of the Qur'an to claim that God can be forced to do something. "God is the Doer of what He wills" (Qur'an 85:16). Thus, one cannot hasten Jesus's return. According to Islamic theology, God alone decides to send Jesus and chooses the time and manner of his descent. The theological principle clearly indicates that both some Shi'ite denominations and some Christian fundamentalist groups who try to create more chaos to hasten the coming of Jesus are going against a central principle of Islamic theology.

Furthermore, the Hadith carries a symbolic meaning indicative of a non-violent struggle against injustice before and after the coming of Jesus, as many prominent Muslims and Christians have been practicing in our recent history. Similar to the famous verses in Isaiah which speak of beating swords into plowshares (2:1–4), one hadith says that when Jesus descends, Muslims will no longer use violence or swords.[6] This hadith avers that Jesus and his Muslim helpers in this eschatological scenario will not use violence in their struggle, since the sword symbolizes the use of force in much eschatological literature and in this hadith the sword is not used. As in the narration from Jabir bin 'Abdillah above, another hadith draws our attention to how the Antichrist "melts" (rather than being "killed") when he meets Jesus: "When the Antichrist sees Jesus, he will melt as salt melts in the water."[7] Despite references to a violent struggle between Jesus and the Antichrist in some Hadith narratives, this particular phrase is very telling regarding the end-time events in Islam. One may arguably conclude that this eschatological scenario in the Islamic tradition, unlike the expectations of some fundamentalist Christians and some radical Muslims, has strong elements of nonviolence that will find its zenith in the descent of Jesus, a symbol of peace foretold by the Prophet of Islam more than 1,400 years ago.

As can be seen in these sayings of the Prophet, the time and the place of Jesus's descent are ambiguous. Any object of faith should be based on the Qur'an or sound and reliable sayings and actions of the Prophet. Just as the text must be reliable, it also must be understandable and unambiguous. Ambiguous texts are not considered valid references for building the principles of Islamic faith, not because they are wrong but because of their ambiguity. Thus, Muslims cannot build their faith in the coming of Jesus upon sayings that specify time and location. Given the ambiguity of the eschatological literature, there is much space for interpretation.

Benefiting from this ambiguity and misusing the expectations of people, many charlatans have emerged to claim that they were Jesus, that their time was *the time*. Ibn Khaldun (d. 1406), a prominent Muslim historian, theologian, and social scientist, warns of the possibility of charlatans who will misuse the message of the Prophet. Although he accepts the reliability of some sources on the descent of Jesus, he strongly criticizes those who attempt to determine a specific date for that event. He says, "There are many similar statements. The time, the man, and the place are clearly indicated in them. But the [predicted] time passes, and there is not the slightest trace of [the prediction coming true]. Then, some new suggestion is adopted which, as one can see, is based upon linguistic equivocations, imaginary ideas, and astrological judgments."[8] Discouraging charlatans and those who follow them blindly, he implies that heralds of the end times have always been a dime a dozen.[9]

## The Place

Different locations for Jesus's return are offered in a number of hadith. The hadith that speaks of the place of Jesus's descent as a "white minaret" of the Umayyad Mosque in Damascus is probably the most interesting.[10] Theologians in general do not accept this hadith literally, instead finding it symbolic. Bediüzzaman Said Nursi's writings about this hadith offer an intriguing allegorical approach. To him the minaret, or the tower attached to a mosque, is a symbol for an announcement that all people of the city can hear. Nursi analogizes this to methods of modern mass communication.

The literal understanding of the hadith led a sixteenth-century Muslim scholar, 'Ali bin Sultan Muhammad al-Qari (d. 1605), to cite various locations for Jesus's descent, including Damascus, Jerusalem, Jordan, and "the camp of Muslims." Al-Qari reconciles these contradictory narratives in an ingenious way: "The narrative that says Jerusalem is my preference. This does not contradict other narratives, because Jerusalem is east of Damascus; that is the camp of Muslims at that time. Also, Jordan linguistically means 'urban' and therefore it includes Jerusalem as well." He goes on to claim that even if there was not a white minaret in his time in Jerusalem, one would be built before the descent of Jesus.[11]

In a hadith narrated by Ka'b al-Ahbar (d. 653), a rabbi who converted to Islam, the focus shifts from a minaret to a bridge. According to this narrative, the place of descent is a white bridge by the east gate of Damascus.[12] This location is no less imbued with symbolic meaning. Why Damascus? Perhaps it is because when these sayings of the Prophet were collected and compiled, Damascus was already a center of Islam. Traditionally, meetings are held in the center of governance, so the meeting of Jesus is accordingly held there. According to this hadith, he is to meet with Muslims and pray with them in Damascus. Despite the fact that the later narration is not authenticated, the analogy of the bridge can be considered a hint about the *goal* of the descent of Jesus. Clearly, this narrative is considerably different from the earlier narrative of the descent; it gives the idea that Jesus does not necessarily descend from heaven to the top of the minaret, as was described in some narratives.

The symbol of a bridge, even if it is not directly put forth by the Prophet, is very significant with regard to the mission of Jesus's descent in Islam, particularly for some Muslims' understanding of the sayings of the Prophet on the subject. Even if this symbol is not accepted as a hadith and even if it is not reliable, the statement by Ka'b al-'Ahbar, when compared with the white minaret narratives, illustrates the richness of discussion about the descent of Jesus even in the first century of Islam. Even if we do not know why Al-'Ahbar used the symbol of a bridge, one can argue that in the modern context, building a bridge can refer to forging a dialogue between adherents of religious traditions and members of different ethnicities. Understanding the descent of Jesus in this manner is compatible with the overall teaching of the Qur'an and the Hadith. The multiplicity of understandings about the nature of Jesus's return gives a sense of the flexibility of interpretation even though some of these interpretations are not found in the major Hadith sources.

Another hadith, indicates the direction from which Jesus comes: "Jesus comes from the west, he acknowledges Muhammad as a Prophet."[13] This hadith draws attention to the manner of Jesus's appearance: he will not descend from heaven but will come from the west. The term "west" has a significant meaning. Although the soundness of this hadith is questionable with respect to the chain of narration, the meanings and interpretations the narrative suggests are important. It is evident that this hadith was known to scholars in the eighth century and in the era of the narrator of the hadith, Ahmad bin Hanbal (d. 903). In interpreting this hadith, one can argue that Christendom may be understood by the term "west," where Jesus's message is widely spread. Therefore, Jesus, in the sense of the spirit of his religious message, lives in the west. Although there is no way to claim with any certainty that the ambiguous terms used by the hadith can be attributed to the Prophet and, in fact, these types of narratives may have been said by some saints or other pious people and wrongly related to the Prophet, the fact that there was much discussion of these ideas in this milieu is of importance.

## Jesus's Physical Appearance

Jesus's physical features are also the subject of some narratives. It is interesting to observe how the body of the Hadith details the description of the face of Jesus. Jesus is described as handsome, beautiful, and clean. He is someone who is beloved. The facial descriptions found in the Hadith are symbolic of his pure message and of the mission to be fulfilled; people must love him and support him in his eschatological role. It certainly can be argued that as Jesus will not be known to many people, the attention to Jesus's appearance can simply be a way of allowing people to be able to pick Jesus out of a crowd. However, given the symbolism involved, a better argument might be what is most important is not actually seeing him and that having a personal acquaintance with Jesus is not something to be sought. Muslims, according to this interpretation, should not seek to find Jesus in person; instead, they should strive to fulfill his message of peace and serenity, a message proclaimed by the Prophet of Islam. Participation in the large-scale project that Jesus fulfills requires tremendous effort and enthusiasm. Muslims and Christians can participate in such efforts even if they never see Jesus or his descent.

These hadith continually describe the physical features of Jesus so that Muslims will not hesitate to accept him when they see him. In some traditions, Jesus's physical appearance is equated to a specific person, one of the most handsome companions of the Prophet. For example, he is likened to 'Urwa bin Mas'ud (d. 630), who was famous for his handsomeness.[14] 'Urwa became a Muslim in the first stages of the life of the Prophet when there were very few Muslims, before the Prophet's arrival in Medina, during his famous *hijra*, or migration. 'Urwa asked the Prophet for permission to go to his people and convey the message of Islam. The Prophet was worried about him and said, "I am afraid that your people will kill you," but 'Urwa said, "O messenger of God, even if I am asleep they will not wake me up. I am beloved to them." In fact he was beloved and highly respected, but the greed and arrogance of his people against the message of Islam led them to kill him while he was trying to convince them of the message of the Prophet.[15] They eventually understood the gravity of their crime, but it was too late. 'Urwa had already been shot with an arrow and killed. Later all the members of his tribe accepted Islam. 'Urwa is one of the first martyrs of Islam. By comparing Jesus's physical beauty to that of 'Urwa, the Prophet was also most likely indicating the common suffering that both experienced at the hands of their own communities. Both of them wanted to convey the message of God to their people and both were rejected. I would argue that the famous hadith "God will send Jesus, son of Mary, who is very much like 'Urwa bin Mas'ud,"[16] which is generally understood by Muslim commentators to refer to physical similarities, can also be considered in terms of the situations of Jesus and 'Urwa vis-à-vis their own communities.

In contrast to the New Testament, many Hadith narratives have been recorded that describe the physical aspects of Jesus, as if the prophet says, "If you see him, don't miss him." Once again the Prophet indicates the importance of the event of the descent of Jesus and the participation of members of his community in the fulfillment of Jesus's pure message. The beauty of the color of his skin and the appearance of his hair are all explicitly stated. The hadith indicates that the Prophet saw Jesus during his night journey when he ascended to heaven and met with him. He mentions that he met Jesus and he describes Jesus to his people, saying, "He was a man of middle stature, reddish, as though he had come out of a bath."[17] The authenticity of these narratives is accepted by Hadith scholars. The accepted interpretation is that the Prophet encouraged his community to recognize Jesus when he comes.

## Attention to the Importance of Prayer

In the hadith narrated by al-Bukhari that I discussed earlier, the Prophet says, "[I am wondering] how would you be when Jesus, the son of Mary, descends among you and your imam [leader] is one of you." The hadith speaks of a leader of Muslims who is also a Muslim or "one of you." The hadith stresses the importance of prayer and again suggests that Jesus will pray behind the leader of Muslims. Indicating the importance of prayer in the time of Jesus's descent and under the same heading, titled "The Descent of Jesus, the Son of Mary," the hadith continues, "One prostration for God will be more valuable than the entire world and what is in it."[18] This emphasizes that one segment of prayer has greater importance than the most significant material thing. This could be seen as an exaggeration, but it could also be understood as a comparison between the transient, worldly life and the world of eternity, the afterlife. Prostration before God is related to the world of eternity, from which even a small amount overweighs all possessions in this worldly life because things of this world are mortal and transient.

One can also see the importance of the prayer through the projected scenario of Muslims and Jesus praying together. The importance of the fulfillment of prayer takes precedence over the killing of the Antichrist. They perform their prayer first. At the request of Jesus, the Muslim leader leads the prayer. Following the example of the Prophet of Islam, whose life was full of prayer, the lives of all Muslims are expected to be full of prayers, the most important of which are the five prescribed daily prayers.

It is noteworthy that Jesus is generally described as coming during one of these daily prayers. Most narratives say he will come in the time of the afternoon prayer, which seems to give a different meaning than one of the other regularly prescribed daily prayers would. The afternoon prayer symbolizes that sunset or the end of human history is near. Prayer is the greatest symbol of piety in Islam and will continue to be so. Jesus's coming in a time of prayer may indicate that he approves of this behavior. The Qur'an contends, "And We have written in the Psalms, after the Torah that My righteous servants will inherit the earth" (21:105). Given the importance of the Psalms in the traditions of prayer for both Jews and Christians, the Qur'anic emphasis on righteousness in reference to the Torah and the Psalms is remarkably significant. Further, if the hadith on Jesus's descent during one of the daily prayers are authentic, they may suggest prayer as a common ground between Muslims and Christians. They may also suggest togetherness between Muslims and Christians on the concept of prayer, rather than the differences some literalist theologians have emphasized in their debates about who would lead a particular daily prayer, Jesus or the Mahdi.

It seems that a literalist approach to this saying of the Prophet, which takes place in one of the most reliable references of the Hadith, would be misleading. In this particular saying of the prophet, "prayer" seems to be the key term. The hadith, by drawing attention to prayer, makes a connection between Islamic piety and the spiritual life of Jesus. Historically and even today, prayer has been the greatest mark of Islamic life and civilization. In every part of the Islamic world, which has a population of 1.6 billion, from small villages to major cities, the call for prayer is announced five times a day from the top of minarets to declare the message of God and His greatness.

Some commentators identify the leader of Muslims mentioned in the Hadith as the Mahdi. However, there is no certainty in the traditions about the name and personality of this leader.[19] In his commentary on this particular hadith, Ibn Hajar al-'Asqalani (d. 1449), a well-known Hadith commentator and historian, prefers the interpretation that this personality is the expected Islamic messianic figure, the Mahdi. He adds that this event of prayer is evidence that the world will always have some scholars or saints who are able to prove their cases and who stand for righteousness.[20] Medieval Muslim theologians concluded that Jesus praying behind the Muslim leader is a sign of Jesus's approval of Islamic law.

## Jesus and Islamic Law

Because the Hadith is the second most important source in Islam, the matter of law and jurisdiction after the descent of Jesus has been a topic of concern for many commentators. Some commentators accept a literal approach and want to complete the scenario by providing already available Islamic laws for him. Jesus's return is certain because the sayings of the Prophet are clear about it. And, according to these commentators, his return is literal. But when he comes, what kind of rules will he follow? Is he going to follow the rules of Islamic law or invent new rules to follow? These are questions that have occupied the minds of some other commentators on the Hadith. Commenting on sayings of the Prophet such as "[I am wondering] how would you be when Jesus, the son of Mary, descends among you and your imam [leader] is one of you,"[21] many Muslim theologians believe that Jesus will take Islamic law as a reference for his ruling system. Al-Suyuti (d. 1505), a noted and prolific Egyptian Muslim scholar, is so confident about this that he wrote a book entitled *Kitab al-I'lam bi Hukm 'Isa 'Alayh al-Salam* [The Book of Declaration of the Rule of Jesus, Peace Be upon Him].[22] Importantly, the ethical teachings of Islam are fully compatible with the ethical teachings of Jesus presented in the New Testament's Sermon on the Mount.

Some scholars give Jesus the role of renewer, or *mujaddid*, of Islam. He will come to renew the religion of Islam.[23] Instead of bringing new laws, he will use Qur'anic law. For example, after recording many hadith on the descent of Jesus in his commentary on the Qur'an, al-Qurtubi says the following: "Our scholars, may God's mercy be with them, have said: This is a proof that Jesus descends as a renewer of the religion of the Prophet [Muhammad], peace and blessings be upon him."[24] Once again the close relationship between Jesus and the Prophet of Islam is emphasized.

Another question that occupied the minds of medieval Muslim theologians is how Jesus will bring about justice and by which kind of knowledge will he do so. Al-Suyuti answers this question by saying: "Jesus will be able to meet the Prophet Muhammad and the other prophets in a vision. Therefore he will adopt their rules and will act according to the rules that the Prophet of Islam has brought." For al-Suyuti, Jesus, as a prominent messenger of God, will also receive revelation from God to guide the community to righteousness.[25]

Some Muslim commentators, perhaps under the influence of certain world religious traditions, have claimed that humankind will no longer have religious obligations when Jesus comes. But Islamic theology clearly underlines that religious obligations will not go away until the day of humanity's resurrection. On this point there is a consensus.[26] In the afterlife, where good and evil are utterly separated, there will no longer be a need for religious obligations. People may want to fulfill those obligations for pleasure but not as a religious duty. In Islamic theology, this worldly life is a test, a place where one works hard to attain eternal bliss, while the afterlife is a place of rewards and not a place of testing. Therefore, religious obligations will continue as long as people live on earth.

## Jesus's Message and His Followers after His Death

Many commentators on the Hadith have carefully crafted the details of the eschatological picture. Jesus will descend from heaven; join with the Islamic leader, the Mahdi, to defeat the Antichrist; and eventually die because he is a human being, even though a messenger of God. How will his death occur? According to one Islamic tradition, Jesus's soul and the souls of his followers will be taken by a comforting breeze. He will neither suffer nor feel the agonies of death. Yet the message of Jesus will continue even after his death through those who help and follow him. These followers will generally be known as "Muslims," but they will not necessarily be only Muslims. They will also be Christians, Jews, and adherents of other religious traditions. The Islamic tradition does not restrict the followers to a certain group. The narrative is inclusive. Helpers of Jesus are praised in Islam, in both a historical and an eschatological sense.

The Qur'an praises the apostles of Jesus, who sincerely helped him and supported his message. The Holy Book of Islam presents them as exemplary personalities for Muslims. The Qur'an narrates their willingness to be Jesus's helpers in the way of God: "O you who believe, be Allah's helpers, even as Jesus, son of Mary, said unto the disciples: 'Who are my helpers in God's cause?' The apostles said: 'We are your helpers in God's cause.' And a group of the children of Israel believed, while another group disbelieved. Then we strengthened those who believed against their foe, and they became the uppermost" (61:14).

The collections of Hadith literature indicate that there will be followers of Jesus in an eschatological sense as well. In some traditions the Prophet of Islam speaks of them and praises them. Although this praise is not found in the major Hadith collections, Hadith experts think it credible. In one of these traditions the Prophet states that some people from *his* community of Islam will be Jesus's disciples. According to one narrative, the Prophet says, "Surely,

Jesus the Messiah will find some people from among my community [as helpers] who are like you or even better than you, [the prophet repeated this three times.] God will not disgrace a community of which I am the beginning and Jesus the end."[27] A group of righteous believers is presented in al-Bukhari, one of the reliable sources of the Hadith, as follows: "There will always be a group from my community steadfast on [the path of] truth until the day of judgment."[28] Some have thought of this group as the helpers of Jesus after his descent.

Like some exclusivist Christians, some Muslim narrators have limited the number of Jesus's helpers to a few hundred at the time of apocalypse. Some hadith were fabricated for this very purpose. This clearly goes against the teachings of Islam, which encourage everybody to believe. This is reminiscent of the prophetic story of the Bedouin who came to the Prophet and said as he prayed with the Prophet, "Lord, give your mercy to me and Muhammad, and do not give it to anyone else." The Prophet, after finishing his prayer, said to the man, "You have narrowed the mercy of God."[29]

Islamic Scholars have commented on the time, the place, and the physical appearance of Jesus frequently. To focus on all these commentaries would go beyond the scope of this chapter. However, it is useful to conclude with an example from a contemporary Muslim scholar who commented on the hadith that tells about Jesus praying behind the imam. Said Nursi is not concerned about the person of Jesus or the specific prayer that is mentioned in the hadith. He puts the idea of leadership in a more global context. One can see why some scholars such as Nursi would go against the classical theologians' understanding, limiting the leadership to daily prayer in a mosque, namely the Umayyad Mosque. This understanding is considerably simplistic when one speaks of Jesus's eschatological descent. Nursi understands that the meaning of the tradition that contends that Jesus will follow "the Mahdi" and pray behind him indicates that Christianity will adopt the principles of the Qur'an.[30] In other words, there will be an alliance between Muslims and Christians. In this alliance the spiritual leaders of Christianity and Islam will be united in their struggle against the nonbelieving or the irreligious. Drawing upon this hadith, Nursi predicts that by this union "the true religion of God will be strengthened."[31] The Republican Brothers movement founded by Mahmud Muhammad Taha in the Sudan considers the return of Jesus to be "the second message of Islam."[32]

But even such an alliance between Islam and Christianity does not mean the end of evil in the world. An axiom of Islamic theology requires the existence of good and evil at the same time. It is impossible to have a world with no sin. Humankind is tested in this world, as the Qur'an says. Even a fully religious society must have some discrepancies so that the exercise of free will can continue. This principle is true with regard to other figures that generally take place in the end-time picture, such as the Mahdi and the Antichrist. In the following chapter I will examine the alliance of Jesus and the Mahdi against the Antichrist as it is depicted in Islamic perceptions of the endtimes.

SIX

# The Mahdi and Jesus as Allies against al-Dajjal (the Antichrist)

In Islamic eschatological literature, there are several important figures. Perhaps the most important of these are Jesus, the Antichrist, and the Mahdi. These three figures are closely related. Although a book could be written about any of these three individually, our focus is Jesus, so it is appropriate to discuss Jesus's relationship with the other two figures. Since the idea of the Mahdi has an especial importance in the Shi'ite tradition, I found it useful to include the Shi'ite theological perspective on Jesus's return in this chapter.

## The Mahdi

The Mahdi is an Islamic messianic figure whose emergence at the end of time is expected to bring justice to the world. He is portrayed as a human being who has the extraordinary power to make such a change. Although the Mahdi is not named in the Qur'an or the highly reliable Hadith anthologies of al-Bukhari and Muslim, belief in the coming of the Mahdi is found both in the Sunni and Shi'ite traditions of Islam.[1] The belief in the emergence of the Mahdi is an essential part of the Shi'ite tradition and doctrines in that tradition regarding his coming and messianic role are considerably different than those found in the Sunni tradition. Although the vast majority of Sunnis believe in the coming of the Mahdi, the figure is not a major part of their theology; that is to say, a belief in the coming of the Mahdi is not one of the pillars of Sunni Islam or its articles of faith.[2] The major role of the Mahdi in the Sunni tradition is to work for justice and to fight with Jesus against the Antichrist and eventually defeat him. In "al-Anbiya," or "the Prophets," a chapter of Muhammad al-Bukhari's al-Sahih, we are taught about a nameless figure who leads a prayer at the request of Jesus. Many commentators on this hadith believe this Muslim leader to be the Mahdi.

Some hadith even suggest that Jesus will meet with the Mahdi at the time of a specific prayer. One hadith says this meeting will take place at a morning prayer while another says it will be during an afternoon prayer. It is believed that Jesus and the Mahdi will pray together but that the leader in prayer will be the Mahdi. Despite the fact that Jesus is among the five elite prophets of God and the Mahdi is lower in spiritual rank than Jesus, some traditions suggest that Jesus will ask the Mahdi to lead the prayer.

Some Muslim commentators take Hadith literature on the Mahdi very literally while other prominent scholars understand the hadith on the subject in allegorical ways. Still other scholars deny that the idea of the Mahdi is found in Islam. For example, Muhammad Rashid Rida (d. 1935), a prominent Egyptian scholar and jurist, argues that neither in the Qur'an nor in the Hadith can one find a reliable reference to the idea of the Mahdi that would support the figure's role in Sunni theology. He warns Muslims of pseudo-Mahdis. In concluding his arguments, he says: "We do not believe in this expected personality. We believe in the harm of believing in him." He also believes that the reason for Muslims' stagnation in technology and military power is their belief in a man with an extraordinary "unseen power and heavenly support," a capacity that can make things right and miraculously bring about justice.[3] It seems that Rida's idea is not the dominant view among Muslims, but his view is shared by a good number of Muslim intellectuals.

There is no doubt that Muslims' expectations for the Mahdi reflect a deep-rooted desire for a just social order and a moral system of governance. Since this ideal is generally future-oriented, it is evident that it has certain eschatological applications. Unlike Jesus, the Mahdi is not mentioned in the Qur'an by name, although many verses refer to the *muhtadun*, or "the guided ones."[4] In the Arabic lexicon, *mahdi* means "the person who is guided by God to the truth."[5] Both words are derived from the same verbal noun, *hady*, which means guidance. Thus, anyone who follows the true path could theoretically be called *mahdi* but without any messianic meaning attached to the term. If we consider hopeful Qur'anic verses to be indicators of the establishment of justice in the future, then we can make a connection between this idea of hope and the Mahdi tradition in Islam.

In the development of the Islamic tradition, many questions arose regarding the persona of the Mahdi and the number of *mahdis*. One prophetic tradition uses the plural form of the term in a context that indicates that the spiritual rank of *mahdis*, or people who are guided to the truth, is quite high. One can understand this from a story narrated in the Hadith collections. When the Prophet prayed for one of his companions, Abu Salama, who had passed away, he said, "My Lord, bestow your forgiveness upon Abu Salama, raise his spiritual rank to the level of the *mahdis*."[6] Since the Prophet used the plural form, it is understood that he did not mean the expected messianic figure. In other instances, the Prophet used the plural form of the term for his four caliphs, or successors, Abu Bakr, 'Umar, 'Uthman, and 'Ali, calling them "the *mahdis*." Collectively, the four caliphs are the highest of the members of the Islamic community in spiritual rank. Irbad bin Sariya, one of the companions of the Prophet, narrates:

> One day after morning prayer, the Prophet talked to us so eloquently that our eyes became full of tears, and our hearts became fearful of God and softened. A man in the group asked the Prophet, "O messenger of God, this is like a farewell speech. How do you advise us?" The Prophet replied, "I advise you to be fearful of God, to listen, and to obey, even if your leader is an Ethiopian slave. Surely, those of you who live longer will see much disunity. I am warning you about changes in the essence of religion. Surely, it is a corruption. If you are alive at that time, stick to my path and the path of my rightly guided successors [the *mahdis*]."[7]

Since the Prophet used the term *mahdis* for his successors, it is very possible that in the mind of most Muslims, the term *mahdi* became associated with a leader who would rule and bring justice to the world, as did 'Umar, the second caliph in Islam, who became a symbol of justice beyond the Islamic world through his practices of just rule.

One of the reasons the Mahdi is not an important element of faith in the Sunni tradition of Islam is because the belief in the Mahdi is not directly mentioned in the two main sources of the Hadith, namely those recorded by Muhammad al-Bukhari and Muslim bin al-Hajjaj. He is also not mentioned among the major signs of the Final Hour. Because of this, Sunni Muslims consider the belief in the Mahdi to be a secondary issue.

Even though it is not an essential part of Islam, belief in the Mahdi is of theological concern to some theologians. Sa'd al-Din al-Taftazani (d. 1390), a prominent medieval Muslim theologian, speaks of sayings of the Prophet on the Mahdi that are not mentioned in the two major sources of Hadith. He draws a distinction between the Shi'ite and the Sunni views on the Mahdi that clearly suggests that the Mahdi issue is a part of Islamic theology. Apparently this remarkable theologian was troubled by the hadith in which the Mahdi leads the prayer when he meets Jesus at the Umayyad Mosque, perhaps because many theologians, including him, have understood the hadith in a literal way. Al-

Taftazani seems not to understand why a prophet, Jesus, would ask a saint, the Mahdi, to lead a prayer when he would be expected to lead the prayer. Therefore, al-Taftazani reiterates that even after his descent Jesus will still remain a prophet of God and will still be higher than the Mahdi. After mentioning several hadith on the Mahdi, al-Taftazani says, "Yes, even he [Jesus] is at that time among the followers of the Prophet, peace and blessings be upon him. Yet Jesus is not stripped of his prophethood. There is no doubt that Jesus, as a prophet of God, is higher than the Mahdi in spiritual rank. That is because the goal of scholars of the Islamic community is the imitation of the prophets of the Israelites."[8] As I shall discuss in chapter eight, al-Taftazani reports others' allegorical interpretations of certain end-time events and seems to have no problem with them. For this specific instance of prayer, however, he has no explanation. It seems that Islamic theology needed to wait until the twentieth century for an allegorical interpretation of the hadith. Bediüzzaman Said Nursi, suggests that this is an indication of a Muslim-Christian alliance based on Qur'anic principles of justice and piety.

The Mahdi and the concept of justice are so intertwined that many Muslims have identified historical figures who struggled for justice and worked against oppression or who brought prosperity for their community as the Mahdi. For example, many considered 'Abdullah bin al-Zubair (d. 692), one of the companions of the Prophet, to be the Mahdi of his time. He fought against the oppression of some Umayyad dynasty leaders, particularly al-Hajjaj bin Yusuf (d. 714), who was notorious for his oppression, especially of the family of the Prophet. Many also considered the Umayyad caliphs Sulayman bin 'Abd al-Malik (r. 715–17) and 'Umar bin 'Abd al-'Aziz, who is known as 'Umar II (r. 717–20), to be the Mahdi for removing all grievances and making "the crooked straight."[9] A modern Egyptian scholar considers 'Umar II to be "a remarkable renewer of Islam foretold by the Prophetic hadith 'surely God sends for this community at the beginning of every century someone who renews for the community its religion.'"[10] He cites several reasons why 'Umar II was the renewer foretold by this hadith. For example, in addition to his piety and ascetic life, 'Umar's just ruling included giving importance to consultation; rejecting oppression; returning wrongly taken property to its owners; protecting minorities, Christians, and Jews; and providing freedom of thought. 'Umar's strong religion and political engagement are also cited as indications that he was a renewer of Islam, though we do not see here a messianic connotation.[11] However, some did see a messianic connotation in giving the Abbasid caliph Muhammad, the son of al-Mansur, the title of al-Mahdi.[12]

From an Islamic theological perspective, those who claim that they are the Mahdi are in fact charlatans. Since the Mahdi is guided by God, any claim to such a spiritual rank negates that rank because humility is an essential part of Islam.[13] Since hadith on the Mahdi assign a highly important task to this eschatological figure—the bringing of justice—the non-Hadith Islamic literary genre has depicted the Mahdi as having supernatural characteristics. The Mahdi has been given the extraordinary power to fulfill those expectations because such a task cannot be accomplished by an ordinary individual. Since this characterization is not found in the Hadith, it lacks theological value. The idea of the Mahdi, however, has affected the social and political life of Muslims and has led to the emergence of many impostors.

It should be noted that because of the similar roles of Jesus and the Mahdi, there has been confusion about the role of each. Some early scholars of Islamic theology have even claimed that there will be no Mahdi, that the eschatological figure called the Mahdi is in fact Jesus himself.[14] Although this view has not received general acceptance among Muslims, some early scholars viewed the concept of the Mahdi in this way. Al-Taftazani tackles this point by referring to a saying related to the Prophet: "there is no Mahdi except Jesus." He interprets the word *mahdi* to mean "guide" instead of the expected messianic figure of Islam. He says, "It is not illogical to interpret this saying of the Prophet to mean that there is no guide [*mahdi*] to lead the annihilation of al-Dajjal and the prevention of his evil actions, as the reliable sayings of the Prophet have indicated, except Jesus."[15]

As did Abu Dawud, some other early Hadith scholars recorded several more traditions about the Mahdi in their collections.[16] One can find a criticism by Muslim historian and sociologist Ibn Khaldun (d. 1406) about the authenticity of these sayings of the Prophet. Generally speaking, he accused many narrators of being unreliable, although one can conclude from his overall approach that he believed some sayings of the Prophet on the subject were reliable, and he affirms that the idea of the Mahdi among Muslims has been a predominant view throughout history. Interestingly, Ibn Khaldun brings the Mahdi, Jesus, and the Antichrist together and explains the sequence of their emergence. In this sequence, the Mahdi comes first, then the Antichrist, and finally Jesus. He also warned that in his time there were some charlatans who claimed they were the expected Mahdi. Summarizing the Sunni understanding of the Mahdi, Ibn Khaldun says,

It has been well known and generally accepted by all Muslims in every epoch that at the end of time a man from the family of the Prophet will, without fail, make his appearance, one who will strengthen the religion and make justice triumph. Muslims will follow him, and he will gain domination over the Muslim realm. He will be called the Mahdi. Following him, the Antichrist will appear with all the subsequent signs of the Hour as established in the sound tradition of the Sahih. After the Mahdi, Isa [Jesus] will descend and kill the Antichrist. Or Jesus will descend with the Mahdi and help him kill the Antichrist, and will have the Mahdi lead the prayers.[17]

A famous hadith explicitly emphasizes the similarity between the Mahdi and the Prophet Muhammad. According to Abu Dawud, who seems to be the Hadith collector most interested in the subject of the Mahdi, the Prophet said: "If the world had no more than one day remaining, God would make that day long in order to send a man from my family, whose name will coincide with my name [Muhammad], and the name of his father will coincide with the name of my father ['Abdullah]."[18] In another narration chain of the same tradition, a similar statement is attributed to 'Ali, the cousin of the Prophet, that emphasizes the fulfillment of justice. 'Ali, referring to his son Hasan, says: "This son of mine is a master, as he was called by the Messenger of God. From his offspring, there will come forth a man who will be called by the name of the Prophet [Muhammad] and who will not resemble him physically, but will resemble him in character." 'Ali then says: "He will fill the earth with justice," the role attributed to Jesus in Hadith literature.[19] This emphasis on character goes against the common understanding of the description of the Mahdi. In most Islamic sources, he is known to have the name of Muhammad and his father has the name of Muhammad's father, 'Abdullah. Also typical are descriptions of facial features of the Mahdi, such as his nose, eyes, and ears, that contradict this emphasis on character.

If the hadith about the Mahdi were proven to be sound and reliable, the promise of the Mahdi was likely a reassuring answer and a comfort to the companions of the Prophet who were asking him about the coming turmoil. For example, the Prophet refers to a caliph who the commentators understand to be the Mahdi: "At the end of my community, there will be a caliph who will distribute countless wealth."[20] The Hadith commentators indicate that this person was believed to have been 'Umar bin 'Abd al-'Aziz, or 'Umar II, the Umayyad caliph whose time was one of prosperity and peace and justice for the Islamic community. Many scholars, poets, and theologians have thought of Umar II as either a *mahdi* or the Mahdi, "whose physical peculiarities foretold that he was the one destined to fill the earth with justice."[21] The word "caliph," or *khalifa*, has the connotation of both religious and political authority. To indicate this, the term *khalifat Allah*, or "deputy of God," was used for the heads of state during the Umayyad dynasty.

Because the term "caliph" was used to indicate both religious and political authority, one can understand how the title of Mahdi in the Shi'ite tradition also came to mean both religious and political authority. If the Hadith commentators are accurate in their assumption that the caliph mentioned in this hadith refers to the Mahdi, then one can claim that the Sunni tradition has a parallel point of view about the position of the Mahdi.[22] Similarly, a hadith about a group keeping the path of righteousness is perceived as a reference to the community of the Mahdi that reasserts the promise of hope in the unseen future. The Prophet says: "There will always be a group of people, following the way of truth triumphantly until the Day of Judgment."[23] These traditions suggest that there is not necessarily just one Mahdi and that there may be more than one. This might explain why historically many people referred to their spiritual leaders, Sufi masters, or just rulers using the title Mahdi.

The idea of the Mahdi also has a significant place in the mystical tradition of Islam. According to Ibn Khaldun, Ibn al-'Arabi, one of the most significant personalities of Islamic mysticism, elaborated extensively on the subject.[24] Ibn al-'Arabi suggests that the idea of the Mahdi has some relationship with the idea of a *mujaddid* (renewer) in Islam. A renewer can be a saint or a scholar. The idea has its roots in a prophetic tradition. The Prophet says, "Surely God sends for this community at the beginning of every century someone who renews for the community its religion."[25] Accordingly, it is believed that although there are difficulties and tumultuous times, God will not leave the community without guidance. The Prophet gave the good news to his community that God will support the community with these selected figures, renewers who possess moral and spiritual power. Many Muslims believe that Abu Hamid al-Ghazali (d. 1111) was the renewer of his time and that Ahmad Sirhindi (d. 1624) was the renewer of the second millennium of the Islamic calendar. Similarly, some consider Bediüzzaman Said Nursi to be the renewer of the twentieth century.[26] There might be others who could be considered renewers of Islam. Theologically speaking, it is not appropriate to make a strict claim in this regard. One should say that God knows best.

Discussion of the Mahdi leads to the place of hope in the Islamic tradition. All this good news from the Prophet about the future should not put out the flame of hard work in the minds and hearts of Muslims. Fatalism and hopelessness are not accepted in Islam. If the idea of the coming of the Mahdi leads to idleness and passivity, it would be because of a misreading of the sayings of the Prophet about future events. It can be argued that for a good period of time, this misreading of the text was the norm. The Qur'an explicitly states that "for human beings there is nothing except through their own endeavors" (53:39). Believers of Islam should combine hope and action. This is true even in difficult times. The faithful are to be hopeful about a better future. The Qur'an mentions the experiences of the prophets before Islam, those who never deviated from justice despite the difficulties they faced. The role of the Mahdi can be understood as a continuation of their belief.

## Jesus

Before discussing the Antichrist in Islamic theology, it is important to elaborate on Jesus's descent as understood by Shi'ite theologians, which is very much related to the emergence of the Mahdi. Essentially, the majority of Shi'ite Muslims, the dominant religious group in modern-day Iran, are in agreement with Sunni Muslims about the descent of Jesus. Yet some Shi'ite theologians may have some different views.

According to the Twelver Shi'ite tradition, Jesus will descend at the end of time and will help establish justice on the earth. Other sects of the Shi'ite tradition are directly influenced by the teachings of Christianity in their religious beliefs. For example, they consider 'Ali, the cousin of the Prophet, to be an incarnation of God and compare Fatima, the daughter of Muhammad and wife of 'Ali, to Mary, the mother of Jesus.[27] They have also developed a religious hierarchy that suggests a Christian influence. According to the scenario that is presented here, Jesus will descend to help the Muslim community fight the Antichrist and will defeat him. We find a parallel between Sunni and Shi'ite beliefs in this regard. However, a slight difference between the two beliefs should be noted: the Shi'ite tradition suggests that although Jesus has died, he will be resurrected and return.

Some Shi'ite theologians, such as Abu Ja'far 'Ali bin Babawayh al-Qummi (d. 991), demonstrate a parallel belief not with the Sunni tradition but with Christianity with regard to the death and the resurrection of Jesus. Ibn Babawayh says, "According to what our opponents [Sunni theologians] narrate, when the Mahdi emerges, Jesus will descend on earth and pray behind him. In fact, Jesus' descent to this world is his return after his death."[28] Two later Shi'ite scholars share this idea of Ibn Babawayh. In his interpretations of the Qur'an, al-Tabarsi (d. 1153) mentions the reliability of traditions concerning the descent of Jesus and discusses different ideas about these traditions. He shares the beliefs found in the Sunni tradition that are narrated in major sources of the Hadith.[29] These Shi'ite Muslims were greatly influenced by pre-Islamic scripture. For example, a seventeenth-century Shi'ite scholar, Fayd-i Kashani (d. 1679), refers to pre-Islamic scriptural references, particularly the Torah, the Psalms, and the Gospels. Kashani quotes "the Gospel" on the coming of the Prophet of Islam to the people of seventh-century Arabia and speaks of Jesus as a precursor of Muhammad: "Jesus said in the Gospel the Reverence [Christ] is going and the Paraclete [Muhammad] is coming after him. He will lighten the bonds and interpret everything for you. He will witness for me as I witness for him. I came to you with parables; he will come to you with interpretation." Kashani continues by narrating a divine revelation to Jesus: "God revealed to Jesus and said, 'O Jesus, believe in Muhammad, and command your community of those who will come after Muhammad's emergence to believe in him. If it were not for Muhammad, I would not have created Adam, and if it were not for Muhammad, I would not have created Paradise and Hell.'"[30] Though Kashani does not give a direct indication of the source for this biblical quote and simply cites "the Gospel" as his reference, the context seems to indicate that he was referring to John 14:16, which says, "I will ask the Father, and He will give you another Helper, that He may be with you forever." The word "helper" as translated here is the Greek word *parakletos*, which is believed to be a reference to Muhammad. It is clear that Kashani is not quoting verbatim from this verse, and he likely took it from some secondary sources of his time.

Some Shi'ite scholars even go further to speak about the conditions in which Jesus lives and whether he is now alive or dead. For example, the prominent contemporary Shi'ite scholar al-Tabataba'i (d. 1981) states that Jesus is alive today. He interprets the verse of the Qur'an about the death of Jesus to mean that God is taking care of Jesus instead of meaning that Jesus died. Therefore, the meaning of the verse "and remember when God said, 'O Jesus, I will cause you to die and raise you to Myself'" (Qur'an 3:55) is "I will take care of you," rather than the literal "I will cause you to die." He also elaborates on Jesus's ascension, saying that it is not just ascension in the physical world. A purely physical ascent would assign a location to God, which is not compatible with the principles of Islamic theology. Here we face the theological problem of confining God to a particular space. In Islamic theology, God is too exalted to have a physical location. If Jesus has ascended to God, does this mean that we should relate God to a particular space?

To respond to these challenging questions, al-Tabataba'i says, "We can say the meaning of ascension to God is the ascension of body and spirit. The apparent meaning of the verse leads to this belief. In this case, Jesus ascended to heaven in the sense that heaven meant the nearest rank to God, the place where people ascend for the glorification of God, the residence of the angels."[31] This view of heaven is shared by some contemporary Sunni theologians, as discussed earlier, and the Shi'ite belief is parallel to the Sunni belief in this regard. Among Shi'ite scholars today, the idea has remained and has kept its vitality. Some modern scholars of the Shi'ite branch of Islam compare Jesus to the Mahdi, perhaps because of the similarity of their roles in bringing justice and rescuing the oppressed.

However, Ibn Khaldun shares the reports of some narrators who give us the impression that the Shi'ite tradition of Islam denies the descent of Jesus. He criticizes some Shi'ite sects for their deification of imams, including the hidden imam, the Mahdi, in the same way that he criticizes Christians for believing in the divinity of Jesus. Ibn Khaldun says, "There are also [Shi'ite] sects that are called 'Extremists' [ghulat]. They transgress the bounds of reason and the faith of Islam when they speak of the divinity of the imams. They either assume that the imam is a human being with divine qualities, or they assume that he is God in human incarnation."[32]

According to Ibn Khaldun, "Some Shi'ites referred to the famous saying of the Prophet: 'There is no Mahdi except Jesus' to claim that there will be no Mahdi except the Mahdi," and some Shi'ites contend that "the Mahdi is the Messiah of the Messiahs."[33] One can argue that Jesus's descent is not denied in Shi'ite theological sources. These sources suggest that Jesus's descent supports the messianic figure of Shi'ites, the Mahdi. If Jesus's descent is acknowledged in the Shi'ite tradition, then why would a prominent Islamic historian, theologian, and sociologist such as Ibn Khaldun have claimed that Shi'ite Muslims do not have such a creed? Here we may make two speculations. First, it is possible that Ibn Khaldun was not aware of some major Shi'ite sects, which have their own creeds and beliefs. Since he lacked this information, he came to the conclusion that Shi'ites do not believe in the coming of Jesus. The second possibility is that Ibn Khaldun knew about this faith of Shi'ites but that since their argument for it was so weak, he just ignored it. Some Shi'ite sects even claimed that 'Ali, the cousin of the Prophet, would return in a manner that is similar to the coming of Jesus. Others claimed that Muhammad, the Prophet of Islam, would return. Sunni Muslims reject both views.

This idea of the return of 'Ali is present in the beliefs of some classical sects in the Shi'ite tradition, including one called the Saba'iyya, an extremist Shi'ite sect. When 'Ali, the fourth caliph of Islam and the most prominent figure in the Shi'ite tradition, died after being wounded while preparing for morning prayer by a Kharijite named Abd al-Rahman bin Muljam (d. 661), the Saba'iyya claimed that 'Ali had not been killed but that Satan had been killed instead.[34] They believed that 'Ali rose to the heavens just as Jesus did and that Ali would return and have his revenge on his enemies.[35] Some of these Shi'ite sects also "greet the clouds," since they believe that 'Ali will come riding on the clouds, a view that is almost identical to some literal readings of the return of Jesus in Christianity. The founder of the Saba'iyya, 'Abdullah bin Saba', claimed that the Prophet Muhammad will also return after his death. Members of the Saba'iyya criticized Sunnis and Shi'ites who do not believe in the return of Muhammad, claiming that "it is strange indeed that anyone should believe in the return of Jesus as the Messiah and deny the return of Muhammad." They claimed that God has announced the return of Muhammad. Reynold Nicholson refers to Julius Wellhausen's belief that the dogmas of this group were derived from Judaic roots rather than from Persian sources.[36] Although the group had an effect on Islamic history, it has not continued into our time.

## Al-Dajjal, the Antichrist

The Mahdi is presented on the side of Jesus in his eschatological struggle as a figure of righteousness.[37] In this understanding, we encounter a figure of evil that is on the opposite side, known as the Antichrist, or al-Dajjal, a fierce opponent of Jesus. In Islam, al-Dajjal is evil personified, along with Satan (Qur'an 2:36, 168, 208, 268), Iblis (Qur'an 2:34; 7:11; 26:95), al-Taghut (Qur'an 2:257; 4:60; 16:36), and the Pharaoh (Qur'an 3:11; 20:60; 28:4). Hadith literature contains a detailed account of the emergence of al-Dajjal, also known as al-Masih al-Dajjal or the Liar Messiah.

Strictly speaking, the word "al-Dajjal" does not appear in the Qur'an. However, some scholars believe that he is mentioned by his character traits. The Qur'anic verses that mention Jesus indirectly make reference to al-Dajjal as well. One verse reads: "Nay, but verily man is rebellious" (96:6). Though the chapter's revelation marks it as a description of a specific historical figure from the time of the Prophet, it goes on to list characteristics that are analogous to those that have been ascribed to al-Dajjal: rebelling against divine revelation and the Prophet; preventing people from worshipping God; and closing houses of worship, in particular mosques, among others. Similar sentiments are found in chapter 68 verses 10–13, which say: "[Muhammad] don't follow the wretch of many oaths, the mischief-making slanderer, the hinderer of good, the wicked transgressor, and the bully who is of doubtful birth." Some argue that verses in the Qur'an about the Pharaoh and false deities such as al-Taghut also set forth characteristics of al-Dajjal.[38] As Bernard McGinn writes, "Some Qur'anic exegetes refer to Chapter 108 in the Qur'an and claim that the verse contains the hallmarks of the Antichrist." The chapter reads: "Lo! We have given you [Muhammad] the *kauthar* [the fountain of paradise, a fountain that permanently quenches the thirst of anyone who drinks of it]; so pray unto your Lord and sacrifice, surely the one who insults you, he is the *abtar* [one who is cut off without posterity]" (108:1–3). McGinn indicates that some Muslim scholars understand the term *abtar* to mean "one who is cut off or defective" and believe that this is a reference to the Antichrist.[39]

In the Hadith collections, al-Dajjal is portrayed as an ugly, dirty person with one eye. A companion of the Prophet, Anas bin Malik, narrates that on one occasion the Prophet told his companions the following: "All of the prophets warned their communities about the Antichrist. Beware, he is blind, and your Lord is not blind. And there will be written on his forehead between his eyes the word 'disbeliever' Kaf-Fa-Ra [or K-F-R, the Arabic letters for the root word for 'disbelief']." McGinn argues that the notion that the Antichrist will have three letters on his forehead parallels a number of Christian beliefs about the physiognomy of the Antichrist, especially those presented in the apocalypse narratives found in the non-canonical texts of pseudo-John and pseudo-Daniel.[40]

The companions of the Prophet asked him about the length of al-Dajjal's stay on earth. The Hadith collections record that the length of his stay is forty days. In a considerably long hadith narrated in one of the two most reliable Hadith collections, Muslim bin al-Hajjaj, the Prophet speaks of the unusual days of the Antichrist: "[He stays for] forty days. One day is as long as a year. . . . And we asked, 'O messenger of God, for the day that is like one year, does it suffice for us to pray a one day prayer?' The Prophet replied, 'No, measure [the time of your prayer] that day according to your [regular] days.'"[41]

Since the Prophet frequently uses figurative language in his talks about future events, we may understand the meaning of these prophetic statements in an allegorical and symbolic way. In the methodology of Islamic theology, when the literal meaning is not reasonable, one should refer to the allegorical and symbolic meaning. This hadith seems to be allegorical in relationship to the Antichrist since the individual this text describes cannot be a human being. It is scientifically implausible for anyone to be born with these letters indicating disbelief or a denial of God inscribed on his or her forehead. However, there are various symbols of disbelief, and perhaps this is what the Prophet meant instead of literal letters. Especially in our time, there are many groups or causes that can be easily recognized by their symbols. For instance, people who sport clothing with the logo of the Coexist Foundation are making a clear ideological statement of the need to understand one another and live together peacefully. Explicit disbelief in God also has its symbols. One can argue that the hammer and sickle have come to represent an atheistic worldview instead of the proletariat and the peasantry that they originally stood for. Here we do not assert that the Prophet of Islam referred in these sayings to certain ideologies of disbelief, but we can assume that the Prophet could have spoken of some future ideologies and movements that might make denial of God a slogan and a symbol.

These are, of course, all possible interpretations and are open to discussion. One cannot determine for sure what the ultimate goal of the Prophet was in making these statements and therefore cannot build a strong faith upon them. The text is open to more interpretations. All of these interpretations are based on our assumption that the Prophet really said these statements because they are mentioned in the reliable sources of Hadith. If the scholars of Hadith prove the unreliability of these sayings of the Prophet, then these interpretations point to what happened after the era of the Prophet. Theologically speaking, the knowledge of these kinds of narratives belongs solely to God because they refer to the future, to unseen events.

Some contemporary scholars have found certain hints in the sayings of the Prophet that help in understanding these ambiguous narratives. One of these hints is the concept of the "long day," according to some contemporary theologians who are much more aware of the geography of the world than earlier generations were. One of these scholars is Said Nursi, who refers to the North Pole as a reference for this hadith, a place where a year is one day. This contemporary knowledge has led him to define the location from which the Antichrist or, in his words, "the ideology of disbelief," emerges. He humbly reminds his readers that "no one knows the realm of the unseen but God" (Qur'an 27:65) to make it clear that his interpretations are not binding. To him, "there are two interpretations of this: the first, the hadith indicates that the big Dajjal (the Antichrist of the world of Christianity) will emerge from the North Pole, because at the North Pole the whole year is one night and one day." In his second interpretation, Nursi says that both Dajjals, the Antichrist of the Islamic world and that of the Christian world, will have three periods of rule. During the first of these, which are called "days," the two Antichrists will accomplish "endeavors" the likes of which a human being could not accomplish in three hundred years. Nursi believed this is what the Prophet of Islam meant by "one day will be like one year." He also suggests that the Antichrist should not be understood as merely a person but as a current or philosophy of irreligiosity that promotes disbelief. For him, a philosophical movement such as Communism can be considered one of these materialistic philosophies or movements.[42]

Unlike Nursi's interpretation, Muslims throughout Islamic history understood the Antichrist to be an individual rather than a movement. Yet Nursi's point shows us that there should be a reevaluation of some historical concepts of Islamic theology. There is no doubt that al-Dajjal, or the Antichrist, is one of these historical themes. His role is a destructive one, and he is purely evil. He is not capable of doing good. He is similar to the evil figure in Islam known as al-Shaytan or Satan.

According to Islamic theology, both Satan and the Antichrist are dedicated to evil. This is why the Prophet mentions refuge from both in God. In his daily prescribed prayers, he used to say the following, which is even today repeated by Muslims as part of their daily prayers: "O my Lord! I take refuge in You from the torment of the grave. I take refuge in You from the chastisement of fire. I take refuge in You from the trial of life and death, and I take refuge in You from the trial of the Antichrist."[43] Muslims are told that the Prophet taught this prayer to his companions as he was teaching them a chapter from the Qur'an.[44]

According to the Islamic tradition, the Antichrist will attack believers until Jesus comes to help them and eventually, with the Mahdi, defeats him. In some later Hadith collections, the situation of believers has been dramatized for maximum effect. According to a saying of the Prophet narrated by one of his closest companions, Abu Huraira, "no one will be able to kill the Antichrist except Jesus, the son of Mary, peace be upon him."[45] After this victory the world will be full of justice and peace. This should not be confused with the Christian understanding of the coming kingdom of God, where evil is totally eliminated. Since this worldly life is a place of testing, it is impossible to eliminate evil completely. Although it is believed that there will be a period of great justice and peace, the struggle between good and evil will continue though evil will be greatly weakened. It is the life of paradise and the realm of eternity where evil no longer exists and the "kingdom of God" is fully established.

## A Case for the Interpretive Approach

At this juncture, we need to discuss and evaluate the reliability of the sayings of the Prophet presented in this chapter. After reviewing the body of Hadith literature on the descent of Jesus, the Antichrist, and the Mahdi, one can conclude that the overall body of the Hadith includes some weak hadith attributed to the Prophet that lack a reliable chain of narration. Hadith authorities have elaborated on those unreliable references one by one. Most likely these weak hadith were wrongly attributed to the Prophet.

Having said this, a good number of hadith on the subject are accepted as reliable and sound. Understanding these sayings of the Prophet in an allegorical way is more compatible with the overall principles of Islamic theology. However, many medieval and modern Islamic scholars have understood these dogmas literally. They rely on a theological principle that avoids allegorical meanings if a literal meaning is possible. In the case of the hadith related to the descent of Jesus, the literalist approach finds the actual descent of Jesus from heaven possible because it is believed to be within God's power to bring Jesus physically from heaven. Because of this possibility, they accept the literal meaning of the text and avoid interpretation.

In contrast to the literalist approach, the contemporary interpretative approach suggests that through his actions in the physical realm, God has shown certain patterns that might be understood by humans. He changes these patterns when it is necessary, though this happens only rarely, such as when he allows prophets to perform miracles. The contemporary interpretative approach, which I argue for, does not see the descent of Jesus as a miracle. The defenders of this approach argue that God is omnipotent, that with God everything is possible. However, God's pattern of action in the physical world teaches us that things happen through the interaction of cause and effect. To expect a person to come in bodily form from the sky, in front of everyone's eyes, and to expect this person to rescue people from oppression and establish justice does not seem plausible, nor does it seem to be in accordance with the divine wisdom or the principles of Islamic theology. God is essentially the "Cause of causes," and no cause can have an effect without the will of God.

Because God's actions in this world are veiled by natural causes, it seems that the hadith containing extraordinary descriptions of future events, including Jesus's descent, the emergence of the Antichrist, and the emergence of the Mahdi, should all be taken in an allegorical way. In this interpretation, God can restore a society with one person in a twinkling of an eye, but even a success such as this was not accomplished by the greatest prophets of God. Therefore, is the Mahdi greater than the Prophet of Islam? All Muslim theologians will answer this question with "No"; why then would the Mahdi be able to restore his society so miraculously when even the Prophet was unable to do this? Therefore, those sayings of the Prophet for which reliability is proven by Hadith authorities can be interpreted in accordance with the Arabic language and the literature of allegory.[46] For example, in Arabic metaphor, when one says, "This person has a long sword," it means that he is a tall man. If he is tall and has no long sword, the statement is still correct. But if he is not tall, even if he has a long sword, the statement is incorrect because the literal meaning is not intended in the phrase. Therefore many hadith on the subject should be understood allegorically. The following hadith by 'A'isha, the wife of the Prophet, which al-Bukhari reported, constitutes a good example of how the Prophet used metaphorical language in his conversations with his companions and the people of his house. After being asked who would be the first to meet him in the afterlife, He said, "The one who has the longest hand." By saying this, the Prophet meant the one who has the longest hand outstretched in charity has the longest hand, not the one with the longest physical hand.[47]

This hadith clearly illustrates that the Prophet used allegorical language in his conversations with his companions and even more so for future events. As in other traditions, particularly in Judaism, there are two tendencies about eschatological events: the restorative-conservative approach and the apocalyptic-utopian approach.[48] In the Islamic tradition one can find similar types of approaches. In the following chapter I will elaborate on what I call the literalist approach.

# SEVEN

# Literalist Approaches to
# Jesus's Eschatological Role in Islamic Theology

After the era of the Prophet, questions concerning certain theological themes developed among Islamic scholars. Encounters with adherents of the religious traditions that were already present in the Arabian Peninsula and in what is today called the Middle East encouraged Muslim scholars and theologians to develop a comprehensive theology that would be able to respond to questions posed by members of neighboring religions. Questions came from adherents of Christianity, Judaism, and Zoroastrianism as well as of other indigenous religious traditions. Because Jesus was central to both the Qur'an and to Christian theology, Jesus's descent to earth, or "Second Coming," was among the themes on which Muslim theologians elaborated.

## The History of Islamic Theology Regarding Jesus's Descent

Since the eighth century, the belief in the descent of Jesus and his eschatological role has been an element of Islamic theology. Early theologians who discussed Jesus and understood the sayings of the Prophet literally did not elaborate on the role of Jesus in a detailed way. Because many sayings of the Prophet were widely known among the audience for early theologians, they may have felt they did not need to elaborate further. It is also possible that they considered the issue to be among those related to the realm of the unseen, *'alam al-ghayb*, or they believed that the only knowledge about Jesus's descent at the end of time comes from the Prophet and that one has to believe what the Prophet has said with no further elaboration or questioning. In most cases, these early theologians cited the belief in the descent of Jesus, as well as many other objects of faith, as a part of the Islamic theological discourse, but only in one or two sentences.

By the tenth century, theologians had begun to elaborate on the possible allegorical meanings of the sayings of the Prophet, and the descent of Jesus became a subject of interpretation among a small number of Muslim theologians. Belying the earlier trend and perhaps due to political and social situations, theologians since the seventeenth century have dedicated significant independent works to the subject of the descent of Jesus. Though for much of the preceding 1,000 years, Islamic power was in ascendency, by the eighteenth century two of the last major Islamic powers, the Ottoman and Mughal Empires, were in decline and full-scale colonization of the Islamic world was under way. The events that followed, including the invasion of Islamic centers such as Cairo by French troops under Napoleon Bonaparte and the gradual breaking up of the Mughal empire by Hindu and later British forces, led some Muslims to believe that the end of time was near.

As theologians became more interested in the details of Jesus's descent and expectations of Jesus's return became dominant in the Muslim community, those who claimed to be the expected Messiah or the incarnation of Jesus also became more numerous. Because such bold claims go against the principle of Islamic theology, literature developed to refute them and reemphasize strict adherence to the sayings of the Prophet. Other theological literature on Jesus aimed to inform Muslims and help them prepare for the life to come, because Jesus's descent indicates that the end is near. This theological literature reinforced that Jesus's descent is a part of the Islamic creed that comes from many reliable sayings of the Prophet. One example of this would be the famous work of Muhammad al-Barzanji (d. 1691), an Islamic scholar from the Kurdish region of Shahrazur in modern Iraq. In his book on the portents of the Hour he dedicates several sections of his book to the descent of Jesus, the coming of the Mahdi, and the emergence of the Antichrist.[1]

## Early Islamic Discourse of Jesus's Descent

It is important to consult these early sources directly in order to have a sense of what Muslim theologians thought about the subject and how they discuss it. These sources give the reader access to the early Islamic theological discourse on Jesus's descent. But any comments on this literature will be incomplete without understanding the essence of the Arabic language and its usage.

Early theologians emphasized the importance of belief in the descent of Jesus without questioning it at all, a trend that continued for a considerable period of time. The theme gradually developed in Islamic theology until our century, when one can find long discussions, interpretations, and questions on the subject. It is puzzling why early theologians did not feel the need to debate this subject and were able to accept Jesus's descent literally. One argument says that in the formative period of Islamic theology the challenging questions were not about Jesus's descent but about God, God's attributes, and human free will. Furthermore, Muslim theologians of this period did not consider themselves as the people of the end-time period. I will return to my evaluations of these views toward the end of this chapter, but first it is important to know how the topic is explicated in the manuals of Islamic theology. The following examples from prominent Muslim theologians demonstrate how Jesus's descent was discussed in theological circles.

One of the earliest scholars of law and theology was Nu'man bin Thabit Abu Hanifa (d. 767). When Abu Hanifa presents major themes that Muslims have to believe in, he includes the descent of Jesus and other signs of the Hour as part of the creed of Islam: "The emergence of the Antichrist, Gog and Magog, the rise of the sun from the west, the descent of Jesus, and other signs of the Hour, as mentioned in the reliable Hadith narrations, are true and will happen."[2] He is very clear and sure that it will happen because the Prophet's narrations in this regard are reliable. Abu Hanifa believes in the descent of Jesus because the Prophet of Islam said it will happen. When the Prophet says something about faith-related matters and that saying is reliable, it becomes a part of faith. Abu Hanifa's assessment of the narrations on the descent of Jesus is positive. His statement is short but gives confidence to the Muslim community about the reliability of the sayings of the Prophet, which makes this topic a part of faith.

Almost a century later another theologian, 'Ali al-Madini (d. 848), added more details to this creed. He says, "It is necessary to believe in the descent of Jesus and his killing of the Antichrist at the gate of Ludd [Lod]."[3] In al-Madini's statement we observe three components. The first element involves the descent of Jesus as a necessary belief since the Prophet said it. The second component provides the reason for his descent, namely his killing of the Antichrist. Thus, Jesus's major role is depicted in this statement. The third component is related to the location of this struggle against the Antichrist. The sayings of the Prophet contain many aspects, as we discussed in earlier chapters. Apparently, however, al-Madini wants to draw to his readers' attention these three aspects.

Following in the intellectual tradition established by Abu Hanifa, a leading Hanafi scholar in tenth-century Egypt, Abu Ja'far al-Tahawi (d. 933), refers to the descent of Jesus as a theme of the Islamic creed in accordance with what is narrated in the reliable traditions. Al-Tahawi says, "And we, [Muslims], believe in the signs of the Hour including the emergence of the Antichrist, the descent of Jesus, son of Mary, peace be upon him, from heaven."[4] He does not refer here to the struggle between good and evil; instead, he refers to two figures that have symbolic importance with regard to the end-time scenario, namely the Antichrist, a personification of evil, and Jesus, a personification of good. Since his predecessor, al-Madini, had already spoken of Jesus's killing of the Antichrist, perhaps the event was already known to most of his audience, which may be why we do not see the details of this struggle. Al-Tahawi's fourteenth-century commentator, Ibn Abi al-'Izz (d. 1390), gives more textual support for al-Tahawi's view of the signs of the Final Hour. Al-'Izz contends that since the descent of Jesus is neither impossible nor irrational, it will happen as it is mentioned in the dogma. This literalistic approach was the way of early theologians, particularly the way of the so-called Ashab al-Hadith, or the People of Hadith, who are more prone to understand the sayings of the Prophet literally. To a certain extent the same path is followed in the works of the founders of the two major schools of Islamic theology.

Abu al-Hasan al-Ash'ari (d. 936), the founder of the Ash'ari school of Islamic thought, and Abu Mansur al-Maturidi (d. 944), the founder of the Maturidi school of Islamic thought, are considered the two poles of Islamic theology. Both have expressed the importance of faith in the descent of Jesus and in his fight against the Antichrist. Interestingly, al-Ash'ari speaks about this in the context of prohibiting defiance of authority. He says, "The people of the Sunnah confirm prayer for the leaders of Muslims for wholesomeness, and confirm the prohibition of an armed revolt against them, and confirm that in the time of the *fitna* [chaos and anarchy when trials happen] they fight not against each other. They also confirm the emergence of the Antichrist and [the coming] of Jesus to kill him."[5] One can conclude from this short statement of al-Ash'ari and the context in which he mentions Jesus's descent that he thinks of Jesus as a public leader who will bring justice. His leadership will coincide with a time when chaos and anarchy are spread in the community. He is clear that in such a period of anarchy, when bloodshed is highly possible, Muslims are not allowed to participate in chaos and defy authority. Their duty is to support Jesus, the just ruler, who in this case represents authority.

For al-Maturidi, it seems that Jesus's descent is not an important part of Islamic theology, at least according to the known sources we have from him. One can argue that if he felt that it was an important part of theology, he would have at least a section on Jesus's descent in his monumental book on Islamic theology, *Kitab al-Tawhid* [The Book of Unity]. Instead this book makes no reference to Jesus's descent, and al-Maturidi criticizes the beliefs of various Christian sects about Jesus and presents theological arguments that no one should ascribe divinity to him. Even though al-Maturidi does not mention Jesus's descent in this famous book on theology, we find his thoughts on Jesus's descent in his monumental commentary on the Qur'an, which remained a manuscript for many centuries and was only recently edited and published.[6] Al-Maturidi mentions the descent of Jesus when he interprets verses regarding the belief of the People of the Book in Jesus before his death. As discussed earlier, the verse "There shall be no one of the People of the Book but left not believing him before his death" (Qur'an 4:159) poses challenging questions for Muslim theologians in general and for al-Maturidi in particular. Al-Maturidi's commentary is important for Sunni Muslims since he is the founder of one of the two most prominent schools of Islamic thought. It seems that al-Maturidi himself prefers the view that the People of the Book—Christians and Jews—will also believe in Jesus when Jesus descends from heaven to earth at the end of time. According to al-Maturidi, because of the temporal proximity and shared spirituality of Muhammad and Jesus, the Prophet states that among all the prophets he is the closest to Jesus. With this knowledge in mind, al-Maturidi makes an interesting prediction: "When Jesus descends from heaven, he will invite all people to believe in Muhammad, peace and blessings be upon him."[7]

There is no doubt that the social environment of these giants of Islamic theology and the available Hadith sources of their time shaped their understandings about Jesus's descent. It seems that they were more concerned about the question of Jesus's deity than his descent. That is why their argument refuting the divinity of Jesus is highly elaborated, but their discussion of Jesus's descent is brief. Because of their brevity on the topic of the descent of Jesus, we do not find that these theologians had a great impact on later generations with regard to Jesus's return and his eschatological role. The only statement that can be related to these theologians on the topic of Jesus's descent is that his descent is a part of faith and that Muslims must believe in it with no further explanation.

A less well-known tenth-century theologian, Abu Bakr Muhammad bin Husain al-Ajurri (d. 970), was most likely the first Muslim theologian to discuss the descent of Jesus in detail. He dedicated a section of his book to the descent of Jesus. Under the subtitle "About the belief in the descent of Jesus the son of Mary, peace be upon him, as a just ruler to administer justice, promote truth, and kill al-Dajjal," al-Ajurri, like some earlier theologians, speaks of the necessity of believing in the descent of Jesus, establishing the truth, and killing the Antichrist. But a challenging question seems to occupy the mind of this great theologian: Who will be Jesus's support when he descends? As he answered this question, he had the Qur'an and the sayings of the Prophet in the back of his mind. He was aware of the praise in the Qur'an for early Christians who sacrificed everything for Jesus. When Jesus was desperately in need of help and said, "Who will be my supporters in the way of God?," a group of Christians who are known in the Qur'an as Hawariyyun, or the people in white garments, said, "We are your helpers in the way of God" (Qur'an 3:52–53). But when Jesus comes again with a new mission to defeat the archenemy of faith, the Antichrist, he will again need help and supporters. In this case the Muslim community will act like Jesus's early disciples and be the greatest support of Jesus in this eschatological mission to defeat al-Dajjal, the Antichrist, about whose deceptions and trials the Prophet of Islam forewarned his community. According to al-Ajurri, eventually, with the support of Muslim helpers, "Jesus will overcome the Antichrist."[8]

## Jesus's Role When He Returns

One problem is still unsolved for Muslim theologians. If the Prophet Muhammad is the final messenger of God, which is a theological principle in Islam, and Jesus is also a prominent messenger of God, which all Muslims must also believe, then wouldn't the coming of Jesus contradict the finality of Muhammad's prophethood? This question has posed a serious challenge to Muslim theologians. Although one can find some hints in the sayings of the Prophet that when Jesus comes he will come to support "the true religion of God" and not with a new prophethood, such an allusion needs further theological clarification. Ibn Hazm (d. 1064), a Cordoban Muslim theologian, philosopher, historian, and jurist, attempted to reconcile this apparent contradiction. Because the Qur'an presents the Prophet Muhammad as the "seal of the prophets," Ibn Hazm, who represented a school of Islamic law that insisted on the literal meaning of texts, the Zahiri school, was certain that Muhammad is the last prophet and that there would be no prophet after him. However, his concluding analysis contends that since reliable narratives from the Prophet of Islam support the descent of Jesus, the coming of Jesus would be an exception to this principle.[9] Many later theologians have also discussed this aspect of Jesus's descent and have come to the conclusion that Jesus will descend from heaven not as a new messenger of God but as a Messiah who will rescue the oppressed and fulfill justice. He will come to support Islam and the Prophet of Islam and not to contradict them. For this reason, Muslim theologians did not find any theological problem in the descent of Jesus as far as the finality of Prophet Muhammad's prophethood is concerned.

One of the most interesting scholars of Islam, the renowned theologian Taqi al-Din Ahmad bin al-Taymiyya (d. 1328) also finds no problem with this. Ibn al-Taymiyya, who led the resistance movement against the Mongol invasion of Damascus in the beginning of the fourteenth century, responded to certain questions about the descent of Jesus. These questions and expectations of the coming of Jesus may have been directly related to the Mongol invasion, when Muslims were desperately in need of a rescuer against the "war machines" of the time. In such a difficult time and under such an oppressive foreign invasion, expectations for messianic help would presumably become more urgent in the community. Muslims might have thought of Jesus, whose coming was promised by the Prophet of Islam, as a rescuer who could come and defeat the Mongols. Our available sources do not make a connection between the discussion of Jesus's descent in this period of time and the Mongol invasions of Islamic lands. However, it is natural that in such times of turmoil, people look for divine grace and mercy and for a redeemer.

In response to a question about whether Jesus was dead or alive, Ibn al-Taymiyya said, "Jesus is alive in heaven, [and] has not died yet. When he descends from heaven he will rule with nothing that is against the Qur'an and the Sunnah [the way of the Prophet]." He makes sure that Islamic references to the descent of Jesus are well rooted and compatible with the Qur'anic teaching. As a remarkable Arabic linguist, he typically refers to linguistic aspects of the texts on which he comments; he interprets the Qur'anic verses and hadith that refer to Jesus's descent through this linguistic lens. Ibn al-Taymiyya contends that the descent of Jesus has been proven in reliable Hadith sources. In speaking about whether Jesus is currently alive in body and spirit, he suggests that Jesus's spirit has not been separated from his body and he will come at the end of time, both bodily and spiritually, because the Prophet used the term *nuzul*, or descent. According to Ibn al-Taymiyya, by using this term the Prophet indicates that Jesus is alive in heaven bodily and spiritually: "Someone who is dead cannot make a descent [*nuzul*] from heaven in his body." In Ibn al-Taymiyya's view, the term *nuzul* indicates that Jesus will come in body and spirit. Because the term *nuzul* cannot be used for a dead person, Jesus is alive.[10]

Ibn al-Taymiyya gives further information about Jesus's rule on earth by referring to him as a just ruler and to his meeting with the Prophet Muhammad in the Prophet's famous Mi'raj, or night journey. Using linguistic analysis, Ibn al-Taymiyya argues that Jesus is closer to the Prophet of Islam than the other messengers of God whom the Prophet met during his night journey, when the Prophet ascended to heaven, reached beyond the realm of physicality, and met with God. Ibn al-Taymiyya singles out Jesus from the other prophets Muhammad met during this journey, saying the Prophet met Jesus in body and spirit, whereas Muhammad met with other prophets only in spirit.[11]

It is interesting that we do not see the dramatization of a war between Jesus and the Antichrist in Ibn al-Taymiyya's writings. Instead, unlike later theologians, he generally attempts to respond to possible theological problems. Under the war circumstances of his time, one would expect an excessive dramatization of the topic; however, he is brief, limiting himself to the frame of questions he receives. We understand from Ibn al-Taymiyya that Jesus's return as described in the Hadith literature is a part of Islamic faith: Muslims have to believe in it, it will happen literally since Jesus is still alive in heaven, and he will return when the time comes. The most notable part of Ibn al-Taymiyya's narrative is his emphasis on the relationship between the Prophet of Islam and Jesus, which is seen as much greater than Muhammad's relationship with other messengers of God.

## The Battle between Jesus and the Antichrist

Some later Muslim theologians focus on the dramatization of a battle between Jesus and his opponent, the Antichrist. They depict Jesus's descent in the context of this dramatic struggle. One can argue that some events in Islamic history, such as the Mongol invasion of Islamic land and the invasion of Egypt by the French, have contributed to the dramatization and the development of detailed narratives of the end-time stories, particularly the descent of Jesus, the coming of the Mahdi, and the struggle of these two against the Antichrist. It is not surprising that those who have detailed these narratives come from these particular turbulent periods of Islamic history. These developments in the Islamic territories have led some theologians to return to the Qur'an and the sayings of the Prophet for reliable scenarios of the end time. It was clear that the Prophet of Islam not only pointed to the end time but also pointed to several other events, including the Mongol invasion. Thus, some Muslim theologians were eager to elaborate and detail the end-time struggle between Jesus and the Mahdi against the Antichrist. These narratives, which have become a popular epic, are found in historical and literary sources as well. Like more recent writers of narratives concerning Jesus's descent, earlier theologians and scholars such as al-Qurtubi (d. 1272), Ibn al-Wardi (d. 1349), and the Egyptian Muhammad al-Hijazi (d. 1625) who authored detailed narratives were most likely influenced by tumults in their own day. Al-Qurtubi may have been responding to the threat the Mongols posed just as Al-Hijazi's narrative of events was likely influenced by the civil unrest in early seventeenth century Egypt.[12] Although such writings are present, it wasn't until much later when Islamic lands became the target of repeated successful invasions and the gradual breaking up of the great Muslim empires was underway, that people in the Muslim world, particularly in Egypt and on the Indian subcontinent, began to believe in earnest that the end of time was near and the topic of Jesus's descent began to figure prominently in theological and popular texts.[13]

In general, tumultuous times are fertile environments for the blossoming of apocalyptic ideas and the emergence of pseudo-redeemers or pseudo-messiahs. The Islamic world is not immune from this trend and within the Islamic world many charlatans have benefited from such an environment. A number of books examining messianic expectations have been written to refute those who claim that they are either the Messiah or the foretold Mahdi. In response to such false messiahs, some Muslim theologians have been prompted to discuss the subject in a detailed manner. Ottoman scholar Muhammad Zahid al-Kawthari (d. 1951) and more recent scholars such as 'Ali al-Herras, 'Abdullah al-Ghumari, and 'Abd al-Qadir have dedicated popular books to the concept of Jesus and his descent. By compiling many sayings of the Prophet, they emphasize that anyone who does not fit the literal descriptions found in the sayings of the Prophet cannot be Jesus, and if any individual claims that he is the expected Messiah he will be considered a charlatan.

It should be noted that in this genre, intellectual analysis of the sayings of the Prophet is not present. Authors of these works generally compile the available sayings of the Prophet and speak of the reliability of those sayings. The reader gets the point that the claimants to messiahship cannot be the true Jesus since they do not fit the criteria mentioned in those hadith. Statements that introduced these works claim that the goal of such writing is to respond to those who had declared that they were the expected Jesus or the Mahdi. Al-Kawthari, for example, defends the belief in the descent of Jesus against those who had made such claims and against the people who deny the return of Jesus, including some Egyptian modernist scholars. Even though he defends the idea in a classical, traditional style, he stresses that there is no doubt that Jesus will descend. According to al-Kawthari, all sayings of the Prophet on the subject state two important points: the descent of Jesus will occur literally and every Muslim must believe in it.

Most of the books that respond to those who deny the descent of Jesus are compiled by scholars and present the sayings of the Prophet on the subject in an inflammatory and literal way. They unquestioningly put forth the Hadith narratives as proof of the inevitable descent of Jesus.[14] Generally the literal approach to the texts about the descent of Jesus is understood as the way of the early generation of scholars of Islam known as the Salaf. Perhaps for this reason today's Salafis, who claim that they follow the way of "Salaf Salih," or the early pious generation, prefer a literalist approach to the dogmas on Jesus's descent.

Adherents of the literalist approach see Jesus's descent as a cosmic event in which the person of Jesus will come from heaven down to earth and will be seen by everyone. Many of those who follow the teachings of the early generation accept the literal meaning and refuse to interpret the verses and the sayings of the Prophet on the subject. They believe that God rescued Jesus from the hands of his enemies and took him to heaven and gave him a different life.

## Jesus as a Sign of the Hour

Mohammad al-Ghazali (d. 1996), an Islamic cleric, scholar, and one of the most popular contemporary authors in Egypt, in his famous book, *Aqidat al-Muslim* [The Creed of the Muslim], writes of the signs of the Hour. He lists Jesus's return first: "Among them [the signs of the Hour] is the return of Jesus. Specifically given this duty among other prophets, he should come to eliminate the superstitions that have been attached to his personality. Even powerful nations have held superstitious beliefs about Jesus. Let the man come and correct by himself what people have attached to him of divinity. He is nothing but a servant of God. Since life is a coherent unity, his descent at the end of time is adequate to indicate this meaning."[15] This view is based on al-Ghazali's belief in the literal descent of Jesus; he finds the return of Jesus to be a necessary event because through his return Jesus will be able to correct some inaccurate beliefs related to him, one of which is the claim about his divinity. The event will literally take place and will be a cosmic one. The idea has become a principle in Salafi thought: "Some of the signs of the final Hour are mentioned in the divine revelation, the Qur'an, and that is the descent of Jesus from heaven to earth as a just ruler, mentioned in the verse 'He is a sign for the Hour. Do not have doubt about it.'"[16]

The same literalist approach is shared by the earlier scholar, Siddiq Hasan

Khan (d. 1890), a founder of the Ahl al-Hadith movement in India, which blends traditional literalist interpretations with reformist ideas and practices. The scenario that he depicts is detailed. According to Khan, the descent of Jesus is proven by the Qur'an, the sayings of the prophet, and the consensus of the community of Islam. He indicates the exact time of day that Jesus will descend. It is possible that his literalist understanding has influenced many contemporary theologians after him, not only in India but in other parts of the Islamic world. We cannot verify how Khan became so specific that even a time of the day is assigned for Jesus's descent. However, Khan is quite confident about his detailed narrative, which is not found either in the Qur'an or in the reliable sayings of the Prophet.

According to Khan's scenario, the descent of Jesus will be in the first six hours of the day. Jesus will come to the Damascus [Umayyad] mosque, speak from the pulpit, and Muslims will enter the mosque. Christians and Jews will enter the mosque as well. Everybody will want to see Jesus. There will be so many people in the mosque that if something drops it will not reach the ground but will fall on the heads of the people.[17] Although some elements of this scenario are found in the sayings of the Prophet, Khan has added his own contribution. He is clear that the descent of Jesus will be a cosmic event since everybody will hear his coming and will want to meet with him. This scenario is interesting because Khan, who had Salafi tendencies, allows for the presence of both Christians and Jews in the mosque. This scenario also draws our attention to the city of Damascus, a political and cultural center for much of early Islamic history, as did some theologians before Khan, based on particular references to Damascus in Hadith narrations.

Other literalist scholars go further to discuss not only the descent of Jesus but also his ascension and the conditions of his life in heaven because the Qur'anic verse states that Jesus was not killed but that God "raised him up to Himself" (4:157). These scholars also debate whether Jesus ascended to heaven in both body and in spirit or only in spirit. In keeping with traditional literalist interpretations, 'Abdullatif Harputi (d. 1916), a late Ottoman Muslim theologian, likened the ascent of Jesus to the night journey of the Prophet Muhammad. Generally Muslims believe that the Prophet's night journey was both physical and spiritual. Harputi, who is known as one of the pioneers of the new science of kalam, would be expected to be more logical and interpretive. However, he does not seem to have a problem with the literalist approach that Jesus will come to the city of Damascus. A brief examination of his position seems to show that he contradicts his literalist approach in this matter. While speaking of the uncertainty about the ascension of Jesus, an uncertainty due to disagreement among Muslim theologians, Harputi makes clear that the descent of Jesus is well documented in the sayings of the Prophet and therefore "theologically [speaking] to believe in it is necessary." Harputi also states: "Jesus will descend from heaven to earth, will kill the antichrist, will follow the religion of Muhammad, peace and blessings be upon him, will stay for seven years, and then will die in Medina and be buried there."[18] Here, he provides answers to important theological questions, such as whether, being human, Jesus will die. Where Jesus will be buried is an important question Harputi addresses. Based on his own sources, he claims that Jesus will die in the city of Medina, although he will come to the city of Damascus. He will be buried in Medina next to the grave of the Prophet of Islam. Another important question is how long Jesus will stay to fulfill justice. Again, this period of time is given as seven years, understood in a literal sense. Unlike some of his contemporaries, Harputi avoids any kind of allegorical interpretations. Basing his view on available Hadith literature, he again suggests a literalist scenario: Jesus will descend in Damascus on the white minaret, and on the morning of his descent he will fight the Antichrist and defeat him. Harputi does not find a contradiction between Jesus's coming and Muhammad's being the seal of all prophets, since Jesus will rule according the Islamic principles of law and will not come with a new prophethood.

## A Possible Reason for the Literalist Approach

Why have so many Muslim theologians adhered to a literal meaning of the texts about Jesus's return? It seems that early generations did not have a problem with accepting the literal meanings of dogmas. Submission to the will of God was strong. Perhaps many early scholars of Islamic theology did not see themselves as authorized to shift from the literal meaning to a figurative one. Throughout the history of Islamic theology, the vast majority of scholars have either cited the descent of Jesus as truth without further explanation or have just ignored it. To ensure that they will be on the safe side of any discussion, they even put some general statements in the literature such as, "We believe in the descent of Jesus as it has come down to us from the Prophet through the reliable Hadith narratives." Accepting dogmas without question was dominant in most of Islamic history. Mainstream Islamic theology was not quick to shift from the literalist approach to a more comprehensive, interpretive approach—one that is recognizable in the "secular age." The following chapter will discuss the interpretive approaches of some Muslim theologians.

# EIGHT

# Symbolic, Allegorical, and Other Interpretive Approaches to Jesus's Eschatological Role

Some Muslim theologians see the descent of Jesus in figurative and allegorical terms. In doing so they employ what I call the interpretive approach. This style of analysis is grounded in the methodological principles of Islamic theology and law and is compatible with the teachings of the Qur'an.[1] Within the methodologies of Qur'anic commentary and Hadith criticism there is a fundamental concept known as *mutawatir*, which can be translated as "recurrently transmitted chain of narration." All verses of the Qur'an are considered to be *mutawatir*. However, scholars have validated only a few hadith as *mutawatir*. Many hadith are still considered sound and reliable, even though they do not reach the level of *mutawatir*. The Qur'an and the reliable Hadith provide the groundwork for Islamic theology and the themes within it, in our case the descent of Jesus. Even though these texts are reliable, they may seem to contradict the known principles of reason. When this is the case, Islamic theologians and jurists say that the texts should be interpreted instead of rejected.

One argument against literalism looks to a methodological principle in the philosophy of Islamic law that clearly says that if there is a conflict between reason and a sound text, either in the Qur'an or the Hadith, reason should be favored and the text should be interpreted in a way that accords with reason. This same principle is stated by the famous Muslim jurist and theologian Abu Ishaq al-Shatibi (d. 1388), who says that the evidence for religious law cannot conflict with reason. A conflict would defy the principle of accountability, which is properly based on the use of free will. One must have reason if one is to be accountable before God in the afterlife; without reason, one is not considered accountable. Therefore, according to Islamic theology, mentally ill individuals are not considered accountable for their actions and are destined for paradise because they do not have a chance to exercise their free will.

God does not place a burden on human beings greater than what they can bear (Qur'an 2:233, 2:286, 6:152, 7:42, and 23:62). In al-Shatibi's line of reasoning, God would not force human beings who have reason and free will to accept what they cannot understand or comprehend. "Islamic Law proofs do not contradict the outcome of reason," al-Shatibi writes. In a few pages he illustrates why dogmas should not contradict reason.[2] Using the legal principle that al-Shatibi emphasizes, if one cannot understand a theological theme, one is not required to believe in it. Blind faith is not accepted in Islam, and even if it were, it would be considered a weak level of faith. Since the literal meaning of the texts about Jesus's descent conflict with reason, they should be interpreted in a way that accords with reason. The descent of Jesus from heaven in his earthly body, in his human form, and in front of people's eyes is a matter that tests the limits of reason. Therefore, two options present themselves: rejecting the texts or interpreting them using reason.

The descent of Jesus is interpreted in a metaphorical way to mean that goodness will prevail or to advocate cooperation between Muslims and Christians. The hadith that mentions Jesus's visit to the mosque and his prayer with Muslims, when he asks the "leader of Muslims" to lead the prayer, symbolizes this cooperation and is most likely what the Prophet meant. As I discussed in the previous chapter, those who support a literal approach to reading the hadith relate it to the power of God. Yet the power of God does not act in a way to compel people to believe, and if Jesus's descent happens as a cosmic event, then everybody will be compelled to believe. This goes against the Islamic theological principle of free will.

## Interpretive Approaches to Jesus's Descent

In what follows I will examine some Muslim theologians' understanding of the descent of Jesus and their preference for an interpretive approach. I will look at the thought of some theologians of our time and that of some early theologians who understood Jesus's descent allegorically.

### Abu 'Abdillah al-Halimi

Abu 'Abdillah al-Halimi (d. 1012), a Muslim theologian, jurist, and ethicist, speaks of the descent of Jesus and his struggle against the Antichrist in a partially figurative way. He points out that Jesus will come but that he will be seen and recognized only by the people close to him. Thus, in al-Halimi's thought, his coming will not be a cosmic event. He also makes the point that Jesus will not descend merely to kill the Antichrist. "God also sends Jesus to die on earth like his brothers, the other prophets," al-Halimi states. This seems to be a notable shift in the Islamic theological understanding of the descent of Jesus and echoes the interpretations of some modern scholars and theologians. Al-Halimi claims, "His matter will run as God has described: God will make him stay on earth for a while, in this period those who are close to him will see him and those who represent him will hear him. Then God will take his soul."[3] Although al-Halimi does not reject the literal approach totally, by mentioning this figurative approach under "another point of view" and thus giving credibility to it, he differs with the literalist approach of many of his contemporaries, who saw the descent of Jesus as a cosmic event.

## Sa'd al-Din al-Taftazani

The interpretation of al-Halimi is an important development in the Islamic theological literature on the descent of Jesus. This trend of interpretation did not find many adherents until the emergence of the fourteenth-century Muslim theologian Sa'd al-Din al-Taftazani (d. 1390). Because al-Taftazani has remained one of the most prominent figures of Islamic theology and his theological works have been used as textbooks in Islamic institutions over the centuries, his views on the descent of Jesus are indispensable.[4]

Al-Taftazani has a unique approach to the subject. He contends that there are many sayings of the Prophet concerning the descent of Jesus that are narrated by just and trustworthy transmitters. Al-Taftazani accepts the sayings of the Prophet and their reliability and does not deny their literal meaning. However, he opens the door for new interpretation; he was not a dogmatic scholar in this matter. Like his predecessor, Abu al-Hasan al-Ash'ari, the founder of the Ash'ari school of thought, al-Taftazani speaks about the emergence of the Mahdi and the descent of Jesus under the section on leadership in his book *Sharh al-Maqasid* [Commentary on Aims]. This gives us a hint that the Ash'ari school of Islamic thought places Jesus's descent within the context of *imama*, or political and religious leadership. Jesus seems to have a role related to the political and religious life of Muslims. Since most political rivalries culminate in uprisings, both theologians emphasize the importance of peace and nonviolence as well as being obedient and avoiding any involvement in chaos and anarchy.

Al-Taftazani carefully clarifies that neither the descent of Jesus nor the emergence of the Mahdi are among the principles of faith but instead are portents that the Prophet referred to as signals of the end time. Although many hadith refer directly or indirectly to the coming of the Mahdi and Jesus, they are not as important as compulsory charity or fasting during Ramadan, and they do not have the same theological weight as the belief in the hereafter. Al-Taftazani places these themes of the signs of the Hour under his section on leadership, or *imama*: "Among the things added to the sections [of manuals of theology] on leadership [of the Islamic community] are discussions of the emergence of the Mahdi and the descent of Jesus, peace and blessings be upon him; both are among the signs of the Hour, and many reliable Hadith have been narrated on these subjects."[5] He opines that the prophetic sayings in this regard are the narratives of individuals or what is technically known as *khabar ahad*; that is to say, they can be reliable, but as far as matters of faith are concerned, they cannot provide textual proof for a belief. It is thought-provoking to see a theologian such as al-Taftazani include Jesus and the Mahdi under the concept of leadership rather than under eschatological matters of Islamic theology. It is clear that he gives certain political roles to these two important figures who are expected to emerge at the end of time. With this approach, al-Taftazani becomes unique both for his figurative understanding and for the social and political roles he ascribes to Jesus and the Mahdi in the eschatological scenario of the end time.

Al-Taftazani then speaks of three sayings of the Prophet on the Mahdi and draws a distinction between Shi'ite and Sunni views of the Mahdi. In the Sunni tradition, the messianic figure is not a central element of faith, but in the Shi'ite tradition he is. He goes on to tackle a saying related to the Prophet, "There is no Mahdi except Jesus," by interpreting the word *mahdi* as "guide" instead of a word that identifies the expected messianic figure of Islam. He says, "It is not illogical to interpret this saying of the Prophet to mean that there is no guide to lead the annihilation of al-Dajjal and the prevention of his evil actions, as the reliable sayings of the Prophet have indicated, except Jesus."[6] After stating that there are many reliable hadith on the subject that were reported by trustworthy transmitters and that there are obstacles to interpreting the sayings of the prophet about the signs of the Hour according to their outward meaning, al-Taftazani mentions the interpretive approach of "some scholars": "And some scholars have interpreted the emergence of al-Dajjal as the dominance of evil and corruption. And they interpret the descent of Jesus, peace be upon him, as the prevention of those who are evil and corrupt, and as the dominance of the good and of wholesomeness."[7] In nineteenth-century Egypt, Muhammad Abduh echoed this view and spoke of the spirituality of Jesus in his interpretation of Jesus's descent.

## Muhammad Abduh

As one of the modern exponents of the interpretive approach, Muhammad Abduh (d. 1905) speaks of the spirit of Jesus that will prevail over a materialistic world. His argument develops as follows: First, he discusses the sayings of the Prophet, the text on Jesus's descent. If these sayings are accurately related to the Prophet, then they have to be understood in an allegorical way. This leads to his view on Jesus's role. It seems that both Abduh and his student Rashid Rida think of Jesus as a renewer of Islamic law. Jesus is expected to come and spark a great renewal of Islam. It is noteworthy that this role has been historically ascribed to some early rulers and other prominent figures, for example 'Umar bin 'Abd al-'Aziz ('Umar II, d. 720), Abu Hamid al-Ghazali (d. 1111), and the famous Indian Sufi Ahmad Sirhindi (d. 1624).

As part of his understanding of Jesus's descent, Abduh asserts that compassion, love, and peace, which are the main aims of Islamic shari'a, will dominate society. This understanding follows Abduh's overall methodology for the interpretation of dogmas: when the literal meaning is logically impossible, the text should be understood in a figurative way. Like early Mu'tazilites, who are also known as the defenders of reason in Islamic theological thought, Abduh, who is often called a neo-Mu'tazilite, is concerned about any contradiction between reason and dogmas. According to Abduh, dogmas should be proven by reason. Reason is a gift from God and is a precondition for an individual's accountability before God. For him, humans were not created to have a bridle; instead, humans were created with free will.

One can conclude from Abduh's viewpoint that the descent of Jesus cannot be understood in a literal way but instead should be understood figuratively. His allegorical understanding of Jesus's decent is that his message of compassion, love, and peace will be dominant toward the end of human history, not that Jesus will physically return. Abduh believes that when the Prophet of Islam spoke of the coming of Jesus at the end of time, he was talking about humanity's return to the noble values Jesus represents and that are found in the core teachings of Islam.[8]

With certain theological principles in mind, Abduh makes two points about the sayings of the Prophet on Jesus's descent: "First, the sayings of the Prophet are narrations of individuals [*khabar ahad*] about a matter that is related to a creed that concerns the unseen themes. Issues concerning creeds cannot be accepted unless we have assured proofs. That is because what is expected in matters of creed is certainty. On this matter, there is not a hadith that is *mutawatir* [transmitted recurrently]."[9] Since a saying of the Prophet that is narrated by an individual does not necessarily cause it to be wrong or inaccurate, Abduh makes a second point. He accepts the Hadith on this matter as real sayings of the Prophet but argues that most Muslims don't understand their meanings. Developing his second point, Abduh interprets the descent of Jesus:

> The descent of Jesus and his ruling on earth can be interpreted as the dominance of his spirit and his enigmatic message to people. This is what dominates Jesus's teachings of commanding mercy, love, and peace, which also emphasize the purposes of the law, rather than what is readily apparent and the shell of it, what does not penetrate into the kernel of the law. Such purpose is the wisdom of the law and the reason why the law is established. Jesus, peace be upon him, did not bring to Jews a new law, but he brought for them something that would move them from being frozen on the literal meaning of the law of Moses, peace be upon him, and lead them to the understanding and the purpose of the law. He also commanded them to follow those purposes, and commanded them with something that attracts them to the realm of spirits through the search for perfect behavior. That is to say, when the people of the last divine law [Islam] became frozen on the literal meaning of the law, furthermore on the literal meanings of those who wrote their own opinions about the law, opinions that were killing the spirit of the law and removing its wisdom, it became necessary for them to undergo a Messiah-oriented renewal that would reveal to them the mysteries of the law, the spirit of the religion, and the true practice of it. All of these purposes of Islamic law are found in the Qur'an but are hidden to a certain extent. They have been veiled even further due to blind imitation, which discourages further investigation. This kind of imitation is a calamity for the truth and the enemy of religion [Islam] in any time. The time of Jesus's descent is a time when people take the spirit of religion and the spirit of Islamic law to heart to reform their inner lives, without sticking to the forms and appearances.[10]

It is clear that Abduh complains about some literalist Muslims who lack the wisdom of Islamic law. He does not specify the time period of such stagnation, but when that time comes, there will be a need for a Jesus-centered renewal of Islamic law and Muslims' behaviors.

## Rashid Rida

Referring to the situation of Muslims in his time, Abduh's student Rashid Rida (d. 1935) emphasized the necessity for reform so that the mysteries of Islamic law, the spirit of religion, and the moral codes of Islam would become manifest. This reform was so urgently needed and so foundational that it could be fulfilled only with a messianic sense of power. According to Rida, who generally follows the path of Abduh, the descent of Jesus means that people will return to the Qur'an and submit to the spirit of Islamic *shari'a*.

Rida does not see his interpretation as a contradiction to the overall meaning of the sayings of the Prophet. He believes that the narrators of the Hadith did not narrate the words of the Prophet verbatim, so possibly the narrators' own words have been included among the words of the Prophet. "These traditions have been narrated not verbatim but by the narration of the meaning of what the Prophet said. The narrator narrated what he understood, not what the Prophet meant," Rida writes.[11]

Blind imitation, which generates a literalistic approach without questioning, has not been a principle of Islamic theology. In fact, some theologians have even claimed that faith through imitation is not real faith. One has to be convinced about what he or she believes in. That is why the notable Muslim theologian Imam al-Haramayn al-Juwayni (d. 1085) commences his well-known book on Islamic theology with the following statement: "The first thing that is compulsory upon any individual who is sane and has reached the age of puberty is to make an effort for right thinking which leads to the knowledge of the creation of the universe."[12] When he was asked why thinking or contemplation is compulsory, al-Juwayni said, "The community of Islam agreed that it is compulsory to know the Creator, exalted be He. And through reason it is clear that there is no way to have such knowledge except via contemplation [*nazar*]. The way to fulfill a compulsory duty also becomes compulsory [because without it the duty cannot be fulfilled]."[13] Despite this strong theology, somehow Muslims became more literalist and accepted the matters of faith more blindly, a trend that came to Muslims under the influence of certain literalist movements that go against the spirit of Islamic theology. A discussion of the factors that contributed to the stagnation of thought in Islamic theology is beyond the scope of this study. To understand Jesus's descent as a revival of the spirit of Islam at the end of time instead of expecting the person of Jesus from heaven is a clear violation of the literalist approach, which expects Jesus to come in person at the end of time.

Perhaps to avoid such a conflict with the literalist approach, Rashid Rida speaks of Jesus's descent in a softer tone without denying the literal coming of Jesus. He suggests that Jesus's case is among the matters related to the unseen world. "What we know for sure is that our master Jesus, peace be upon him, is in the realm of the unseen like his other brothers, the prophets. And he is doing well, since he is among the divine messengers who possess steadfastness. . . . We do not know anything in detail about his situation, as is our situation with regard to other matters related to the realm of the unseen. That is because there is no space for the use of reason and opinion in such matters."[14] Because he is a student of Islamic rationalistic theology, one would expect more philosophical and theological comments from Rida. It is possible that the debates on the subject in his time were closely tied to certain political polemics and perhaps he did not want to amplify those polemics among his peers in Egypt.

Tantawi Jawhari

Rida's ambiguous approach is clarified by an important twentieth-century scholar, also from Egypt. After referring to the difficulties humanity faces because of wars and weapons, Tantawi Jawhari (d. 1940), a renowned commentator on the Qur'an, speaks of the coming of Jesus as an ideal time for humanity. He is squarely among the group of theologians who prefer the interpretive approach. Like some earlier scholars and theologians, he speaks of the time of Jesus's descent as a time of peace, and in contrast to those who claim that wars or even Armageddon are needed to pave the way for the coming of Jesus, Jawhari argues that battles delay the coming of Jesus. He refers to a part of a Qur'anic verse, "Until the war lays down its burdens" (47:4).

Jawhari speaks of the descent of Jesus as symbolic reflection, of the cooperation of nations. He is clearly aware of the fact that as human beings we live in the realm of the laws of nature and the realm of cause and effect. Like physical phenomena, social changes are also subject to certain laws. He does not expect that the time of peace will happen as a miracle. Instead, if there is something called the coming or descent of Jesus, it can be understood as cooperation among nations such as the development of positive relationships between Christians and Muslims who are working hard for peace.

The issue of the theology of human free will is brought up again. None of these events will happen spontaneously; instead, they will depend on the exercise of people's free will. Consequently, Jawhari does not believe that such a beautiful period will come abruptly. He contends that Muslims have to work for peace and that they will have to work to make such prophetic promises possible. He compares humanity in this era to bees anxiously working in a honeycomb to make honey available. Just as bees are cooperating and working hard, human beings should also work to reap the fruit of peace and harmony.

Regarding the descent of Jesus, he asks this question: "Will Jesus descend personally or is his descent a symbol of the end of hatred, jealousy, and the unification of all nations, their cooperation and harmony?"[15] When one evaluates his assessment of the coming of Jesus, one can come to the conclusion that because he witnessed the emergence of certain pseudo-messiahs, including one in India and one in Iran, he favors the idea that the descent should not be understood in a literal sense. In this commentary he assigns a meaning to the text that is so esoteric that it is open to challenges from other Muslim scholars. Perhaps because of his highly regarded position in the field, scholars have not challenged his authority: "The important thing in this matter is not the personality of Jesus, nor his coming personally. The important thing is global peace, truthfulness, and sincerity. This is what to be taken from the descent of Jesus and this is what the great scholars have interpreted. Therefore, what is meant by Jesus, the Messiah, is not his personality. . . . The goal is the happiness of all nations and not the coming of an individual. The coming of Jesus is possible, but what is meant is all-encompassing brotherhood."[16] Being aware of the Islamic theological principle that this is an event related to the future and that no one can be sure about some unknown future events, he carefully speaks of the possibility of the descent of Jesus spiritually and physically. It seems that although he does not want to deny the physical, bodily descent of Jesus from heaven, he prefers an allegorical meaning.

## Bediüzzaman Said Nursi

A modern Islamic scholar from Turkey, Bediüzzaman Said Nursi (d. 1960), also emphasized Muslim-Christian interaction and cooperation in his comments on the descent of Jesus. With Nursi, this interpretive trend takes a new direction: a dialogue and cooperation between Muslims and Christians. Nursi's interpretation seems very significant to me because he had the seeds of this idea in an early period of his life. For example, in his famous Damascus Sermon, which he delivered in 1911, while addressing nearly 10,000 people in the Umayyad Mosque, Nursi spoke of cooperation between Islam and Christianity.[17] Later, in the 1950s, he elaborated further on this in his other writings and in his correspondence with his students. He believed that dialogue between Muslims and Christians who have dedicated themselves to justice and spiritual life will fulfill the meaning of the coming of Jesus, that is, to bring justice and peace to our world. Therefore, it can be argued that Bediüzzaman Said Nursi should be seen as a leading advocate of the interpretive approach, at least as it relates to the coming of Jesus.

Nursi's interpretation seems to be based on a long history of interaction be-tween Muslims and Christians and seems to have a mystical dimension as well as a theological one. He does not indicate a rejection of the literalist approach, but he speaks confidently of his interpretations. He does not give a linguistic explanation, as some of his predecessors did. His approach is quite unique and seems to be empowered by his spiritual strength. His understanding is especially important in our time because of the need to overcome the spread of religious hatred. Nursi interprets the descent of Jesus in the sayings of the Prophet as a renewal of Christianity and a return to the original message of Jesus, something that will promote cooperation between Muslims and Christians. According to Nursi, through this interaction and cooperation, Muslims and Christians will come together and work shoulder to shoulder for the betterment of humanity and against the challenges of materialistic philosophy that are presented in the form of militant atheism or irreligiosity.

The idea of faith or belief in God is a theme in Nursi's work, and his inter-pretation centers on belief and disbelief. Nursi understands from the Prophet's statement that Jesus will defeat the Antichrist and that the message of Jesus, which is divine revelation, will overcome the message of nonbelief personified in the concept of the Antichrist. "This is the meaning of the Prophetic statement 'Jesus will kill the Antichrist,'" Nursi explains.[18] Therefore, Nursi does not take this prophetic statement literally; he reads it metaphorically.

Considering the previously mentioned hadith narratives, it certainly makes sense to assume that many of the Prophet of Islam's sayings concerning Jesus's descent are reliable. That being said, reliability is one thing and accurate under-standing is something else. For Nursi these sayings of the Prophet need a new interpretation if we are to understand what the Prophet really meant. As was his typical style, Nursi does not speak too much about the scholars of the past; rather, he confidently puts forward his own opinion. Jesus and the Antichrist are symbolic representations of collective personalities of belief and disbelief. Nursi does not look for extraordinary events. He has great trust in the nature of human beings, of whom he says, "human beings are by nature honored." For Nursi, such an honored human nature will look for spiritual satisfaction and will eventually find it. The struggle between faith and disbelief will end with the victory of faith over disbelief at the end of time. In other words, spirituality will overcome materialism. Muslims and Christians will take a greater role in this spiritual success. This will be possible through a Muslim-Christian alliance that will bring peace and harmony to the world. Nursi believes that this was foretold by the Prophet of Islam as good news for believers in particular and for all human beings in general when he spoke about the coming of Jesus at the end of time. This is one way that God shows His mercy to human beings—a mercy that is personified in both Muhammad and Jesus.

If one is to make a meaningful theological deduction, it is vitally important that one understands the prophetic sayings in a figurative and not just a literal sense. Jesus represents the true religion while the Antichrist represents nonbelief. This struggle between Jesus and the Antichrist as described in the Hadith narratives is metaphorical rather than literal and physical, as is attested by Nursi's use of the phrase "the sword of Revelation." Revelation is made of words and cannot be established by the sword. But the words of the revelation of the Qur'an have greater power than the sword, so the sword in this case becomes a spiritually powerful metaphor for convincing rather than fighting and killing people. That is to say, in the hadith, when the Prophet uses the word "sword" he means the "Word" or the convincing power of divine revelation, the Torah, the Gospel, and the Qur'an, not a literal sword. Another example is the Prophet's statement when the Antichrist sees Jesus, he will melt as salt melts in water. If a physical sword was meant, how could one use a sword against someone who melts like salt in water? These hints from the Prophet help us to give preference to the interpretive approach.

## The Interpretive Approach as a Middle Way

The interpretive approach is a middle way to understanding the text. This approach avoids the extremism of solely literalist understandings as historically represented by a heretic group in Islam known as al-Hashwiyya and the extremism of solely esoteric understandings as historically represented by a heretic group in Islam known as al-Batiniyya. Both depart from the Sunni understanding of the text. Al-Ghazali would consider these groups as misguided. One has to balance the inner and the outer meaning of the text.

In interpreting the Qur'anic passage about God's address to Moses, al-Ghazali says that there is a deeper meaning in the Qur'anic verse when God says, "Moses, I am your Lord, take off your two sandals, you are in the holy Valley of Tuwa" (20:12). The verse can be understood literally, but it has also a further and deeper meaning. The apparent meaning is clear. According to al-Ghazali, the esoteric meaning of this verse is that we should "abandon the two worlds when in the presence of God"[19] Thus, a full understanding of the text requires us to merge the two interpretations, both esoteric and literal. In addition to the literal meaning here, the sandals represent two worlds, the visible life in this world and the invisible world of the afterlife. Similarly, al-Ghazali refers to a well-known hadith that says, "The angels do not enter a house that has a dog in it." Without denying the literal meaning, al-Ghazali focuses on a deeper interpretation: "The outward sense is not meant; on the contrary, what is meant is removing the dog of anger from the house of the heart because it prevents the entrance of knowledge, which derives from the lights of angels, since anger is the ghoul of the rational faculty."[20]

This trend of interpretation of the text and seeking a deeper meaning are central to Islamic theology. Nursi and other scholars who see a deeper meaning in the sayings of the Prophet present their interpretations regarding the descent of Jesus as essential to the Sunni understanding of the text. Therefore, understanding Jesus's descent as the strength of spirituality, as Abduh suggests, or the alliance of Muslims and Christians, as Nursi understands it, is very much compatible with and even fundamental to Islamic theology. With this we come to the question of how this cooperation and spiritual development can be achieved.

## Cooperation and Dialogue between Muslims and Christians

Human effort is necessary for great spiritual achievement. Nothing in our world can be achieved without labor. To tackle this aspect of the story, Nursi refers to certain Christian communities who want to follow the true teaching of Jesus and reconcile it with the truth of Islam. He called these communities "dedicated and devoted." He also mentioned that members of these communities could be called "Christian Muslims," or Muslims who are the followers of Jesus, a phrase Nursi coined. Some Christian theologians, such as Karl Rahner, use the concept of the anonymous Christians.[21] Similarly, Nursi states that "Christian Muslims" are Muslims in the sight of God but are not known as Muslims per se. It is believed that under the spiritual leadership of Jesus and in cooperation with Islam, these communities will defeat the idea of nonbelief and rescue humanity from the ideology of the denial of God.[22]

In fact, the idea of cooperation and dialogue between Muslims and Christians can be traced back to the revelation of the Qur'an and the early period of Islam. Historically, with the exception of the eras of the Crusades and the Spanish Inquisition, Muslims and Christians have lived together and cooperated in many areas. The same is true for Islamic-Jewish relations, both in Spain and in the Ottoman Empire. Since my topic here is Muslim-Christian cooperation and the descent of Jesus, my focus is on this aspect of the story. The Islamic civilization of Andalusia is a great example of cooperation between Muslims and Christians.[23] Recent scholarship has explored this cooperation and chronicled how the civilizations of Islam and Christianity are intertwined.[24]

This intertwining of Islam and Christianity is a way to understand certain statements in the Hadith that are believed to be related to Jesus's descent. For example, although many Hadith commentators and theologians have understood the hadith describing Jesus breaking the cross and killing a swine in a literal sense, it would be overly simplistic to accept this without interpretation because this would disregard the Islamic understanding of human free will and accountability. If we consider the literalist approach, the hadith means that Jesus will take the cross and break it into pieces and take a swine and kill it. Theologically speaking, however, this event would not warrant that the Prophet would refer to it as one of the events with paramount importance in the end times. To make theological sense of the hadith and to have the complete meaning of it, we need an interpretive approach. Even though scholars who focus on the interpretation of Hadith did not state a specific symbolic meaning, one can make certain conclusions. Jesus is following principles that are compatible with the teachings of Islam, and these teachings, as described in Islamic theology, are not compatible with the acceptance of pork and the symbol of the cross, which indicates the killing of Jesus by his enemies. One possible interpretation is that since Jesus will not come with a new message from God, he will come to restore the messages of the Gospel and the Qur'an. For this reason some contemporary Egyptian Muslim theologians consider Jesus to be a *mujaddid*, a renewer of Islam. The hadith can be understood as a renewal of Christianity, allowing it to be freed of elements that have been added over the centuries and are not necessary or compatible with the core teachings of Jesus.

For this saying to be fulfilled, it is not necessary for Jesus to physically destroy symbolic objects of Christianity such as the cross. One possible understanding of this hadith is that the message of renewal will be voluntarily accepted by Christians out of their free will and their contemplation of Jesus's message would fill their hearts and convince their minds enough to break their internal identification with practices and symbolic objects that are not compatible with or central to the original teachings of Jesus. For example, upon reflection on the teachings of Jesus, Christians may decide to stop participating in some secular practices that are affiliated with religion, such as many activities that are part of celebrating Christmas.[25] For a Christian, breaking the cross is challenging because of the affection and comfort derived from this symbolic object. Genuinely breaking one's affection for and ties to the symbolic meaning of an object is much more difficult and challenging than breaking a physical object. To genuinely break this bond, those affective ties would need to be supplanted by something even more powerful and fulfilling, which ultimately can be found in a peaceful, just community. This internal struggle is compatible with the teachings of both Jesus and Muhammad.

Many scholars and theologians have presented commentaries on the descent of Jesus that one can find valuable and that fit well with Islamic theological methodology. The question of whether the literal meaning of the text on Jesus's descent is possible remains valid. This question has been tackled by many Muslim theologians both directly and indirectly. One literal interpretation says that even if Jesus were to come, people would not recognize him as Jesus because he acquired certain angelic qualities after his ascension to heaven. In this case only people who are highly spiritually developed, may be able to recognize him. In Islamic mysticism it is not unusual to see connections between individuals and angels, hence Muslim mystics would not deny that some communication with the personality of Jesus in a spiritual realm is possible. Some medieval and contemporary Muslim theologians opine that Jesus will not be known by everybody; only Jesus's close friends and companions will recognize him, and they will do so by "the power of belief."[26] Although some scholars who take an interpretive approach to understanding the texts defend the importance of figurative language used by the Prophet, they also speak of some possible literal meanings. Yes, Jesus will descend as the Prophet said, such scholars say, but he will not descend in the way that people generally understand. This group accepts the message of the Prophet about the descent of Jesus, but they do not accept it literally. They do not feel that the physicality of Jesus is necessarily indicated in the hadith.

All the interpretations mentioned here and the conclusions that some theologians have acquired from the sayings of the Prophet are worthy of consideration. It seems that by witnessing the social upheavals of our age, particularly the two world wars in the twentieth century, one should read the spirit of this age of secularity carefully, as Charles Taylor indicates in his book *A Secular Age*. Muslim-Christian cooperation is a necessity and is vital in efforts to stop more violence and wars in the world.

## Sufis and the Descent of Jesus

Any study of the eschatological role of Jesus in Islam is incomplete without mentioning Sufis and Islamic mystics, who are open to and interested in an interpretive approach and are largely in agreement with mainstream Sunni Islam. Throughout the history of Islam, Sufis have adopted the ascetic lifestyle of Jesus and see him as a prototype for their lives in this world. Further, they have definite views about the subject of Jesus's descent. A large number of Sufi commentaries on the Qur'an address this topic, a few of which are presented and analyzed here. It is not surprising to see that their understanding of Jesus's descent is highly esoteric and allegorical. A thorough investigation of the subject of Jesus's return in the mystical tradition of Islam is beyond the scope of this study and perhaps is the topic of another book. The discussion that follows is limited to several examples from eminent Muslim mystics, including Muhyi al-Din ibn al-'Arabi and Jalal al-Din Rumi, the renowned Sufi poet.

## Muhyi al-Din ibn al-'Arabi

Ibn al-'Arabi (d. 1240) frequently speaks allegorically by using the metaphorical language of mysticism. The style of his writings on the subject is considerably different from any legalistic text. As a Sufi, Ibn al-'Arabi speaks of a high level of spirituality, and his language can be quite ambiguous. The following paragraphs contain careful translations that I made from his monumental book *al-Futuhat al-Makkiyya*, which can be translated as "The Meccan Conquests." It can be difficult to understand Ibn al-Arabi because he frequently writes of his spiritual experiences as if they are real. If the reader is not aware of his style, he or she may misunderstand Ibn al-Arabi and even accuse him of being unrealistic and untruthful. We will see in the following responses of Ibn al-'Arabi to several ambiguous points related to the descent that he has his own terminology. Even when one understands this terminology, one can still find ambiguities in his statements.

In his account of the descent of Jesus, Ibn al-'Arabi responds to some points that may occupy the minds of many mystics. First, to whom does Jesus come? His answer is that Jesus comes to Muslims and his addressees are Muslims. Therefore, Ibn al-'Arabi concludes, Jesus's return at the end of time directly relates to Muslims; Jesus comes to rescue Muslims from oppression. Second, why does Jesus come? Although Ibn al-'Arabi speaks of the necessity of the return of Jesus, he does not speak about why such a return is necessary. Here one can infer several possibilities: (a) The return of Jesus is necessary because the Prophet of Islam said so and the Prophet does not speak in vain; (b) If Jesus comes to the oppressed, it is necessary for him to come. It is the way of God's dealings with humanity to send a rescuer for the oppressed. The coming of Jesus in this regard is the fulfillment of the divine will to protect and rescue the oppressed. The third question is related to the path Jesus follows. Ibn al-'Arabi is very clear in his response to this question: Jesus will follow the path of the Prophet of Islam just as early successors of the Prophet did. He will not bring a new law but will practice the law that was brought by the Prophet of Islam.

What is the spiritual rank of Jesus? Usually Muslim mystics are concerned about the spiritual rank of those they admire. It is known that the highest in rank in the Islamic community after Muhammad is his first successor, Abu Bakr (d. 634). Thus, is the rank of Jesus higher or lower than that of Abu Bakr? Ibn al-'Arabi draws a comparison between the spiritual rank of Jesus, who will descend at the end of time, and Abu Bakr, the first caliph, who Sunni Muslim theologians accept as the highest in spiritual rank after the Prophet: "Surely, it is known that Jesus, peace be upon him, is higher in religious rank than Abu Bakr." He continues, "It is necessary that Jesus will descend in the community of Muhammad at the end of time. He will rule according to the path of Muhammad, peace be upon him, as rightly guided caliphs ruled." Interestingly, Ibn al-'Arabi states that many People of the Book will enter Islam by following the path of Jesus, who will rule according to the path of Muhammad.[27]

Regarding the descent of Jesus, Ibn al-'Arabi speaks of a consensus among Muslims that Jesus is both a prophet and a messenger of God and that he will descend at the end of time as a just ruler. The question of whether Jesus's descent contradicts the finality of the Prophet Muhammad occupied Ibn al-'Arabi's mind as well. According to him, the descent of Jesus does not contradict the Islamic principle that there will be no prophet after Muhammad.[28] It is fascinating to see how Ibn al-'Arabi develops a new Sufi terminology. Sainthood and prophethood are evidently distinguished in this account. He describes Jesus as the seal of general sainthood, whereas Muhammad is the seal of the prophets. Ibn al-'Arabi uses the terms "general sainthood," "seal of the saints," and "general prophethood," terms that are not commonly known by theologians. These special terms are uniquely used by mystics, particularly Ibn al-'Arabi. When he speaks of Jesus as the "seal of the saints," one can infer that any saint who comes after Jesus will be within the frame of Jesus's sainthood since Jesus is both a prophet and the seal of the saints. Ibn al-'Arabi says, "The seal of the general sainthood is Jesus, peace be upon him. He is the saint and a prophet in the time of the community of Muhammad. . . . Jesus will descend at the end of time as a seal and heir. Although Jesus comes after Muhammad and is among the steadfast and elite prophets, there will be no saint after Jesus with all-encompassing prophethood as there is no prophet after Muhammad with prophethood that brings new laws." He then says, "Muhammad and other saints will join Jesus. Jesus is from us and our master. Therefore, at the beginning of this matter [the journey of humanity] there was a prophet, Adam, and at the end of it is a prophet, Jesus." Ibn al-'Arabi refers to the Qur'anic verse that says that the story of Jesus is similar to the story of Adam in the sight of God (3:59). He continues, "Among the principles found in what was revealed to Muhammad is that God will end the general sainthood that started with Adam with Jesus. Therefore, the end will be similar to the beginning. God will end this adventure of humanity in a way similar to the way He started it."[29]

Regarding the final destination of humanity, Islamic theology states that every human being will be resurrected and sent by God's judgment either to paradise or hell. Prophets, saints, and all good people are among the people of paradise. Generally speaking, like other messengers of God, Jesus will also be resurrected and sent to paradise as his final destination. Ibn al-'Arabi has a different approach than that of other Muslim theologians to the resurrection of Jesus. He speaks of two resurrections of Jesus. According to Islamic theology, all people will experience one resurrection:

> Among the saints there is one who is called al-Khatm [The Seal]. He is the only one in the world. God seals with him the sainthood of the Prophet Muhammad. Among Muhammadian saints there is no one greater than him. There is another Khatm by whom God seals the general sainthood, and that is Jesus, peace be upon him. He is the seal of all saints. Jesus will have two resurrections on the Day of Judgment. One with the community of Muhammad and the other as a messenger of God with other divine messengers, peace be upon them all.[30]

Ahmed Avni Konuk (d. 1938), a prominent Turkish commentator on Ibn al-'Arabi, relates in his discussion of *The Bezels of Wisdom* a famous hadith narrated by Abu Hudhayfa, one of the companions of the Prophet who cites ten signs of the Final Hour, including the descent of Jesus. Konuk also refers to another saying of the Prophet that is not very well known and is not found in the major sources of the Hadith, a saying that can be translated as follows, "Blessed are those who live after the descent of Jesus. The sky is given permission to generously give its rain, the earth is given permission to generously put forth its plants to the extent that if you plant a grain on a rock it will grow. A man will pass by a lion. The lion will not harm him and will step on a snake, but the snake will not harm him."[31] Most likely this hadith, which is not from the reliable sources, is borrowed from the book of Isaiah, which speaks about the end of time: "And the lion will eat straw like the ox. The nursing child will play by the hole of the cobra, and the weaned child will put his hand on the viper's den" (Isa. 11:7–8).[32] Narrators might have confused the words of the Prophet of Islam with the words of prophets before Islam, such as Isaiah.

Konuk's commentary on the hadith that indicates that Jesus will kill a pig suggests that Jesus will not kill the innocent pig just because its flesh is prohibited in the Qur'an. According to Konuk, this saying should be understood as referring to "pig-like human beings" who are believed to be harmful to humanity and have no capacity to be saved because of their deviation from the right path; these people will be punished by Jesus.[33] In these commentaries, the descent of Jesus is a symbol of an ideal life and purity in the Sufi literature.

## Jalal al-Din Rumi

Jalal al-Din Rumi (d. 1273) speaks of the purity of the life of Jesus and his being among the angels in that pure life. In the context of speaking of the purity of Jesus, Rumi addresses someone who claims to have memorized many prayers but does not have the purity of heart that the prayer requires: "You may remember a (life-giving) incantation derived from the Messiah [Jesus], [however] where (in you) are the lips and teeth of Jesus, O abominable man?"[34] A person may have the prayer of Jesus, but if he fails to have the mouth of Jesus, the prayer itself will not be very helpful. This echoes Jesus's address to his contemporaries: "Woe to you, scribes and Pharisees, hypocrites! For you clean the outside of the cup and of the dish, but inside they are full of robbery and self-indulgence" (Matt. 23:25).

Rumi expresses the view commonly accepted by Muslim theologians and commentators on the Qur'an that someone else was mistakenly taken by those who intended to kill Jesus. Rumi speaks of this in the context of the lovers of God who are always being saved by God: "The knowers of God are safe for ever because they have passed through a sea of blood." He cites Jesus as an example of this. He speaks of an amir, probably referring to Judas Iscariot, who betrayed Jesus for thirty pieces of silver (Matt. 26:14–16). This amir entered the house where Jesus was hiding, but he turned into Jesus and was captured by the authorities. He cried out that he was not Jesus, but the crowd shouted to hang him "with all speed, for he is Jesus: (he is) seeking to escape from our hands by impersonating another."[35] According to Rumi, because Jesus was the "knower of God," he was saved. Rumi also gives an example from the famous historical story of Abraha, the king of Yemen who in 570 CE, a year before the birth of Muhammad, attempted to destroy the Ka'ba, the holy shrine of Islam in

Mecca with a huge army that included many elephants. The event is mentioned in the Qur'an in chapter 105, "The Elephant."[36] Abraha's goal was to make all pilgrims gather around him and worship toward his own Ka'ba in Yemen. But God again defeated him. Abraha and his Ka'ba were eclipsed. The war matériel of Abraha and his men became spoils for the poor Arabs of Mecca.[37] According to Rumi, God always saves the knowers of God and thus God saved Jesus from his enemies.

Rumi draws a comparison between the spiritual individual and Jesus, saying, "The table of the spiritual is (like) the cell of Jesus: O afflicted one, beware, beware! Do not forsake this door!" Rumi then recounts how those who were blind and lame would come to Jesus and were healed.[38] In another context, Rumi speaks of a conversation between a man and Jesus, who is escaping hastily into the mountains. The man recognizes Jesus's divine qualities and asks the reason for his fearful escape. And Jesus responds that he is the one who, with the help of God, cured all diseases but that the only disease that he could not cure was the disease of stupidity.[39] On another occasion, Rumi refers to the power of God to create fifty earths in a moment but says that God creates gradually to teach people to be patient. Rumi contends that God creates a man in forty years so that the man will become a complete human being over time. "Jesus by means of one prayer was able to make the dead spring up (to life) without delay: Is the Creator of Jesus unable, without delay, to bring (full-grown) men in manifold succession (into existence)?"[40] In these examples, Rumi refers to the Islamic understanding that Jesus had the ability to perform miracles through the power of prayer, that Jesus was not God but was created by God, and that God supported Jesus by giving him the ability to raise the dead.

In a similar verse of poetry, Rumi speaks again about the power of the breath of Jesus, not the physicality of that breath but the power hidden in it that raises the dead. Rumi likens a human being to the breath of Jesus. The physical aspect of that breath is weak, but there is a very strong inner aspect of both the breath and the human being: "Man is like the rod of Moses; Man is like the incantation [breath] of Jesus."[41] On another occasion, Rumi compares the nature of Jesus to that of angels: "Jesus and Idris [Enoch] ascended to heaven, since they were homogeneous with the angels."[42] Abdulbaki Gölpinarli, a prominent Turkish interpreter and commentator on Rumi, speaks of an anonymous individual whom he calls "the Jesus of the time." He refers to the Qur'anic verses that speak of Jesus as a messenger of God to the children of Israel, when Jesus says,

> Surely I came to you with a sign from your Lord. I create from clay the likeness of a bird, then I breathe into it and it becomes a bird by God's

permission. I heal those born blind and the leper, and I resurrect the dead by God's permission. I announce unto you about what you eat and what you store up in your houses. Surely in all of this there is a sign for you if you are believers. And I confirm the Torah, which came before me, and I am to make lawful for you something that is forbidden unto you, and I came with a sign from your Lord, keep your duty to Allah and obey me. Surely God is my Lord and your Lord, so worship Him. This is a straight path. (3:49–51)

After mentioning these verses, Gölpinarli interprets them allegorically to indicate that the resurrection of the dead is not always to be understood as the resurrection of a dead human being but instead as the idea that dead hearts can also be brought back to life. Gölpinarli says, "The Jesus of the time and the Khidr [a mysterious, saintly figure] of the time each opens the eyes of those whose hearts' eyes are blind. They heal the spiritual diseases of those who cannot hear the truth. They resurrect the dead hearts."[43]

When Rumi speaks of the miracles of Jesus, he clearly shares the view of Muslim theologians that Jesus performed miracles in the name of God and with God's permission. Rumi wrote that the "miracles which Jesus had performed he was performing by pronouncing the Name of God. . . . When the soul has been united with God, to speak of God is to speak of that soul and to speak of that soul is to speak of God."[44] This couplet echoes the Qur'anic verse about the Prophet of Islam. When the Prophet's companions gave their hands to him in allegiance, the verse says, "Surely those who give allegiance to you, Muhammad, give allegiance to God" (48:10). This verse has never been understood to bestow status as a deity on Muhammad but has always been understood by Muslim theologians to mean that the Prophet was representing God and speaking on behalf of God. The Prophet was not an incarnation of God but was sent by God to represent God's message. Because he so thoroughly represented God or, using Sufi terminology, he was so united with God, giving allegiance to him was giving allegiance to God. For the same reason, Muslim theologians and mystics such as Rumi would understand Jesus's similar statements about his representation of God to mean that Jesus represents God but is not God, and thus they would not call Jesus or Muhammad a deity. As evidence of this representation, God gave them miracles. But these miracles were aimed to show their truthfulness rather than their status as deities.

In another verse Rumi speaks of what he calls "the dyeing-vat of Jesus," from which a hypocritical king who wanted to corrupt Christianity could not take any positive thing. Rumi writes, "He [the king] had no scent (perception) of the unicoloration of Jesus, nor had he a disposition from (imbued with) the tincture of the dyeing-vat of Jesus. From that pure vat a garment of a hundred colors would become as simple and one-colored as light."[45] With this, Rumi indicates that doctrines may differ but the nature of the way is one.

## 'Abd al-Wahhab al-Sha'rani

Some mystics were concerned about the life of Jesus in heaven and how he would survive without eating and drinking. These mystics were asked by their pupils about Jesus's eating and drinking in heaven. An important Egyptian mystic and theologian 'Abd al-Wahhab al-Sha'rani (d. 1565) gives an interesting answer to the question: How can Jesus live in heaven without eating and drinking? His answer: "Jesus's body has become an angelic body. Therefore, he does not need to eat and drink in the heavenly world. His sustenance is glorifying God, praising God, and saying, Holy, Holy, Holy! as angels do."[46] He also mentions Sufis and saints whose bodies become like light. They do not feel the need to eat and drink. Therefore, al-Sha'rani contends, one should not be in doubt about Jesus's eating and drinking. Later scholars discuss the idea that Jesus did not breathe as humans do, saying that God has the power to allow people to breathe without air. According to Muslim mystics, Jesus can live without eating, drinking, and breathing in heaven because all of these are merely conditions of our worldly life.

Al-Sha'rani goes further and speaks about the necessity of a firm belief in the descent of Jesus: "Surely the descent of Jesus, peace be upon him, is proven by the Qur'an and the sayings of the Prophet. . . . The truth is that Jesus was raised to heaven, bodily as well. And belief in this is necessary." He then refers to a view of his mystic predecessors: "Know that the way of his ascension, and his descent, and his stay in heaven without eating and drinking is something that reason cannot comprehend. There is no way for us, except to believe in it and submit to the wide power of God."[47]

## Ismail Hakki Bursevi

Ismail Hakki Bursevi (d. 1725), a noted Turkish mystic and the author of a well-known commentary on the Qur'an, puts forth a scenario of the descent of Jesus that describes in literal terms the time of the descent and also describes his marriage. His narratives and his presentation of the scenario give an impression that he is not concerned about the reliability of the sources from which he quotes. Perhaps for this reason we see him quoting from much less reliable Hadith sources. Unlike some other Sufis mentioned earlier, he generally seems to be quite literalist regarding Jesus's descent, although not always.

According to Bursevi's scenario, "Jesus will descend as a just ruler in the time of al-Dajjal." Most likely in order to indicate the unknown nature of the time of Jesus's descent, he intentionally describes it as the time of the emergence of the Antichrist. An unknown is described with another unknown, but at least both are known as the signs of the Hour and their coming is known to be at the end of time. One can assume that when he speaks of the time of al-Dajjal it is another way to say at the end of time. Bursevi also narrates that "Jesus will marry an Arab woman, he will have children from her, and then after living forty years on earth he will die. Muslims will perform his funeral prayer. That is because Jesus prayed to God to be a member of Muhammad's community, and God has accepted his prayer."[48] Bursevi's addition to what we already know of the scenario of Jesus's descent is his marriage with an Arab woman. Fascinatingly, he takes this marriage literally. Since he narrates the scenario as a future fact, he does not leave a space for further symbolic interpretations. The marriage addition to this eschatological scenario is not found in the reliable Hadith sources, although one can find it in the less-known Hadith collections from which Bursevi quoted with no hesitation.

When one examines Bursevi's view on the descent, several points draw one's attention. The first thing is Jesus's relationship to celibacy. According to Bursevi, unlike his original celibacy, after his return Jesus will not advocate for celibacy and will instead marry and encourage marriage. If this is taken literally, as Bursevi claims, it will mean an important shift in the Christian tradition. Second, Bursevi speaks of the duration of Jesus's stay as forty years. It is very well known in the Arabic literature that the numbers forty and seventy are indications of multiplicity. In this case, it indicates the long duration of Jesus's time on earth. Third, Bursevi speaks of the end scenario of Jesus's death. This clearly indicates that Bursevi believes that Jesus is mortal, and everything that is mortal cannot be God. This Muslim mystic once again emphasizes the Islamic view that Jesus is God's messenger and cannot be God.

Many Sufis use symbolism when they speak of Jesus's descent, similar to Muslim theologians who take an interpretive approach. This symbolism can be found in a Turkish Sufi poem written in the Mathnawi style (characterized by the use of couplets) and presented to the Ottoman sultan Murad II. In this poem, the author presents the sword of Jesus as one made of light, a weapon that does not harm but heals.[49] This relates to the struggle between the Antichrist and Jesus, which many Muslim theologians including Nursi understand to be a nonviolent struggle.

# NINE

# Jesus's Descent and Theologies
# of Muslim-Christian Cooperation

So far I have examined various Islamic theological understandings of Jesus's eschatological role and Islam's rich theological engagement with Jesus. This chapter will explore this theology in light of its implications for Muslim-Christian cooperation, pluralism, and world peace. In this regard, the focus of this chapter is twofold: it first highlights the textual aspects of the Islamic approach to interreligious dialogue and then addresses the praxis of dialogue between Christians and Muslims.

## The Roots of Dialogue in Islamic Theological Thought

If one is to read contemporary Muslim commentators who view Muslim-Christian cooperation as part of their understanding of the descent of Jesus, it is necessary to first examine the roots of dialogue in the Qur'an. Within the Qur'an and the sayings of the Prophet one finds many references to Christians and Jews, "the People of the Book." Among the world's major religions, Judaism is the closest to Islam in terms of laws and practices, particularly dietary restrictions. As far as the personality of Jesus is concerned, Christianity is the closest religion to Islam. The Qur'an instructs Muslims to love all prophets equally, however for many Muslims, there is a special love for Jesus. This is because, according to Muslims, Jesus spoke both in the Qur'an and in the Gospel about the coming of the Prophet of Islam. Also, the Prophet Muhammad frequently spoke about Jesus and his descent. These references have contributed to Muslims' unique love of Jesus. In fact many Muslims name their children after him with his Arabic name 'Isa, just as they name their children after other prophets such as Abraham, Moses, Isaac, Ishmael, and David.

The Qur'an was revealed in a multicultural and multireligous environment.

The Prophet of Islam had already been exposed to diverse societies before his first experience of revelation; His family life, and particularly his later marriages, is a good example of the multicultural environment in which the Qur'an was revealed. The Prophet married a Jewish woman named Safiyya as well as an Egyptian Christian, Maria. Among Muslims, the wives of the Prophet are considered the mothers of the Islamic community. Thus, when Muslims refer to the wives of the Prophet they say, "Our mother Safiyya" or "Our mother Maria." The Qur'an brought a new understanding to the people of Arabia, yet its message was not limited to one segment of human society. Instead, it was given to *all* human beings. In fact, the Qur'an frequently refers to its audience as *al-nas* (the people) and *al-insan* (the human being).[1]

A deep examination of Qur'anic passages reveals that the scripture was in dialogue with its diverse society. The primary listeners of the Qur'an were the Muslims who followed its teachings. However, the Qur'an addressed Arab polytheists known as *mushrikun* as well as Christians and Jews, known as Ahl al-Kitab, or the People of the Book. The Qur'an even refers to a group known as the Sabi'un, an esoteric group that some believed worshipped stars and angels in addition to the one God. In the midst of such cultural diversity, the Qur'anic revelation came to the Prophet in the year 609 CE.[2] Since this revelation constitutes the most holy reference for Muslims, a verse, a word, or even a hint in the Qur'an is substantially important for any theological discourse. Therefore, even an allusion in the Qur'an to the descent of Jesus or to the promotion of dialogue between Muslims and Christians is significant. The Qur'an clearly states its preference for such dialogue.

The Holy Book of Islam instructs its audience to initiate dialogue with others by showing a way of greeting, the same way Jesus used to greet his disciples: "When you are greeted, respond with an equal or better greeting" (4:86). By using such a general statement, the Qur'an in fact opens a wide door for dialogue and understanding. This is the first step to establishing good relationships with others, regardless of differences between people. After establishing this relationship, the Qur'an addresses pagans, polytheists, idol worshipers, Christians, and Jews. The language of the Qur'an regarding polytheists is strong and engaging. The Qur'an considers the denial of God's existence to be a great error, so the verses regarding polytheists are highly critical but also contain a strong invitation for them to understand the message of the Qur'an from a logical basis. For example, the Qur'an asks of disbelievers, "Will they [the people who do not believe in God, pagans of Mecca] not look at the camels and how they are created, and the heavens, how it is raised, and the mountains, how they are set up, and the earth, how it is spread. [O Muhammad] remind them [of this] for you are only a reminder. You are not a coercer of them" (88:16–20).

It is evident that the Qur'anic address to Arab idol worshippers is uncompromising. The Qur'an challenges them by citing what the Scripture contends is the work of God, such as the creation of natural phenomena, and even the skill of idol worshippers, such as their eloquence. For example, one verse says, "Are you harder [for God] to create or is it the heaven that God built? He raised heaven thereof and ordered it. And He made dark the night thereof. And He brought forth the day thereof. And after that, He spread the Earth" (79:27–30). In another verse the Qur'an says, "If you are in doubt concerning that which We reveal unto our servant [Muhammad] then produce a chapter of the like thereof and call your witnesses beside God if you are truthful. If you cannot do it, and you can never do it, then guard yourselves against the fire the fuel of which is of men and stones prepared for the disbelievers" (2:23–24). In the Qur'anic narrative, the polytheists of Mecca are presented as *kafirun* (disbelievers) and *mushrikun*, those who associate their idols with God. The Holy Book complains of this group's stubbornness, saying that Arab polytheists (al-A'rab, or Arab Bedouins) are the strongest in disbelief and hypocrisy (9:97). Despite this, the door of dialogue has been kept open with them. The Qur'an uses emphatic language to invite even these disbelievers to think about their environment and the beauty around them and to recognize the Creator. Thus the Qur'an justifies dialogue not only with Christians and Jews, who are members of the Abrahamic family to which Muslims also belong, but also with atheists. The Qur'an invites all deniers of God into dialogue about basic beliefs. Therefore today's atheists, agnostics, humanists, and so on, are invited into dialogue in the same way.

Occasionally dialogue between the Prophet and the polytheists would turn into a heated debate; however, the Qur'an prohibits insulting the gods of polytheists because the polytheists in turn might insult God (6:108). The Prophet engaged in a respectful debate over resurrection with the disbelievers of Mecca. A leading personality among them came to the Prophet with some rotten bones in his hand and crumbled the bones to dust, asking the Prophet, "Who will resurrect these rotten bones?" In response to this, divine revelation instructed Muhammad to say that "the One who first brought them into being will resurrect them again" (36:77–80).

Muhammad, as God's messenger, engaged in an instructive dialogue with the people around him. When Meccan polytheists used physical force against him, he did not respond with force but instead preferred migration; he also practiced nonviolence when persecuted.[3] After he visited the city of Ta'if to seek refuge for himself and his community and was, in modern parlance, violently run out of town, the angel Gabriel came to him and said that God would destroy the entire city if he wished. He said, "Lord, there may be some believers from the offspring of these people. They do not know what they are doing." This is similar to Jesus's famous statement "Father, forgive them; for they do not know what they are doing" (Luke 23:34).

The Qur'an describes Muhammad as a "mercy for the universe" (21:107). This quality is observed in his relationship with the polytheists of Mecca. On one occasion, some of Muhammad's companions asked him to pray that God would send a plague upon the disbelievers. The Prophet replied, "Surely I am sent by God only as a mercy for all people." Instead he asked God to forgive the disbelievers of Mecca. In another version of this hadith, the prophet says, "I am not sent to curse people, but sent only as a mercy for people."[4]

Christians and Jews are both important groups in the intended audience of the Qur'an. The Prophet's dialogues with Christians and Jews took place on a higher level. The Christian king of Abyssinia, modern-day Ethiopia, was a constant ally of the Prophet against Meccan polytheists. Throughout Islamic history, generally speaking, Jewish and Christian minorities lived peacefully in Islamic communities and flourished within Islamic civilization, including such notables as Yahya bin 'Adi (d. 974), a prominent Christian theologian who translated numerous Greek philosophical works into Arabic, and the Jewish polymath Moses Maimonides (d. 1204). Muslim theologians and jurists have developed specific rights, responsibilities, and protections for the People of the Book based on the Qur'an and the sayings of the Prophet.[5] Historically, starting in the era of the Four Caliphs through the end of the Ottoman Empire, Christians and Jews living under Islamic law were called the people of the *dhimma* and received special legal protections. Even today, Islamic law impels a government to be responsible for the protection of its Christian and Jewish citizens.

A well-known story among scholars of Islamic law illustrates this protection and gives it further support in the legal tradition. A famous Muslim jurist, Qadi Abu Yusuf (d. 798), sent a message to the Abbasid caliph Harun al-Rashid (r. 786–809), advising him to be compassionate toward the people of the *dhimma* under his rule:

O Leader of Believers, may God protect you, surely it is necessary that you deal with the people of the *dhimma* with compassion. They are under the protection of your Prophet and your cousin Muhammad.[6] It is your responsibility to make sure that they are not wronged or harmed or bothered. Also you make sure that nothing beyond their capacity is asked from them. Also you need to make sure that nothing is taken from their wealth, except the rightly assigned required tax."[7]

Then Abu Yusuf reminded Harun al-Rashid of 'Umar, who said before his death, "I advise the caliphs after me to protect the people of the *dhimma*. They are under the Messenger of God's protection. And I advise the caliphs to give the people of the *dhimma* what they promise them. The leader of Muslims is to fight on their behalf, and not to put upon their shoulders something that is beyond their capacity."[8] The Prophet's compassion and mercy were codified in Islamic law as a guarantee of protection for the rights of minorities, especially Christians and Jews.

Just as the Prophet was a mercy for humankind, he was also humble in his dialogue and relationships with others. The humility of the Prophet contributed to this dialogue. When mediating a conflict between a Jew and a Muslim over whether Moses or Muhammad was the paragon of humanity, the Prophet responded, "Do not elevate me over Moses."[9] That the Prophet did not consider himself to be higher than Moses in the sight of God demonstrates his humbleness. On another occasion he said, "Do not compare me to my brother Jonah."[10] This humility set an example for Muslims and contributed to respectful dialogue with other religious traditions because he always spoke positively about the messengers of God who came before him. In addition, he brought beautiful ethics to the community and valued relationships within the multireligious community. An important hadith recorded by al-Bukhari reads "'Abdullah bin 'Amr narrates that a sheep was slaughtered for and brought to the Prophet. The Prophet twice [indicating its importance] said to his servant 'Have you shared this with our Jewish neighbor?'"[11] Muhammad also had financial interactions with members of this community. For example, he used his shield as collateral for a loan from a Jewish neighbor. He valued good qualities in others whether they were Muslims or not, and this was his understanding of the Qur'an. He would say, "People are like minerals, the one who was good pre-Islam is good after Islam too."[12] Therefore, people were praised because of their good qualities, regardless of their race, ethnicity, or religious background. The Qur'an was the foundation of the Prophet's ethics.

## Finding Common Ground with the People of the Book

Christians and Jews are mentioned more than forty times in the Qur'an. The best-known term for them collectively in the Qur'an is the tender phrase Ahl al-Kitab, the People of the Book. The Qur'an also uses the term *ahl* in describing the family of the Prophet: Ahl al-Bayt, "the People of the Family." The Qur'an speaks of the beliefs of the People of the Book, their holy scriptures, and their prophets, and in some cases narrates their conversations and describes them as examples for Muslims. The God of Islam, Allah, is the same as the God of Abraham, Moses, and Jesus; the Qur'an says, "Our God and your God is one" (46:29). The People of the Book share many of the beautiful names of God in the Qur'an: the Creator, the Merciful, the Compassionate, the All-Powerful, the All-Wise, the All-Knowing, the Eternal, the Vigilant Guardian, the One Who Answers All Our Needs, the Very Loving, and many others. These constitute a common ground between Muslims and Christians, the adherents of the two largest world religions.[13] Since they share the same God, they share the most important aspect of faith, and therefore dialogue between them is much easier. Although there may be differences in interpretation of doctrines that sound irreconcilable, a shared humanity and a common Creator are more fundamental.

In Islamic teaching, Allah is the God of all, not just the God of Muslims. The Qur'an states, "We [God] have advised those who received the Scripture before you. We also advised you [Muslims] that you should be respectful to God. If you disbelieve, beware! All that is in heaven and earth belongs to God. Allah is All-sufficient and Worthy of Praise" (4:131). In Islamic theology, God does not need the belief and prayers of humankind. If people reject prayer, they do not harm God; they harm only themselves. Islamic theology holds that people can neither harm nor benefit God. To describe God's role in the Islamic tradition, there is a well-known analogy of a medical doctor who insists that patients take their medication. The doctor insists upon this for the sake of her patients because they need the medication. Similarly, humans need worship for their own spiritual betterment.

The Qur'an encourages dialogue and cooperation with the People of the Book. As great messengers of God, Moses is mentioned more than 150 times and Jesus is mentioned over 100 times, including twenty-five times by his Islamic proper name, 'Isa, and thirty-three times by the epithet "Son of Mary." The Qur'an esteems biblical prophets highly. Likewise, the Qur'an praises the People of the Book for their good deeds and faith in God: "As for those who believe in God and remain steadfast in their faith, God will enter them in His mercy and grace. He will lead them to the path of righteousness, the straight path" (4:175). Therefore, the Qur'an encourages coexistence, cooperation, and harmony among the People of the Book in order to bring common good to society. Wherever there is something good, the Qur'an considers it Islamic.

In fact, the Qur'an invites and encourages all human beings, no matter what their backgrounds are, to strive to better themselves and to contribute to the betterment of others through good deeds. The Qur'an very clearly considers diversity a part of the divine will, and it clearly teaches that to urge uniformity goes against the divine will. The Qur'an says, "If God willed, He could have made you one community, but [He has not] in order to test you with what He has given you. Therefore, vie with one another for good deeds. All of you will return to God. He will then inform you about what you have differed on" (5:48). This verse indicates that diversity functions as a test for humanity, to try mankind's ability to overcome bigotry and prejudice. In passing this test, humankind will accomplish the common good to which the Qur'an calls all people.

Two Qur'anic verses include not only Muslims but also Jews and Christians among those who will be rewarded by God as long as they believe in God and the afterlife and do good deeds (2:62, 5:69). This is possible if, as some Muslim theologians have understood it, belief in the prophets, including the Prophet Muhammad as the final messenger of God, is a necessary result of the belief in God. In fact, the Qur'an itself makes belief in the prophets inseparable from belief in God (4:150). The Qur'an therefore enables the building of bridges between Muslims and Christians.

Today, if oppositional feelings develop between Muslims and Christians, it is not because of the Qur'an or the Gospel. It could be because of political circumstances or a lack of understanding of the Holy Scriptures, but the scriptures themselves are not to blame. How unfortunate it is when a fringe group of Christians wants to burn the Qur'an without having even read it. Those who are promoting violence in the Islamic community are fringe groups as well, and their disruptive actions bring them more attention than positive actions bring to the mainstream Muslim community. Distraction often makes noise while good things are quiet. In the Qur'anic passages regarding the People of the Book in general and Christians in particular, one often finds a tender tone. The various discourses of the Qur'an and the styles it uses in addressing non-Muslim audiences encourage dialogue and cooperation.

The Qur'an mandates a positive dialogue with the People of the Book. This means that the debate between Muslims and Christians must be based on kindness: "Do not argue with the People of the Book unless it is in the best way, save for those who do evil. And say 'We believe in that which has been revealed to us and what was revealed to you. Our God and your God is One and to Him we submit'" (29:46). Any debate must be, as the Qur'an states, a friendly one. The

Qur'an is realistic and does not negate the differences. However, even discussing those differences can cause a certain level of enmity. To prevent any animosity, the verse commands Muslims to only debate with the People of the Book, including theological debates, in the kindest way. The foundation of healthy debate should focus on the dimensions upon which both traditions agree.

In addition to a shared belief in one God, and in fact the same God, another important theological principle shared by Muslims and Christians is the concept of prophethood.[14] The Qur'an presents prophethood as an indispensable element of human history and a common theme between Muslims and Christians. There is no doubt that Jesus, as a messenger of God, is one of the most important prophets in Islam. Similarly, Moses is a touchstone for both Jews and Muslims. The Qur'an narrates the struggle of Moses against Pharaoh and casts Moses as a predecessor of the Prophet of Islam. One cannot find a Muslim named Pharaoh. However, one can find many Muslims named Jesus ('Isa) or Moses (Musa). This social fact clearly demonstrates that the feelings of Muslims are inherently positive toward Christians and Jews. In fact, many biblical prophets are mentioned in the Qur'an. The Qur'an describes believers in God and His messenger Muhammad as those who do not distinguish between God's messengers (2:285, 4:152). Muslims are required to believe in all of God's messengers. In Islamic teaching, Noah, Abraham, Moses, Jesus, and Muhammad are all in the same chain of prophethood, and belief in one of them entails a belief in all of them. Such an approach paves the way for mutual understanding and positive relationships between Muslims and Christians.

In a multicultural society, it is important to have a respect for individual voices in order to stimulate good feedback through dialogue.[15] This allows individuals to talk freely and to be engaged in the process of decision making. The Prophet Muhammad and his companions were a great example of such engagement. He had great respect for individual thought and allowed others to speak freely, including women and children, without silencing them. Even if he occasionally was frustrated, he was always patient and compassionate. The Qur'an describes him in the following way: "It is because of a mercy from Allah that you were lenient with your people, O Muhammad, for if you had been stern and fierce of heart they would have dispersed from around you. Forgive them, and then ask forgiveness for them from God. And consult with them in your affairs, and trust in God" (3:159). When the Prophet was frustrated by questions and extraordinary requests from his audience, the Qur'an consoled him by mentioning that previous prophets endured the same frustration, and even worse (3:184). Multiple passages strike the same chord: "If they deny you,

[O Muhammad,] surely many Messengers of God before you were denied as well and everything will ultimately return to God" (35:4). This empowered the Prophet to remain patient and merciful; it kept Muhammad in alignment with the prophetic tradition and thus the Qur'an describes him as "the seal of the prophets" (33:40).

In addition to the common prophetic tradition, the Qur'an further encourages relationships between Christians and Muslims by presenting Islam as the religion of Abraham, the common ancestor of Jews, Christians, and Muslims. The verse says, "Say, we [Muslims] believe in Allah and in that which is revealed unto us, and which is revealed unto Abraham, Ishmael, Isaac, Jacob, and the tribes, and which is also revealed to Moses, Jesus, and in what the prophets received from their Lord. We do not differentiate between any of them, and to God we have surrendered" (2:135–36). This verse connects Islam with the Jewish and Christian traditions via the chain of prophethood. As the verse states, Muslims believe in all that was revealed to Jesus and Moses and to the other prophets. Muslims believe that when Jesus speaks, he speaks truthfully. According to the teachings of Islam, Jesus never lied. The only difference between Muslims and Christians with regard to the sayings of Jesus is in their interpretation. In Islamic theological thought, Jesus was the most important human being on earth in his time; the message Jesus taught was the true message of God and a renewal of the Abrahamic tradition. According to the Qur'an, the essence of the message of God to all prophets is the same. Any difference is based on the conditions and needs of the people to whom each prophet was sent. God chose to send Muhammad within the same tradition as Jesus, and He made Muhammad the seal of the Prophets.

## Admonitions and Instructions for Muslims and Christians

Although the need for dialogue between Muslims and Christians is important in the Qur'an, this idea can sometimes turn into admonition and instruction. There is no doubt that the Qur'an criticizes some Christians and Jews for their bad deeds or false beliefs; however, this criticism is motivated by a desire for the people of Abrahamic faiths to take the right path, as it is presented in the first chapter of the Qur'an. In their daily prayers, Muslims ask God for guidance on the path. The Qur'an criticizes the Christian understanding of the metaphysical presence of Jesus and asks Christians to avoid exaggeration in regard to Jesus. The verse says, "Say [Muhammad]: O People of the Book! Do not exaggerate in your religion, excepting the truth. Do not follow the desires of people who went astray before and have misguided many people and have themselves strayed from the right path" (5:77). The "people who went astray before" in this verse can be interpreted as a reference to the Greco-Roman religious tradition. In another verse, the need to question the trinity is underscored: "O People of the Book! Do not exaggerate in your religion. Do not say anything about God except truth. Surely, the Messiah, Jesus, son of Mary, is God's messenger and God gave His word through Mary and he [Jesus] is a spirit from Him. Therefore believe in God and His messengers and do not say God is 'three.' Avoiding this is better for you. There is no doubt that God is but One God. He is too exalted to have a son. Whatever is in heaven and on earth belongs to Him and God is all sufficient as the Trustee" (4:171). According to Islamic theology, monotheism is the message of both the Qur'an and the Gospel and is therefore a common value that Muslims and Christians share.

The Qur'an instructs Christians to avoid exaggeration. Even though most Christians consider Jesus's divinity a truth of revelation, Muslims consider this an exaggeration of the personality of Jesus, which is not found in the essence of his message. Forgoing exaggeration is an important principle for Muslims to consider as well. The Prophet responded in a similar tone to his companions who wanted to pursue an ascetic lifestyle. They sought to reject marriage, fast throughout the year, and pray day and night. The Prophet asked them to avoid extremism. As a moral example and the Islamic ideal, the Prophet reminded them of the middle way, exhorting them that marriage is in accordance with human nature and should not be rejected. He instructed them to fast sometimes but not to go to extremes.

The Prophet Muhammad exemplified this exhortation to avoid exaggeration by modeling it in his own life. From the beginning of his calling to the end, he resisted every desire to inflate his own status. One example of how the Prophet rejected exaggeration about himself can be seen when Muhammad gave the same warning to his companions when they wanted to exaggerate the status of his prophethood. He reminded them that he was only a human being and not a deity, that the only difference between him and other men was that he was receiving a revelation from God. The Qur'an instructs him to proclaim this principle of Islamic faith: "Say [Muhammad] 'I am only a human being like you. It has been revealed to me that your God is only One God. Therefore, whoever hopes to meet his Lord, let him do righteous work, and associate none with God in worship'" (18:110). Once again, the Prophet Muhammad is asked to confirm his status as a human being: "Say [Muhammad] 'I do not say to you that God's treasures are with me, and I do not know the unseen, and I do not say to you that I am an angel. I only follow what is revealed to me.'" (6:50). Again, "Say [Muhammad], O people, I am a messenger of God to you all" (7:158).

Being a messenger of God also indicates the Prophet's servanthood. The Qur'an presents Muhammad as a servant of God in the same way that it presents Jesus as a servant of God. The Qur'an says, "The Messiah will never disdain being a servant of Allah" (4:172). In Islamic teaching, the highest rank that one can attain is to become the closest servant of Allah. Therefore, when the Qur'an relates the Prophet Muhammad to God with phrases such as "Our servant" (2:23) and "His servant" (17:1, 18:1, 25:1. 39:36, 53:10, 57:9), it alludes to two important points. First, the Prophet Muhammad is a human being and a servant of God; his position therefore should not be elevated to the level of a deity. Second, while he is not a deity, his close relationship to God is indicated in the pronouns "His" or "Our." Therefore, when God describes someone as His servant, He gives that person the highest spiritual rank an individual can attain. For this reason, God may even change the course of the natural laws for this servant's sake, yet this individual is a servant and cannot be an object of worship. Keeping these two points in mind, Muslims would never imagine worshipping Muhammad. Therefore, Orientalists' description of Muslims as "Muhammadans" or Islam as "Muhammadanism" is considered offensive because it implies that Muslims worship Muhammad.

Muhammad always humbled himself and drew people's attention to his humanity so that no one would consider him a deity; he was a preacher of God's word and a conveyor of God's message to mankind, not a deity. The verses of the Qur'an state this in a powerful way. It is well known that the Prophet did not allow his companions to rise and stand before him, as some people did to show respect to their king.[16] One companion of the Prophet narrates that he knew no face more honorable and precious than the face of the Messenger of God but that the Prophet's companions would not stand up before him because they knew that he had forbidden the practice.

One of the important traits that Jesus shares with Muhammad is humility. In contrast, the Qur'an criticizes Pharaoh and his arrogance because he claimed that he was God. The Qur'an indicates that a pious, humble, messenger of God such as Jesus would never be so arrogant as to claim that he was God. For all servants of God, humility is essential. The Qur'an praises Christians who are humble: "You will find the closest in affection to those who believe [Muslims] are those who say, 'We are Christians.' This is because among them there are priests and monks and they are not arrogant" (5:82). Mahmoud Ayoub, a leading scholar of Islam in the United States, finds two crucial points in this verse. First, there is amity between Christians and Muslims. Second, Christian monks and learned priests accept the truth when they hear it because of their humble character.[17] In fact, the next verse continues in the same style, praising the piety of some Christians: "When they hear what is revealed to the Messenger of God, you see their eyes overflow with tears because of their recognition of the truth, and they say, 'Our Lord, we believe. Include us among the witnesses'" (5:83).

The occasion of the revelation of this verse is significant with regard to Muslim-Christian interaction. The verse was revealed after a group of the Prophet's companions, some seventy men and women, had migrated to Abyssinia and met with King Ashama bin Abjar (known in the Islamic sources as al-Najashi, meaning the Emperor) to ask for refuge in his kingdom so they could escape the torture of Meccan pagans. In an effort to extradite the Prophet's companions, these Meccan polytheists sent a delegate to the king. While the king considered returning the Prophet's companions to the Meccans in order to improve diplomatic relations with Mecca, the leader of the group, Ja'far bin Abi Talib (d. 629), who was also a cousin of the Prophet Muhammad, objected to the decision by saying that they were sent by the Prophet because they believed in the same God that the king believed in. After Ja'far made a remarkable defense by reciting the Qur'anic verses from chapter 19 on Jesus's birth and on Mary, the king's eyes and those of his companions filled with tears. The king turned to the Meccan delegate and said, "Not for a mountain of gold will I return them to you."[18] Then the king asked the group to stay in Abyssinia as long as they wished.[19]

This verifiable historical event is considered a landmark in the history of Muslim-Christian cooperation. The Qur'an praises this king and his associates because of his fear of God and their favorable reaction to the Qur'anic revelation. Although the Qur'an speaks of a particular historical event, the significance of that event is not limited to that time period. We also know that when King Ashama passed away, the Prophet felt sorry and said: "Today the wholesome servant of God Ashama [al-Najashi] died. Stand up and perform [funeral] prayer for him." The companion of the Prophet who narrates the story continues, "We stood up and the Prophet led us in the Prayer."[20] The Prophet performed a funeral prayer for al-Najashi in the city of Medina, which set the precedent in Islamic law for what would later be called by scholars of Islamic law the "funeral prayer in absentia."[21]

To contribute to the overall cooperation between Muslims and Christians, the Qur'an avoids generalizations and stereotypes about certain negative behavior and beliefs of Christians. While the Qur'an is positive overall toward People of the Book, in those instances where it ascribes negative characteristics to the People of the Book, it uses adjectives such as "some" or "many," as opposed to "all," to show that these characteristics are not common to all the People of the Book.[22] Since the Qur'an opens the door to interaction with the People of the Book and invites them to a common ground, some Islamic scholars have been impelled to consider the descent of Jesus in a more universal and allegorical way, as is discussed in previous chapters, to devise an interpretation that lays the groundwork for the future of Muslim-Christian collaboration. Before moving on to discuss contemporary dialogue efforts, it is important to give a brief account of the history of Christian-Muslim relations.

## Christian-Muslim Relations after the Era of the Prophet

Since the era of the Prophet, Muslims and Christians, more often than not, have lived peacefully side by side. During the Umayyad Caliphate, Christian scholars and scribes were able to attain significant positions in the government and Umayyad leaders allowed Christians, as well as Jews and other religious groups, a high degree of autonomy. In the same way, the Abbasid period of Islam was an era when Muslims were able to coexist with Christians, Jews, and even atheists. Most notably, under the rule of Harun al-Rashid (r. 786–809), these groups were able to debate their theological differences in the palace of the caliph. This period of harmony generally continued until the height of the Crusades. Even during the era of the Crusades, religious harmony continued to flourish in Islamic Spain, where through mutual cooperation Muslims, Christians, and Jews created a culture of intellectual and spiritual development that can be scarcely rivaled elsewhere in human history. By the fifteenth century, the Ottomans had established a new era of peaceful coexistence between Muslims, Christians, and Jews. Ottomans were known for their tolerance toward adherents of different religions. Their ideas came from the teaching of the Qur'an, which for them was considered the most authoritative reference for dealing with minorities.

The Ottoman Empire left behind a remarkable legacy of harmonious interreligious relations and cooperation. One example is its *millet* system, the legal framework that allowed Christians and Jews to continue their religious and legal traditions. Until the emergence of modern nationalistic movements in the mid-nineteenth century, Muslims, Christians, and Jews managed to live together more peacefully and productively in Ottoman times than has been possible in the twenty-first century. This legacy of mutual recognition between members of different faith communities in the Ottoman era was at least partially the result of the teachings of Sufi masters such as Ahmed Yesevi (d. 1166), Jalal al-Din Rumi (d. 1272), Yunus Emre (d. 1321), Haci Bayram-i Veli (d.1429), and Akşemseddin (d. 1459).[23] All of these Sufi masters espoused ideas of tolerance and understanding. Later figures such as Bediüzzaman Said Nursi (d. 1960) and Fethullah Gülen (b. 1941) have continued this tradition. Nursi was so interested in dialogue with Christians that he visited the patriarch of Eastern Orthodox Christianity in Istanbul and sent his writings in the 1950s to the Vatican desiring dialogue with the Catholic Church.

This practice of tolerance and dialogue by Muslim mystics and scholars did not find a similar response from Western Christians during the Middle Ages, with some exceptions such as St. Francis of Assisi (d. 1226). The behavior of the Catholic Church toward the Prophet of Islam under Pope Innocent III (r. 1198–1216) was quite hostile, to the point of calling Muhammad the Antichrist.[24] I do not want to suggest that throughout its history Christianity has been antagonistic toward Islam; from both a Christian and a Muslim point of view the historical relationships between the two religions have been very complex and multifaceted. Instead, I want to suggest that there have been important positive developments in the relationship between followers of these two religions in the past half-century.

## Christian-Muslim Relations Today

The world is changing rapidly. In the beginning of the 1960s, the Second Vatican Council expressed a more respectful attitude toward Islam and Muslims, and extremism on both sides has faded, even if its volume has not. The *Nostra Aetate* of the Second Vatican Council accepted Islam as a religion sent by God and announced the following:

> Upon the Moslims [*sic*] too, the Church looks with esteem. They adore one God, living and enduring, merciful and all-powerful, Maker of heaven and earth and Speaker to men. They strive to submit wholeheartedly even to His inscrutable decrees, just as did Abraham, with whom the Islamic faith is pleased to associate itself. Though they do not acknowledge Jesus as God, they revere Him as a prophet. They also honor Mary, His virgin mother; at times they call on her, too, with devotion. In addition they await the day of judgment when God will give each man his due after raising him up. Consequently, they prize the moral life, and give worship to God especially through prayer, almsgiving, and fasting.[25]

During my conversations with some Muslims, I have found doubt in their minds about the Vatican's intended rapprochement with Muslims. Because of certain negative events, both historical and contemporary, the speeches of some Catholic religious leaders evoke suspicion. However, as time passes, positive steps by the Vatican will remove such suspicion and increase cooperation between the two faiths. The decision to make such a statement about Islam is believed to have been directly influenced by participants who were missionaries to different parts of the Islamic world and were impressed by the theological strength of Islamic belief and the common ground between Islam and Christianity. In early 2013, Jorge Mario Bergoglio, a Jesuit priest, was made pope. Eschewing tradition, he took the name Francis in honor of St. Francis of Assisi, who undertook a great leap of faith and met with the sultan of Egypt during the Crusades. One can only hope that a similar leap will be taken today and that this new pope will work with Muslim religious leaders to further the cause of Muslim-Christian cooperation. With his Jesuit background and history of humility, the current pope has received a positive reaction from Muslims. In his personal message to Muslims at the end of Ramadan in the first year of his papacy, Francis underscored the role of both education and respect in religious dialogue. "This year's theme is intended to underline the importance of education in the way we understand each other, built upon the foundation of mutual respect. 'Respect' means an attitude of kindness towards people for whom we have consideration and esteem. 'Mutual' means that this is not a one-way process, but something shared by both sides."[26]

The Second Vatican Council represented a great shift in understanding on the part of Roman Catholic Christians toward Islam and Muslims and is only one example of strengthened communication. This trend toward increasing cooperation may also be seen in Western Christian academic and lay religious circles. Despite, and perhaps because of, the hostile events of September 11, 2001, and its aftermath, Muslim-Christian dialogue continues to grow. This growth in dialogue includes other religious traditions as well.

An important element toward the creation of an environment for dialogue has been present since the beginning of Christianity. Most Christians share the first part of Islam's testimony of faith, which states that there is no deity but God. Some Christians even accept the second part of the Islamic testimony of faith, which states that Muhammad is God's messenger. This was historically demonstrated by an important patriarch of the Nestorians of Iraq, Catholicos Timothy I (d. 823), who believed that Muhammad was "worthy of all praise . . . he walked in the path of prophets," and has some resonance in our time.[27]

It seems that there has been an increase in cooperation between Muslims and Christians of late. In the United States and Europe, goodwill between Muslims and Christians is flourishing. Noting this development, and despite the obstacles of extremism on both sides, one can hope and expect that the future of Muslim-Christian relations is bright and that this may bring the family of Abraham—Jews, Christians, and Muslims—together and further the divine message of Abraham, Moses, Jesus, and others. Despite the fact that some Muslim groups oppose interfaith dialogue, several Islamic institutions and personalities are engaged in dedicated efforts to make Muslim-Christian cooperation possible in countries such as Jordan, Egypt, Pakistan, Indonesia, and Turkey, with some success.[28]

In February 1998, Fethullah Gülen, a prominent Turkish scholar of Islam, met with Pope John Paul II to develop interfaith relations with Christians.[29] As the leader of the prominent movement that takes his name, Gülen is highly respected in the Islamic world; he has approximately eight million admirers and sympathizers both within and outside of Turkey. Many people, including Fr. Thomas Michel, SJ, believe that the Gülen movement is the largest, most well-organized, and most effective systematic investment in interfaith dialogue in the world. Gülen has been a champion of dialogue between adherents of the major world religions, especially the Abrahamic faiths, for over two decades. This substantial engagement of Muslims in interfaith cooperation has resulted in a broad rapprochement among civilizations. In 2005, the prime ministers of Turkey and Spain and the UN secretary-general co-founded the United Nations Alliance of Civilizations. Since then the alliance has grown and has established a variety of academic and social programs and events. Despite the claims of Samuel Huntington (d. 2008) that there would be a clash of civilizations, such efforts seem to suggest the opposite.[30]

Gülen is highly involved in spiritual life as a "Sufi in his own way."[31] In an era of materialism, Gülen focuses on the importance of the spiritual life and brings spiritual prosperity to the service of dialogue, understanding, and peace among human beings. This resembles the message of Jesus in his time, to which Gülen frequently refers in his writings. In recent decades, Gülen's innovative efforts have fostered interfaith dialogue and cooperation in Turkey and throughout the world.[32]

According to Gülen, cooperation between the two great world religions of Christianity and Islam is not an option but an imperative. Gülen believes that efforts at cooperation and toward mutual understanding and other endeavors based on commonly held values are duties of Muslims to be undertaken along with adherents of other faiths and that these will lead to a more peaceful and safer world. Gülen does not see any problem with Christians reading the Qur'an with Muslims and Muslims reading the Bible with Christians. Gülen often refers to Bediüzzaman Said Nursi, who advocated cooperation between Muslims and Christians at the beginning of the twentieth century. Muslims and Christians, as active participants in interfaith dialogue, should focus on their common values and common message rather than focusing on points of contention. Gülen refers to the letter that Nursi sent to the Vatican and the meeting he had with the patriarch of the Eastern Orthodox Church.[33] Gülen inspires millions with his understanding and openness, and he leads the way toward the future of Muslim-Christian cooperation.

Christian-Muslim cooperation should continue despite memories of historical conflicts between Muslims and Christians. Gülen's response to historical conflicts is very clear: since those events are history, they have to stay buried in the past. Gülen contends that there is no need to rehash violent historical events. Such efforts only produce renewed hatred. Instead of dwelling on the events of the past, Muslims and Christians should work together on new projects that will bring harmony and peace to their communities and to the world. According to Gülen, "one cannot sing the songs of love with hatred." Among the greatest virtues is "to love love and to hate hatred."[34] Gülen complains that this idea, which Nursi put forth almost a century ago, has not been heard enough. Addressing Muslims, Gülen echoes the message of Jesus: "The Muslim's duty is to breathe new life into the spirit of the hopeless people who have come to believe that humanity will never resurrect again."[35]

Gülen also says, "Close the doors of greed, abhorrence, and hatred. They may be a small seed, but by opening the door they could grow and become a huge tree of evil."[36] If this door is not closed, the social environment will remain open for the "clash of civilizations" that Samuel Huntington predicted.[37] Gülen believes that dialogue and cooperation between Muslims and Christians can prevent this conflict. To achieve this, Gülen promotes the idea of compassion, a value Jesus and Muhammad shared and projected on a large scale in the works of Christians and Muslims. While the Qur'an presents God as the "Most Just" when it speaks of morality and ethics, other divine names, the Most Compassionate and the Most Merciful, are used as often, if not more often, when morality is the topic. In fact, 113 chapters of the Qur'an, including the opening chapter, start with the Islamic formula "In the name of God the Compassionate, the Merciful." According to Gülen, people must be compassionate and merciful in their relations with fellow human beings and with nature:

Compassion is the beginning of being; without it everything is chaos. Everything has come into existence through compassion and by compassion it continues to exist in harmony. . . . Everything speaks of compassion and promises compassion. Because of this, the universe can be considered a symphony of compassion. All kinds of voices proclaim compassion so that it is impossible not to be aware of it, and impossible not to feel the wide mercy encircling everything. How unfortunate are the souls who don't perceive this. . . . Man has a responsibility to show compassion to all living beings, as a requirement of being human. The more he displays compassion, the more exalted he becomes.[38]

Sometimes ideology blinds people. For this reason, Gülen asks Muslims to be self-critical and maintains that they should not make the religion of Islam an ideology because "ideologies are divisive rather than unifying."[39] Gülen says that since the Holy Book of Islam both presents all humankind as a family and says "knowing each other" is one the main goals of the creation of human beings, cooperation among adherents of different religions works to achieve this Qur'anic goal.

Toward this collective goal, various Islamic, Christian, and Jewish institutions are actively involved in dialogue. The Islamic Society of North America is an important participant in dialogue with Christians and Jews. They cohost annual meetings such as the Midwest, West Coast, and Mid-Atlantic Catholic-Muslim Dialogues and the National Baptist-Muslim Dialogue; they also sponsor regular events with the National Jewish Center for Learning and Leadership. All of these efforts are steps to fulfilling a Qur'anic message for all human beings. The Qur'an says: "O humankind, we have created you from a male and a female and have made you nations and tribes that you may know one another" (49:13).

The verse also shows the universal message of Islam to humanity. In the Islamic tradition, as the Qur'an frequently says, all humans are the creatures of God and all humans are servants of God regardless of their ethnic or religious background. Because of such instructions, Muslims should overcome another obstacle of dialogue and cooperation, the idea of nationalistic and ethnic superiority. Similar to the teachings of Jesus, Islamic teachings denounce the idea of superiority on the basis of color, nationality, race, geography, or profession. The Prophet of Islam says that there is no superiority of Arabs over non-Arabs and vice versa.[40] The superiority for which we should strive is sincerity in good conduct, a quality that is only known fully by God.

These universal principles of Islam contribute to the initiatives for dialogue and cooperation between Christians and Muslims. Since these principles are also within the framework of the messages that Jesus and Muhammad taught, theological interpretations that lead to the understanding of the descent of Jesus in the context of cooperation between Islam and Christianity, as some scholars have interpreted it, are not only reasonable but essential. Efforts to strengthen relationships between Muslims and Christians bring hope to humanity. Muslims, Christians, Jews, Hindus, Buddhists, Taoists, and adherents of other religions can come together over mutual concerns and common values. This dialogue should help us understand the "common word" the Qur'an has extolled for 1,400 years.

## Building a Common Word

The Qur'an's invitation to the People of the Book to find common ground has become necessary in our time, as if the verse in question were newly revealed. It is true that since the beginning of Islam, Muslims and Christians have lived and cooperated with each other. Demonstrating contemporary cooperation, for example, John Paul II met often with Muslim scholars, intellectuals, and youths in an effort to develop a positive relationship between Islam and the Catholic Church. Even the devastating terrorist attacks of September 11, 2001, in the United States were unable to destroy the relationship between the two faiths that these efforts have nourished.[41]

All the efforts that Muslims have made to build a strong relationship with Christians are echoes of the Qur'an's invitation to the People of the Book to come together with Muslims over common ground.[42] This idea was the basis for the Common Word initiative started by a group of Muslim scholars and intellectuals as a reaction to a lecture Pope Benedict XVI gave in 2006 at Regensburg University in Germany. The pope quoted a statement from Manuel II Palaiologos, one of the last Byzantine emperors, that was very negative about the Prophet of Islam. The pope's words caused a firestorm of protest in the Islamic world. But, as indicated by statements the pope and the Vatican later made, his lecture was not meant to defy the Prophet of Islam. In fact, the quote was part of a historical example used to make a larger point against religious violence in general. Despite this, damage was done. The pope attempted to repair this damage by visiting Turkey and praying in the Blue Mosque with the Mufti of Istanbul. As a result of these tensions, a group of thirty-eight prominent Muslims sent a letter titled "A Common Word between Us & You" to the pope and many other leaders of Christian denominations, inviting them to participate in a common word, inspired by a Qur'anic verse that invites the People of the Book to a common ground (3:64). This proposal, the Common Word initiative, has become well known among scholars of interfaith dialogue.[43]

"Common word," is a Qur'anic term commanding the Prophet to invite the People of the Book to participate in dialogue and cooperation. Since the People of the Book worship the same God, they have shared ground. While the Qur'an describes the common word as "to worship only one God," it also implies that this concept can be an example of common ground in other areas. The Qur'an, addressing the People of the Book, says, "Our God and your God is One" (46:29). Despite the significance of this verse, extremist groups in the West constantly propagandize that the Muslim God, Allah, is a different God, ignoring the facts that "Allah" is merely the Arabic name for God and that Arab Christians use "Allah" to refer to God.

Some Muslim exegetes limit the Qur'anic invitation to dialogue to Jews and Christians. Others, however, argue that this limitation was because of the social environment in which the Qur'an was revealed. Thus, some commentators interpret the expression "People of the Book" to include adherents of religions other than Judaism and Christianity, most notably Hindus and Buddhists. The Qur'an commands the Prophet as follows: "Say [this, Muhammad]: 'O People of the Book, come to a common word between us: that all of us worship none but God, that we ascribe to God no partners, and that we take no one as Lord except God.' If the people reject your invitation, [Muhammad,] you shall say to them, 'Be witness, then, that we are submitting ourselves to God'" (3:64).

This verse is a straightforward invitation to dialogue. The ostensible meaning of the verse is that worship is only to be directed to God. Many Muslim commentators understand this verse to be a rejection of a foundational tenet of Christianity, as they see it, that Jesus possesses a status equal to that of God.[44] With regard to the occasion of this revelation, a tenth-century scholar and commentator on the Qur'an, Ibn Jarir al-Tabari (d. 923), reports an early encounter between the Prophet and a group of Christians that eventually resulted in the Christians' alliance with the Prophet of Islam. According to this story, a group of Christians who came to the Prophet from the region of Najran in Arabia debated with the Prophet about the nature of Jesus and were unwilling to accept the Islamic understanding of Jesus because the Qur'anic Jesus is "a messenger of God and a *word* from God" but not God himself. According to al-Tabari, God asked the Prophet to suggest to the Najran Christians that they join Muslims at a common ground between them: the belief in one God.[45]

Despite the fact that this story refers only to a particular group of Christians, al-Tabari argues that the verse pertains to all Jews and Christians: "It is necessary that by 'the People of the Book' every individual member of the People of the Book is meant. That is because having God as the sole object of worship and believing sincerely in the oneness of God is a requirement of all responsible creatures of God."[46] A contextual reading of the Qur'anic revelation suggests that for the sake of cooperation, modern-day Muslims and Christians should focus on shared ideas and common values.

Furthermore, some commentators on the Qur'an focus more specifically on the concept of justice as a common theme between Muslims and Christians. The same theme of justice is found in the prophetic sayings describing Jesus's descent. The Prophet gives good tidings of the descent of Jesus and states that he will be a just ruler. Therefore, by helping to bring justice to people around the world, Muslim-Christian cooperation fulfills this prophetic mission of justice, a justice that brings freedom and equality.

Bediüzzaman Said Nursi's commentary on this verse is much more inclusive. To Nursi, in our time this invitation is addressed more relevantly to *ahl al-maktab*, or "the people of the school," that is, educated people. It is noteworthy that *kitab*, book, and *maktab*, school, are derived from the same Arabic root k-t-b which connotes writing, books, education, and so forth. By issuing such an invitation, the Qur'an presents its message to them in particular. Nursi contends that the Qur'an invites all educated people, be they religious or not, to come together on common ground in a civilized way to bring justice and equality to their communities.

Nursi also addresses the question of dialogue between Muslims and Christians more broadly. In one of his commentaries on the first verses of the Qur'an, he says that the Qur'an does not invite the People of the Book to reject all beliefs of their previous faith but invites them to build on the scripture in their own traditions. According to Nursi, the following can be concluded from the Qur'an: "O People of the Book, as you believe in the past prophets and the divine books, believe in Muhammad and the Qur'an as well. Believe because the early prophets and their scriptures give good news of his coming. The proofs that show the truthfulness of those prophets and their books are truthfully and spiritually found in the Qur'an and in the personality of Muhammad."[47] By saying this, Nursi indicates that the essential message of the Qur'an, the Torah, and the Gospel is one.

As noted earlier, many individual leaders and scholars are working for the improvement of Muslim-Christian relations. An exhaustive list is beyond the scope of this study, but a brief look at some of the events and organizations working toward Muslim-Christian cooperation is informative. Limiting myself to some examples from the United States, the Midwest Catholic-Muslim Dialogue (with which I have been involved), the West Coast Catholic-Muslim

Dialogue, and East Coast Catholic-Muslim Dialogue are all organizations that work extensively in both academia and in the public sphere to further the cause of dialogue and cooperation.[48] Many American universities have created excellent dialogue and research centers. The Macdonald Center for the Study of Islam and Christian-Muslim Relations at Hartford Seminary, the Tuohy Chair of Interreligious Studies at John Carroll University, and Georgetown University's Center for Muslim-Christian Understanding are among the oldest such centers in the United States. The Claremont School of Theology, a Christian seminary, offers not only Christian-based degrees but also degrees in Muslim leadership and interfaith chaplaincy, and many other seminaries and theological training institutions have brought seminarians and clerics from the Abrahamic traditions together. Numerous other organizations have been formed to promote interfaith dialogue, including the Rumi Forum for Interfaith Dialogue in Washington, DC; the Niagara Foundation in Chicago; the Interfaith Youth Corps; Abrahamic Alliance International; Abraham's Vision; and the Peace Islands Institute. Finally, undergraduate students at many American universities have created religious outreach organizations and interfaith dialogue projects, and religious studies programs at American colleges and universities commonly incorporate multiple religious perspectives, including Muslim-Christian relations. Beyond these academic programs, events connecting the faithful at local churches, mosques, and synagogues are common throughout the United States. I have personally been involved in many such events, where one can see individuals truly coming together to learn from one another and promote well-being and harmony in their communities.

Coming together for the betterment of society is highly compatible with the spirit of Islam and the teaching of the Prophet. From an Islamic perspective, an eschatology that is concerned about the present rather than the future is more compatible with the action-oriented teaching of Islam. It is not appropriate for a Muslim to stand idle and wait for the coming of Jesus or the Mahdi; a Muslim must do good deeds throughout his or her life. Fatalism does not reflect the main teachings of Islam expressed in the Qur'an: "For human beings there is nothing except the result of their actions" (53:39).

Even before his prophethood, Muhammad was a very active participant in social justice efforts. He actively participated in the famous organization known as Hilf al-Fudhul, "the alliance for virtue," which was established by three famous figures of Mecca. The Prophet joined this civic organization, whose main purpose was to support the weak against the strong and the oppressed against the oppressor. Even after his emergence as a messenger of God, he praised the establishment of this alliance by saying, "If I were invited to join such an alliance today, I would again respond affirmatively."[49] To be on the side of positive action is a necessary part of the teachings of Islam, which encourage all people to participate in the betterment of their community and make our planet a cradle of kinship.

# Conclusion

There is a great need in the West to better understand the place of Jesus in Islam, particularly his eschatological role. Jesus's descent from heaven, his personality, and his eschatological role have been vibrant themes in Islamic theology throughout history. This book has explored the place of Jesus in the Islamic eschatological vision and has elaborated on the Qur'anic Jesus because of his importance to Islamic faith. Muslims cannot be considered Muslims if they do not believe in Jesus as a messenger of God who brought the revelation of God to humanity. Islam's Jesus is neither God nor just a saint. He is one of the greatest messengers of God, and his message is God's message; denying Jesus as a messenger of God is denying a part of the Qur'an.

Both Christians and Muslims believe in the descent of Jesus, even if there are points of disagreement. The majority of Muslim theologians are in agreement that Jesus is a sign of the nearness of the Final Hour and that he will descend from heaven to earth to bring justice and peace. In Islam, Jesus is the only prophet whose return is expected. The Prophet Muhammad both directly and indirectly spoke of the coming of Jesus at the end of his community. One of his famous statements reads: "God will not disgrace a community of which I am the beginning and Jesus the end."[1]

The Qur'an makes plain many aspects of Jesus and his message. Many Qur'anic verses speak of Jesus as a messenger of God and of Jesus's own message. The Jesus of the Qur'an and his message are compatible with the Jesus found in the original Gospel, which emphasizes the common ground between Christians and Muslims. Christians and Muslims constitute over half of the world's population, and if they can work together, this will help bring peace on earth, which is one of the main goals of Islam for humanity.

The Hadith sources of Islam also contain more than 100 sayings of the Prophet on Jesus, his message, and his eschatological role; these sayings indicate Jesus's importance for Muslims. Interpretation of some of the sayings of the

Prophet that speak of Jesus's descent at the end of time is necessary because the literal meaning of these hadith seems to be impossible and interpretation has become a part of mainstream Islamic understandings of the texts. It is clear that the Prophet used allegorical language when discussing future events.

Because there are many fabricated hadith on the subject, one must be careful to use only the most reliable ones as references. This study has attempted to do just this. To a certain extent, a careful examination of even reliable sources is needed to find the real meaning of the text. Muslim theologians since the beginning of Islam have striven to ensure the reliability of the sayings of the Prophet as a source for legal and theological understanding. But understanding the allegorical sayings of the Prophet is not easy. Understanding the real message of any saying of the Prophet, especially when it contains allegorical and figurative language, is a great task. Because of this difficulty, an intense debate has been ongoing as to whether the prophetic sayings on end-time issues, including Jesus's descent, should be taken literally or allegorically. Sharing the view of some contemporary scholars, I find the approach that allows for an allegorical interpretation of the sayings of the Prophet more accurate and compatible with the overall theological principles of Islam.

There are three major approaches toward understanding the eschatological role of Jesus in Islam. One approach, influenced by modern Western philosophy, denies all narratives that come from the Prophet about Jesus's descent. They consider these narratives to be a product of the influence of Christianity on Islam. The second approach, which I call "literalist," accepts all texts as they are, with no interpretation and no questioning. The literalist approach refers to the power of God when asserting the possibility of the literal truth of the Hadith. The third approach, which I call "interpretive," contends that sound and authenticated hadith should be accepted not in a literal way but allegorically. My rationale for the allegorical approach is based on my understanding of the way the Divine Will deals with humanity—namely, that God has put natural laws in place and they do not change, theologically speaking, except during the miracles of the prophets. To keep the free will of people active, God does not compel people to believe in something beyond their reason and capacity. Therefore, descriptions of the descent of Jesus in a cosmic way, a person coming from the sky and bringing justice, do not seem compatible with the overall teaching of the Qur'an. Another argument for the interpretive approach is that both the Qur'an and the Prophet spoke in an allegorical language and that therefore the sayings of the Prophet about Jesus's descent should be interpreted accordingly.

More important to understanding the interpretive approach is the theological principle that even the prophets do not know the future if God does not permit them to know it. The Prophet seemed to accurately foretell some events that were later understood from his descriptions, such as the civil war between Muslims and the Mongol invasion of the Islamic world. Even these two events were mentioned only briefly and to a certain extent in a veiled way. For example, he described a prominent feature of the Mongol invasion: you will fight against a nation whose faces are like shining shields. Similarly, when he spoke of the descent of Jesus, he did not specify a time or method of the descent; therefore, I feel, such a text by the Prophet is in need of interpretation.

Furthermore, in Islamic theology one should put each source in its proper context. The future events that are mentioned in the sayings of the Prophet are important, but for an individual adherent they are not as important as the five pillars of Islam or the six articles of faith. The Prophet used ambiguous and veiled language to describe future events, but he did not use ambiguous language about the five pillars of Islam: belief in God and His Messenger Muhammad, the five daily prayers, fasting in the month of Ramadan, charity, and pilgrimage to Mecca are all clearly stated in the Qur'an and the Hadith because they are the essence of the religion. Since these are essential to the Islamic faith, there is no space for allegory. However, when it comes to future events, which are not essential parts of Islamic faith, interpretation is possible and even appropriate.

The Prophet intentionally used allegorical language. Occasionally people would question the Prophet and he would respond in a way that in fact was not based on the intent of the questioner. This is the Qur'anic method. The Qur'an says, "They ask you [Muhammad] about new moons." Two of the Prophet's companions were asking about why the new moon had different shapes. In response to this question about the physical reason for the moon taking different shapes, the Qur'an says, "Tell them that they are time measurements for people and for human beings, and [in particular] for pilgrimage" (2:189). The Qur'an responded to their questions in a way that underscored that the movements of the sky are a gift from God that reveals the mystery of time. If the Qur'an had explained the physical aspect of the event, it would have been beyond their capacity to understand or perhaps they might have even denied it. This is, in Arabic literature, called "al-uslub al-hakim," or "the wise method." Following the path of the Qur'an, when someone asked the Prophet, "When is the time of the Hour," instead of giving a specific time, the Prophet said, "What did you prepare for it?"

One can see an even stronger case in the narrative of 'A'isha, the wife of the

Prophet, when the wives of the Prophet asked which of them would die first after his death. He responded that the one with the longest hand would die first. 'A'isha narrates that they started measuring their hands. Yet they realized later that the Prophet meant the one who loved charity the most, with charity symbolized by outstretched hands. This hadith clearly illustrates that the Prophet used allegorical language in his conversations with the people of his family and with his companions. Both examples of allegorical language also convey the same meaning, which is central to understanding the text.

In the Islamic middle ages, submission without questioning was so strong that people and theologians would not have difficulty accepting texts literally even if they sounded beyond the limits of reason. In our day there is a trend toward more questioning derived from a need to understand these texts within the boundaries of finite physical existence, and this makes interpretation necessary. Needless to say, these interpretations should always be within the methodology of Islamic sciences, as Abu Hamid al-Ghazali practiced in many of his writings, especially his mystical writings. Thus, it would be unfair to consider all medieval Muslim theologians as literalist regarding the descent of Jesus. The minority of medieval Muslim theologians who held an allegorical understanding paved the way for later theological commentaries including interpretations of narratives about the eschatological descent of Jesus. Jesus's descent to the Umayyad mosque means that Christianity, through renewal, will become closer to the real teachings of Jesus and will bring the teachings of Islam and Christianity into alliance. It is believed that if this interpretation is the most accurate one, it will pave the way for Muslim-Christian cooperation and world peace, which is indicated as one of the goals that Jesus will fulfill after his descent.

Islam is not about waiting for Jesus to fall down from the sky; that is incompatible with the overall teaching of Islamic theology. The interpretative approach does not eliminate the possibility that Jesus will come in person because many Muslims believe Jesus has an angelic quality and can come and go without even being noticed. However, this understanding of the descent of Jesus deemphasizes the person of Jesus in favor of focusing our attention on cooperation toward bringing peace on earth.

The idea of Muslim-Christian cooperation has paramount importance both practically and theologically. In our world, where human beings suffer from a variety of problems, such as war, violence, poverty, drugs, and corruption, cooperation between Muslims and Christians is essential. This book has attempted to bring to the scholarly discussion a connection between the Islamic theological creed on the descent of Jesus and the idea of dialogue and cooperation between Muslims and Christians. Such cooperation and alliance will benefit not only Muslims and Christians but also the other member of the Abrahamic family, Jews, as well as Hindus, Buddhists, and adherents of other traditions.

The current trend of interfaith solidarity is a great step toward a peaceful future for humanity. It can be argued that when the Prophet said that Jesus will come as a just ruler, he emphasized the importance of justice and peace on earth. If the trend toward dialogue and cooperation leads to justice and peace in our world, it will mean the fulfillment of the messages of both Muhammad and Jesus, peace and blessings be upon them.

# Appendixes

These two appendixes provide examples of contemporary Islamic scholarship related to the descent of Jesus. The first appendix presents Fethullah Gülen's thoughts regarding Jesus as a common ground between Muslims and Christians, and the second is a translated commentary from Muhammed Hamdi Yazir.

# APPENDIX 1

## Fethullah Gülen on Jesus and Interfaith Dialogue

Because this book argues that the Islamic understanding of Jesus and his eschatological role can lay the groundwork for interfaith dialogue, it is important to show how this can be put into practice. Fethullah Gülen, a prominent contemporary Muslim scholar who is highly involved in interfaith dialogue and has significant influence and spiritual authority, should be considered an important example in this regard. In response to a series of questions I posed, Gülen offered these thoughts on Jesus and interfaith dialogue, and he kindly allowed me to include these previously unpublished musings here. I have made slight editorial revisions to the text I received.

In order to better understand and explain the messianic mission attributed to Jesus in the relevant sayings of the Prophet Muhammad, upon him be peace and blessings, we should consider the following event: After the victory of Badr (624), and since no divine commandment had been revealed about how prisoners of war should be treated, the Prophet of Islam consulted with his companions on this question, as he always did when there was no specific divine commandment. 'Umar argued for their execution, but Abu Bakr gave the following opinion: "O God's Messenger! They are your people. Even though they did you and the believers great wrong, you will win their hearts and guide them well if you forgive them and please them."

The Prophet turned to Abu Bakr and said: "You are, O Abu Bakr, like the Prophet Abraham, upon him be peace, who prayed to God about his people: 'He who follows me is of me, as is he who disobeys me—but You are indeed All-Forgiving, All-Compassionate'" (Qur'an 14:36). The Prophet continued, "You [Abu Bakr] are also like Jesus, who prayed: 'If You punish them, they are Your servants. If You forgive them, You are the All-Mighty, the All-Wise'" (Qur'an 5:118).

Then the Prophet turned to 'Umar and said: "O 'Umar! You are like Moses, who said [of the Pharaoh and his chieftains]: 'Our Lord, destroy their riches and harden their hearts so that they will not believe until they see the painful chastisement'" (Qur'an 10:88).

The Prophet of Islam also compared 'Umar to the prophet Noah, who prayed for the punishment of his disbelieving, obstinate, and unjust people.

Muslims believe that Islam is the last universal form of the divine religion and the consummation of all previous religions. Muslims believe Islam contains all the perennial values and truths in those religions, and Islam compels its followers to believe in all the prophets. However, this does not mean that Islam dictates a certain type of behavior in all circumstances. To the contrary, just as its universality and applicability in completely different times and circumstances caused the emergence of different schools of law, Islam's consummation of all previous religions requires acting differently in different times and conditions. Adherents believe that God bestowed special favors on each prophet according to his mission within the circumstances surrounding him (Qur'an 2:253). For example, the prophet Noah was endowed with steadfastness and perseverance. The prophet Abraham was honored with intimate friendship with God and with being the father of numerous prophets. The prophet Moses was given the capability of administration and was exalted through receiving God's speech from beyond a veil, and the prophet Jesus was distinguished with tolerance, compassion, and profound spirituality. All the prophets have shared in the praiseworthy qualities mentioned, but each of them surpasses, on account of his respective mission, the others in one or more of those qualities.

While each prophet was distinguished with certain excellent characteristics in a greater degree than the others, the Prophet Muhammad, upon him be peace and blessings, who was charged with conveying Islam in its universal form, had all the qualities mentioned above at their most perfect level, except that of being the father of prophets. He had, because of the universality of his mission, the distinction of being like Moses in that he warned mankind, brought and established a law, and fought against his enemies. He was like Jesus in that he was a bringer of good news who preached mercy, forgiveness, love, charity, altruism, modesty, sincerity, purity of intention, and moral values of the highest degree. This means that the Prophet Muhammad, and therefore Islam, had the mission both of Noah and Abraham, and of Moses and Jesus. That is, Islam requires that Muslims act like the prophets Noah and Moses when they find themselves in circumstances like those in which

Noah and Moses found themselves, and like Abraham and Jesus in circumstances that are like those experienced by those prophets. This explains why
the Prophet Muhammad and Muslims sometimes had to fight against their
enemies for defensive purposes.

We see in the reliable books of the Hadith many sayings of the Prophet Muhammad indicating that Jesus will come back to the world before the end of
time to kill al-Dajjal (the Antichrist). He will meet the Mahdi (the Guide, or
Muslim messiah) who is promised to come at the end of time to call people to
Islam and serve for the right guidance of people. The Mahdi will ask Jesus to
lead a prayer. This may also mean that the Mahdi will offer Jesus leadership in
the Islamic guidance movement. However, Jesus will answer, saying: "Some of
you are leaders of some others in the Prayer" and prefer the Mahdi's leadership
in the prayer.

The Qur'an also mentions Jesus as a means to the knowledge of the last Hour
(43:61). It cannot be wrong to interpret these revealed reports as meaning that
before the end of time the sincere followers of the prophets Muhammad and
Jesus will and should cooperate in calling people to God's way and in struggling
against corruption and irreligion, or that Islam must manifest itself mostly in
that dimension represented by Jesus. That is, the main aspects of the messengership of Jesus must be given prominence in representing, practicing, and preach-
ing Islam.

Chief among these aspects is the contention that Jesus came to the world
and fulfilled his mission in an utterly materialistic environment. This environment was also one in which religious hypocrisy was widespread. God's religion
embodies and demands balance in everything. The Qur'an says: "The sun and
the moon move by an exact calculation [of the All-Merciful]. And the stars and
the trees both prostrate themselves [before God in perfect submission to His
laws]. And heaven—He has made it high [above the earth], and He has set up
the balance, so you must not go beyond [the limits with respect to] the balance;
and observe the balance with full equity, and do not fall short in it" (55:5–9).

The Qur'an also declares: "Surely We have sent Our Messengers with manifest truths, and We have sent down with them the Book and the Balance so that
humankind may live by equity" (57:25).

Like a lever that requires a lifting force that is equal to the object to be lifted,
the balance in religion and social life requires the exertion of a spiritual and
moral force that will counter materialistic inclinations. In an atmosphere where
people were drowned in materialism and hypocrisy, Jesus came as a spirit from
God. His message was based on pure spirituality and the highest morality:

You have heard that people were told in the past, "Do not commit murder; anyone who does will be brought to trial." But now I tell you: whoever is angry with his brother will be brought to trial. You have heard that it was said, "Do not commit adultery." But now I tell you: anyone who looks at a woman and wants to possess her is guilty of committing adultery with her in his heart. So if your right eye causes you to sin, take it out and throw it away! It is much better for you to lose a part of your body than to have your whole body thrown into hell. . . . It was also said, "Anyone who divorces his wife must give her a written notice of divorce." But now I tell you: if a man divorces his wife for any cause other than her unfaithfulness, then he is guilty of making her commit adultery if she marries again; and the man who marries her commits adultery also. (Matt. 5:21–32)[1]

It should never be thought that Jesus, who taught such things, rejected, negated, or neglected the law. Before these teachings, he taught about the law as follows:

Do not think that I have come to do away with the Law of Moses and the teachings of the Prophets. I have not come to do away with them, but to make their teachings come true. . . . So then, whoever disobeys even the least important of the commandments and teaches others to do the same, will be least in the Kingdom of heaven. On the other hand, whoever obeys the Law and teaches others to do the same, will be great in the Kingdom of heaven. (Matt. 5:17–19)

Jesus stressed that the commandments of the divine religion were not like dead bodies without a spirit or covers without an essence. As the essence or spirit of the commandments, he always emphasized pure spirituality, high morality, mercy, compassion, sincerity or purity of intention, and love, utmost chastity, and peacemaking in society. He was a bringer of good news. Modern times or circumstances are like the environment in which Jesus began and fulfilled his mission. The world today needs spirituality, moral values, justice, mercy, love, altruism, forgiveness, and peace more than at any other time in history; most of the problems of the modern world arise from excessive worldliness, scientific materialism, hypocrisy in religion, a great erosion in spiritual and moral values, injustice, and the ruthless exploitation of nature. By declaring that Jesus will descend toward the end of time, the Prophet Muhammad drew our attention to this important point. He suggested that at the end of time Muslims should give prominence to the points or teachings that Jesus emphasized in his message, that they should never forget that the Prophet Muhammad was sent as a mercy for all the world, for the whole of existence (Qur'an 21:107). This good news must be conveyed to all places, and people should be called to the way of God with wisdom and fair exhortation (Qur'an 16:125). The faithful must never repel others (Qur'an 41:34, 42:43). A Muslim scholar describes this as the highest degree of piety, righteousness, and God's consciousness, the highest degree of pious asceticism and abstinence, and the highest degree of saintliness and striving in God's cause with the diamond principles of the Qur'an.

Moreover, Jesus was the child of the Virgin Mary and was without a father. The Qur'an tells us that while the Virgin Mary stayed in the sanctuary, she ate of the food sent to her by God: "Whenever Zachariah went in to her in the Sanctuary, he found her provided with food. 'Mary,' he asked, 'how does this come to you?' 'From God,' she answered. Surely God provides to whomever He wills without reckoning" (3:37). It could be deduced from this that the biological origin of the prophet Jesus was not fed with any unlawfully obtained food. This teaches us that we must refrain from all forms of illicit earning, from theft, usurpation, and plundering. This is especially important for pure spirituality.

Jesus's birth without a father also alludes to the fact that scientific materialism is sheer delusion and that God is absolutely able to create without any physical means, and that these means and what we call natural causes are only veils before God's acts.

In the Qur'an, Jesus says the following when introducing himself: "God has enjoined upon me the Prayer and the prescribed purifying alms for as long as I live. And [He has made me] dutiful towards my mother, and He has not made me unruly, wicked" (19:31–32).

Both this verse and Jesus's teachings about divorce and adultery suggest that toward the end of time children will not be obedient to their parents, the rights of women will be violated, and chastity will not be given its due importance. Therefore, as the Qur'an enjoins (17:23), Muslims (and the followers of Jesus) in our age, in addition to performing their prayers, worshipping correctly, and helping the poor and needy, must be very careful about showing due respect to their parents and elders. The Qur'an also warns men about piety, righteousness, and God's consciousness of their treatment of women (2:231–37, 240:12; 4:1, 6–14, 19–22, 34).

Jesus's miracles included healing diseases and reviving the dead by leave of God. Respect for life was very important in his message. The Qur'an attaches the greatest importance to life and regards one who kills a person unjustly as if he had killed all humankind, while one who saves a life is as if he has saved the life of all humankind (5:32). Islam also teaches that the rights of a person cannot be sacrificed, not even for a whole community. If there are nine criminals and one innocent person on a ship, this ship cannot be sunk to punish the criminals. So those who have dedicated themselves to the cause of Islam and the message of Jesus must attach the utmost importance to life, particularly in this age, when human life is treated like some extremely cheap, common commodity; only in this way can we try to prevent wars and find cures for illnesses. We should also know that reviving a person spiritually is never less important than healing physical diseases.

While discussing Jesus's promised descent from heaven and the emergence of the Muslim messiah, or the Mahdi, it should not be forgotten that there will always appear those who claim that they are the Messiah or Mahdi. Particularly in times when the world has suffered great tragedies and been shaken by worldwide calamities, the followers of three great religions—Muslims, Christians, and Jews—have awaited the emergence of the Messiah or Mahdi. These times have also witnessed the emergence of many who have claimed to be the Messiah or Mahdi. This should be viewed as a natural phenomenon, particularly when we consider that there have been many who claim prophethood or messengership. However, every prophet was endowed, equipped, and supported by many clear signs from God that they were prophets. Perfect truthfulness, trustworthiness, conveyance of God's religion, freedom from sin, perfect intellect, intelligence, and sagacity, and freedom from mental and abhorrent physical shortages were the basic characteristic of every prophet. Prophets were also supported with many clear miracles, so that those who did not believe in the prophets did not fail to believe because they could not recognize those prophets; rather, they did not believe mainly because of sectarian considerations, sheer obstinacy, haughtiness, or tribal or racial reasons, as well as the fear of losing their social status or wealth.

Just as the prophets had distinguishing marks showing that they were prophets, as is declared in the Qur'an, chapter 4, verse 69, the leaders on God's straight path are also distinguished by certain characteristics. They are perfectly righteous, honest, sincere, truthful, and have deep spirituality and sufficient knowledge of religion. There is an hour every Friday when prayers are acceptable, but so that Muslims will spend the morning of Friday praying, God has concealed that hour. He has concealed the "Laylatu'l-Qadr" (the Night of Power and Destiny) within Ramadan so that Muslims spend the nights of Ramadan worshipping him. Also, so that all believing people should be paid due respect, God has usually concealed his saintly people among humans. Saints do not usually know themselves to be so, and the Mahdi and the Messiah may not know themselves to be the Mahdi and the Messiah. However, they may be known through the light of sincere belief, due to their distinguishing marks.

As for the claims that the world will be destroyed in 2012 or some other year, Muslims believe that no one except God knows the exact time of the destruction of the world. We hope and even believe that before the end of the world humankind will universally experience a paradisiacal period when almost all wars, exploitations, and injustices will come to an end.

## Common Points between Islam and Christianity as Cures for Present "Diseases" of Humanity

Despite the significant differences between Islam and Christianity in creed, the common points between them are important in offering solutions to the modern problems of humankind. Social events, both within a community and at the global level, are manifestations of the more substantial aspects or dimensions of human existence. They are like symptoms of a disease. Doctors say that coughing is not a disease but rather the symptom of a disease in the respiratory system. So what should be treated is the disease itself, not the cough. Today's main problems—wars, proliferation of armaments, environmental pollution, economic collapses, poverty, plagues, injustices, and deep rifts in the distribution of income—are in fact dangerous symptoms of certain deeper and fatal diseases that humankind has been suffering from for centuries. Dazzled and defeated by our unparalleled victories in science and technology, we have forgotten and neglected our true nature, our essence, the basic, deep dimension of our existence, our main purpose in life, our position among other beings, and the duties that this position has placed upon us.

Viewing the matter from this perspective, we see that the common points between Islam and Christianity impose grave and urgent duties on the followers of both religions for the present and future of the globe. These duties are enough to solve almost all the problems of humankind. Consider the following injunctions.

### On Life and the Prohibition of Murder

He who kills a soul, unless it be [in legal punishment] for murder or for causing disorder and corruption on the earth will be as if he had killed all humankind; and he who saves a life will be as if he had saved the lives of all humankind. (Qur'an 5:32)

You have heard that people were told in the past, "Do not commit murder; anyone who does will be brought to trial." But now I tell you: whoever is angry with his brother will be brought to trial. (Matt. 5:21–22)

## On Chastity and the Prohibition of Adultery

Do not draw near to any unlawful sexual intercourse; surely it is a shameful, indecent thing, and an evil way. (Qur'an 17:32)

You have heard that it was said, "Do not commit adultery." But now I tell you: anyone who looks at a woman and wants to possess her is guilty of committing adultery with her in his heart. (Matt. 5:27–28)

## On Politeness and the Good Treatment of Others

Do not turn your face from people in scornful pride, nor move on earth haughtily. Surely God does not love anyone proud and boastful. (Qur'an 31:18)

And say to My servants that they should always speak [even when disputing with others] that which is the best. Satan is ever ready to sow discord among them. For Satan indeed is a manifest enemy for humankind. (Qur'an 17:53)

Whoever is angry with his brother will be brought to trial, whoever calls his brother "You good-for-nothing!" will be brought before the Council, and whoever calls his brother a worthless fool will be in danger of going to the fire of hell. (Matt. 5:22–23)

## On Modesty and Humility

Be modest in your bearing, and subdue your voice. For certain, the most repugnant of voices is the braying of donkeys. (Qur'an 31:19)

Do not strut about the earth in haughty self-conceit; for you can never split the earth [no matter how hard you stomp your foot], nor can you stretch to the mountains in height [no matter how strenuously you seek to impress]. (Qur'an 17:37)

Happy are those who are humble; they will receive what God has promised! (Matt. 5:5)

## On Peacemaking

Come in full submission to God and peace, all of you, [without allowing any discord among you], and do not follow in the footsteps of Satan, for indeed he is a manifest enemy to you. (Qur'an 2:208)

Do not cause disorder and corruption on the earth, seeing that it has been so well ordered, and call upon Him with fear [of His punishment] and longing [for His forgiveness and mercy]. God's mercy is indeed near to those devoted to doing good, aware that God is seeing them. (Qur'an 7:56)

The believers are but brothers, so make peace between your brothers. (Qur'an 49:10)

Happy are those who work for peace; God will call them His children! (Matt. 5:9)

## On Honesty and Trustworthiness

And do not consume your wealth among yourselves in false ways [such as theft, bribery, usurpation, gambling, and usury]; nor proffer it to those in authority so that you may sinfully consume a portion of other people's goods, and do that knowingly. (Qur'an 2:188)

Do not covet that in which God has made some of you excel others. Men shall have a share according to what they have earned, and women shall have a share according to what they have earned. (Qur'an 4:32)

Give full measure [in all your dealings], and be not one of those who [by cheating and giving less] cause loss to others. And weigh with a true, accurate balance. Do not wrong people by depriving them of what is rightfully theirs, and do not go about acting wickedly in the land, causing disorder and corruption. (Qur'an 26:181–83)

You shall not covet your neighbor's house. You shall not covet your neighbor's wife, or his manservant or maidservant, his ox or donkey, or anything that belongs to your neighbor. (Ex. 20:17)

On Forgiveness

And vie with one another, hastening to forgiveness from your Lord, and to a garden whose breadth is as the heavens and earth, prepared for the God-fearing who give alms in prosperity and adversity, and who restrain their rage and pardon the offences of their fellow men; and God loves the good-doers who, when they commit an indecency or wrong themselves, remember God, and pray forgiveness for their sins—and who shall forgive sins but God?—and do not persevere in the things they did, and do that wittingly. The recompense of such people is forgiveness from their Lord, and gardens beneath which rivers flow, therein dwelling forever; and how excellent is the wage of those who labor!(Qur'an 3:133–36)

Addressing the Prophet and his relationship with his companions, the Qur'an says, "It was by some mercy of God that you were gentle to them; had you been harsh and hard of heart, they would have scattered from around you. So pardon them, and pray forgiveness for them, and take counsel with them in the affair [a public concern]; and when you are resolved, put your trust in God; surely God loves those who put their trust [in Him]" (3:159).

This verse echoes a conversation between Jesus and Peter. Peter came to Jesus and asked, "Lord, if my brother keeps on sinning against me, how many times do I have to forgive him? Seven times?" "No, not seven times," answered Jesus, "but seventy times seven" (Matt. 18:21–22).

On Nonresistance to Ill Treatment and Avoiding Vengeance

Goodness and evil can never be equal. Repel evil with what is better [or best]. Then see: the one with whom you had enmity has become a bosom friend. (Qur'an 41:34)

You have heard that it was said: An eye for an eye and a tooth for a tooth. But now I tell you: do not take revenge on someone who wrongs you. If anyone slaps you on the right cheek, let him slap your left cheek too. (Matt. 5:38–39)

On Love, Compassion, and Altruism

A people whom He [God] loves, and who love Him. (Qur'an 5:54)

There has come to you, O people, a Messenger from among yourselves; extremely grievous to him is your suffering; full of concern for you is he, and for the believers, full of pity and compassion. (Qur'an 9:128)

O you who believe! Let not some people among you deride another people; it may be that the latter are better than the former. Nor let some women deride other women; it may be that the latter are better than the former. Nor defame one another; nor insult one another with nicknames [that your brothers and sisters dislike]. Evil is using names with vile meaning after the faith. Whoever [does that and then] does not turn to God in repentance, those are indeed wrongdoers. Avoid much suspicion, for some suspicion is a grave sin [receiving God's punishment]; and do not spy [on one another], or backbite [against one another]. Would any of you love to eat the flesh of his dead brother? You would abhor it! Keep from disobedience to God in reverence for Him and piety. Surely God is One Who truly returns repentance with liberal forgiveness and additional reward, All Compassionate. O humankind! Surely We have created you from a single [pair of] male and female, and made you into tribes and families so that you may know one another [and so build mutuality and cooperative relationships, not so that you may take pride in your differences of race or social rank, or breed enmities]. Surely the noblest, most honorable of you in God's sight is the one best in piety, righteousness, and reverence for God. Surely God is All Knowing, All Aware. (Qur'an 49:11–13)

They love those who emigrate to them for God's sake,[2] and in their hearts do not begrudge what they have been given; and [indeed] they prefer them over themselves, even though poverty be their own lot. (Qur'an 59:9)

No one is a true believer unless he desires for his brother [and sister] that which he desires for himself. Believers are like a body; when one member of it ails, the entire body ails. (Prophet Muhammad)

Jesus replied [to a teacher of the law]: "The most important one [commandment] is this: 'Listen, Israel! The Lord our God is the only Lord. Love the Lord your God with all your heart, with all your soul, with all your mind, and with all your strength.' The second most important commandment is this: Love your neighbor as you love yourself." (Mark 12:29–31)

Love one another. As I have loved you, so you must love one another. (John 13:34)

## On Justice and Equity

O you who believe! Be upholders and standard-bearers of justice, bearing witness to the truth for God's sake, even though it be against your own selves, or parents or kindred. Whether the person concerned be rich or poor, [bear in mind that] God is nearer to them [than you are and more concerned with their well-being]. So do not follow your own desires lest you swerve from justice. If you distort [the truth] or decline [to bear truthful witness], then know that God is fully aware of all that you do. (Qur'an 4:135)

O you who believe! Be upholders and standard-bearers of right for God's sake, being witnesses for [the establishment of] absolute justice. And by no means let your detestation for a people [or their detestation for you] move you to [commit the sin of] deviating from justice. Be just: this is nearer and more suited to righteousness and piety. Seek righteousness and piety, and always act in reverence for God. Surely God is fully aware of all that you do. (Qur'an 5:8)

You shall not give false testimony against your neighbor. (Ex. 20:16)

Follow justice and justice alone, so that you may live and possess the land the Lord your God is giving you. (Deut. 16:20)

As seen in the examples given above, both Islam and Christianity exhort us to virtuous deeds and a righteous, pious life. They exhort us to believe in God and the afterlife, to practice honesty, truthfulness, trustworthiness, modesty, peace, love, justice, moderation, purity, chivalry, charity, benevolence, altruism, self-control, chastity, and uprightness. Both faiths condemn falsehood, debauchery, dishonesty, hypocrisy, cruelty, pride, wrongdoing, treachery, all kinds of illicit relations, fraud, selfishness, hatred, and violence. The basic rules of Christianity and Islam aim to protect the fundamental freedoms and rights of humanity. Both aim to protect and guarantee the freedom of faith and the right to life, personal property, mental and physical health, and reproduction. So both must cooperate to encourage these virtues and try to prevent vice. And, as was predicted by the hadith concerning the final descent of Jesus, this cooperation will hopefully take place.

Excerpts from Muhammed Hamdi Yazir

These two passages from the work of noted Turkish commentator on the Qur'an Muhammed Hamdi Yazir have been unavailable in English until now. Because they represent relevant source material from a contemporary Muslim Qur'anic commentator, I thought it would be helpful to give them as examples of Qur'anic commentary on the descent of Jesus.

What follows is Yazir's interpretation of Qur'anic verses 3:45–51, translated from Yazir's *Hak Dini Kur'an Dili* [The True Religion and the Qur'an's Language], 2:1100–1105. The translation is mine. After giving the Qur'anic verses in Arabic, Yazir begins by translating the verses into Turkish.

And the angels said, "O Mary, God gives good news to you with a word from him whose name is Jesus the Messiah, son of Mary, who is honorable in both this world and the afterlife, and at the same time he is among the closest to Allah. He will talk to people from his cradle and when he is an adult, and he will be among the righteous." Mary said, "O my Lord, how can I have a baby without being touched by any human being?" And God said, "God creates what He wants. When He wants the creation of something He only says, 'Be,' and it happens immediately." God teaches Jesus the book [reading and writing], wisdom, the Torah, and the Gospel. God will send him as a messenger who will say to Israelites the following, "Surely I have brought to you a sign [a miracle or a document] from your Lord. I make for you out of clay something in the shape of a bird and I breathe into it. With the permission of God it becomes a bird. I heal the blind and the lepers, and with the permission of God I resurrect the dead. I inform you about what you eat at your homes and what you store there. Surely in this there is a sign for you if you will believe. And confirming what is of the Torah in front of me and to make lawful some of that which has been prohibited to you and I came with a sign from your Lord to you. Therefore be fearful of God and follow me. Surely God is my Lord and your Lord and therefore always worship only Him. This is the right path" (3:45–51).

[After the verse, Yazir gives etymological information for the Turkish words *Mesih* (Messiah), *kelime* (word), *vecih* (noble), and *kehl* (adulthood). He goes on to interpret Mary's conversation with the angel.]

After the good news from the angels, Mary, who had no doubt about herself in her heart and conscience, returned directly to her Lord after hearing the unusual word and said with great bewilderment and in supplication, "My Lord, how and where can I have a child without being touched by any human being?" And her Lord said, "God creates what He wants. When He wants the creation of something He only says, 'Be,' and it happens immediately." With this God taught her that for those who have faith in their hearts and know the divine plan and His power there is nothing strange or far from truth. This, "Be," was the explanation of the mystery of the Word. God taught this and mentioned the following as well: he taught Jesus the book and the wisdom. Here the word "book," *kitab*, is a verbal noun meaning *kitaba* [which means "to write"]. This means that Jesus was a wise man, literate and knew how to write. With regard to his miracles, the frequent use of the phrase limiting Jesus's power, "with God's permission," shows that these miracles do not indicate the divinity of Jesus, as Christians have claimed, but rather powerfully explain the divinity of his Creator.

Thus, Jesus in the divine plan was such a word. As is understood from the verse "God creates what He wants. When He wants the creation of something He only says, 'Be,' and it happens immediately," the divine power, which relates to the oneness of God, cannot be under the control of any cause. As words indicate meanings, Jesus, with his creation and ethics, his knowledge and wisdom, his book and writing, his actions and words, was a sign of God and a true portent who came as a messenger to Israelites and showed them four types of miracles involving the laws they thought were unchangeable. He came to invite them to faith in God, to confirm the Torah, to allow and support certain things that had been prohibited. There was one reason for his coming and for all his miracles, that people would understand one verse. The verse is this: "Be fearful of God and follow me. There is no doubt that God is my Lord and your Lord. Therefore accept only Him for your worship and worship only to Him and be a servant of Him. Thus this is the straight path." Consequently this verse would be the meaning of Jesus, who was a word.

Now, have the good news of angels from God and the divine plan and promise been fulfilled? Has the word moved from potentiality to reality? Did Jesus with these situations and qualities come and declare this message? There is no need for these questions because the answer to these questions is within these verses. First of all, God said, "God never breaks His promise" (3:9). Then, it is clear that angels never lie. It is clear that Mary received a response to her supplication from her Lord. . . . Therefore Jesus came with this identity, with these conditions, and these qualities, with this religion and calling as a messenger of God [as indicated in the following verse]: Jesus said "I came to you with a sign. Therefore be fearful of God and follow me. Surely God is my Lord and your Lord and worship Him. This is the right path" The entire life and message of Jesus was the meaning of this verse. When Jesus said, "Obey me," he was not saying, "Recognize me as Allah" or "Worship me." He was saying, "My Lord and your Lord is God. Be a servant of Him and recognize Him only for your worship, the right path is this." The straight path that Jesus invited [people] to was nothing but the true religion of Islam. Jesus was not inviting anything other than that. [As the verses of the Qur'an say]: "If you really love God, follow me and God will love you" [3:31]; "Be obedient to God and to His messenger" [5:92]; "I have submitted myself to God and those who have followed me [also submitted themselves to God]" [3:20]; "Be muslims [those who submit themselves to God]" [22:34, 39:54]. Jesus was doing nothing but inviting people to these messages of the Prophet Muhammad. Jesus's message was exactly the reality that is mentioned in this verse. "Surely the religion in the sight of God is islam [the submission to the will of God]" [3:19]. He was not doing any testimony except this: "God has testified that there is no deity but Him and so do the angels and the sages, testify that [God is] fulfilling justice and that there is no deity but Him. He is the Mighty. He is the Wise" [3:18]. In summary, the word of Jesus did not have any other meaning than the word of *tawhid*, the oneness of God. In response to divine scriptures and powerful texts, those who run after ambiguous verses by saying, "We are searching the verse's spirit and we are looking at that spirit" should know that the real spirit of the Torah and the Gospel is solely this *tawhid*.

Jesus, with this meaning and with regard to this spirit, was a spirit of God. In this word and in this meaning and in this spirit John the Baptist came and confirmed Jesus and gave good news of his coming as Jesus in the same way confirmed Muhammad—peace and blessings be upon him—and gave good news of his coming. And then Muhammad, also with this book, this *Furqan* [another word for the Qur'an, the one which distinguishes between the truth and what is false], came as an encompassing confirmer [of all of the above messages]. When Jesus said, "Surely Allah is my Lord and your Lord, therefore worship only Him," if Moses would have come he would not deny this statement; as he confirmed the coming of Jesus, he would accept Jesus again. Now Muhammad, the Messenger of God, by conveying this truth of "Obey God and the Messenger" would have the support of Jesus and all other prophets. If they came, they would agree with Muhammed. They would accept him and would not do anything contrary to his message.

Yazir on the Interpretation of the Qur'anic Verse on Jesus's Death and Rising

The following is Muhammed Hamdi Yazir's commentary on the death of Jesus as found in the Qur'an, chapter 3 verse 55, translated from *Hak Dini Kur'an Dili*, 2:1111–15. Yazir begins by quoting the verse:

> Then God said as follows: "O Jesus, surely I will cause you to die and I will raise you to Myself and I will cleanse you from the disbelievers. Also I will make superior those who follow you over the disbelievers until the day of resurrection. And then your return is to Me. I will judge you [all people] with regard to the things you have disagreed on." (Qur'an 3:55)

Thus, God made his plan known to those who were plotting against Jesus. Despite the plot to assassinate Jesus, God told him, "O Jesus, I am the one who will cause you to die [*tawaffi*] and raise you to Myself." The word *tawaffi* comes from the root *wafa* [w-f-y], the original dictionary meaning of which is "to take something completely." However, when this word is used in the context of creatures with souls, particularly human beings, it is evident and well known that it indicates a taking of the soul [*ruh*, meaning both soul or spirit but translated here as soul] of an individual when the determined time comes. Accordingly, without having a proof of another meaning, an interpretation of *tawaffi* that draws on a different meaning [other than a taking of the soul of an individual] is not accurate. However, in the chapter "Al-Nisa," in relationship with the concept of "plot," we find the following verse: "They did not kill him. They did not crucify him. But it was made to appear so to them" (4:157). This verse openly states that they neither killed the Messiah, the son of Mary, the messenger of God, Jesus, nor did they crucify him, but they were made doubtful or confused about the death of Jesus. Also, because many sayings of the Prophet [say something] similar to the prominent saying "Jesus did not die. He will return before the day of resurrection," it is necessary to interpret the phrase "I will cause you to die" or *mutawaffika*, in a way that is rather different than the literalistic dictionary meaning. Because of this, commentators have offered seven to eight meanings in this regard. Let's discuss some of them.

1. *Tawaffi* means death. However, because the conjunctive Arabic letter *waw* that comes after it does not present either togetherness or consecutiveness, there is a meaningful transposition in this verse. [In other words,] rising will be first and death will be later. This meaning is narrated from Qatade [a companion of the Prophet]. This is to say that Jesus was raised to God during the assassination plot and the plotters assumed that they had killed him and crucified him, but in fact he had not died. Nonetheless, he will die before the Day of Judgment because God has said, "Surely, *I* will cause you to die." Among Muslims, this is the [most] well-known meaning [of the verse] and the creed. This is because in this there is not any interpretation that goes against the literal meaning [of the verse]. To us, the summary of this commentary and creed is as follows: the soul of Jesus, the Messiah, who is a word from God and is supported by the holy spirit, has not been taken yet. The appointed time of his soul has not come yet. The word has not returned to God. He has more works to do on earth. This [the case of Jesus] is an eternity of soul. But this eternity of soul is not something in the afterlife, as Christians say. This eternity is related to the realm of *barzakh* [the period from death until the time of final resurrection]. His appointed time will come before the day of resurrection, he will die and his spirit will be taken [by the angel of death, Azrael]. In the afterlife, [for Jesus] there will be a resurrection, a new restoration after death.

Since the soul of Jesus has not been taken, in that regard his rise to God is his departure from earth. What was taken away and risen to God and what will return to earth is his soul. Therefore, one should not confuse the characteristics of the raising of Jesus to heaven as mentioned in some narrations and the raising of Jesus to God as mentioned in the Qur'an. That is because heaven is not one of the divine names. Although Christians call heaven God and God heaven, this is not allowed in Islam.[3]

Therefore, the statement "I will raise you to Myself" should not be interpreted as "I will raise you to heaven." Because of this point, we can say that it is Jesus's body which is raised to God and his soul which is raised to heaven and has not been taken yet [by the angel of death]. This heaven is not the earth's [physical] heaven but it is the fourth spiritual heaven in which the Messenger of God—peace and blessings be upon him—saw Jesus in his Night Journey. He also saw Aaron in the fifth heaven, Moses in the sixth, and Abraham in the seventh. Therefore, the ascent of Jesus to heaven and his descent from heaven before the day of resurrection in the narrations and Hadith should not be understood [as statements] about his body, which is raised to God.

As the soul of Jesus became temporarily eternal [by God's raising him before he became fully eternal in Paradise], the souls of other prophets are also the same. That is why the prophets in their graves are alive, as is explained in the books of Islamic jurisprudence. The appointed time for the soul of each messenger of God is the appointed time of his community. [The soul of each prophet will depart when his community comes to an end.] The souls' appointed time has come for many prophets, and they have not been mentioned in the Qur'an. Based on the above-mentioned verse about choosing [Abraham; Qur'an 2:130] and the verse "They were descendants of one another" [Qur'an 3:34], the great messengers who are included in this chain of being chosen continue their existence in the spiritual heavens according to their levels. The family of Abraham and the family of Imran are among this [group of prophets]. The body of Jesus has been raised to God but his soul has not been taken; that is to say that the appointed time of his community has not yet come [and so it is ongoing].

Despite the Israelites' plots and tricks, Christianity did not vanish and survived those plots and continued its existence with the spirit of Moses.[4] That is why the small group of followers of Jesus, who were thought to have vanished, in a short period of time benefited from this spirit and reached a level in life over the Jews [the population of Christians became greater than the population of Jews] and finally, with the coming of Muhammad as a prophet, all [Jews and Christians] have become together with the spirit of Muhammad. After that, Jesus, together with other prophets, is with the Prophet Muhammad.

A day will come when the community of Muhammad will be in a difficult situation. The spirit of Jesus, who is an unusual word of Allah, will emerge and will serve with the soul of Muhammad, yet it [Jesus's soul] will die before the day of resurrection. The reason why this case [of Jesus's spirit being raised to God] was explained specifically about Jesus is that Jesus is an unusual, abstract word of God. That is to say, it is because of his ability to miraculously resurrect the dead, a blessing from God that is mostly denied by people. A similar blessing is found in all prophets and is particularly found in the truth of Muhammad; it is a highly recognized reality. His [Muhammad's] path, or Sunnah, extraordinarily encompasses this complete truth [of Muhammad's reality]. Jesus, like Adam, is an unusual beginning of perfection; Muhammad is a reality that is the goal of perfection. For this reason, the soul of Muhammad, with God's permission, in the miracle of the resurrection of the dead, uses the soul of Jesus. With Jesus, the resurrection of the dead is an abstract miracle; with Muhammad, it is a principle.[5] In the purification of the soul of Muhammad, there is continuity with the soul of Jesus as well. Every extraordinary thing relates to the first blessing. The miracle of Muhammad is a perfect attribute that is added to the continuity of the miracles of other prophets. "God has elevated the level of some of them over others" [Qur'an 2:253].

2. "O Jesus, I will allow you to live until your appointed time. I will not allow the murderers to kill you. I will cause you to die and raise you to Myself."

3. "I will take you and take your [physical] person from earth and raise you to Myself."

4. "I will cause you to sleep and then raise you to Myself." The second and third meanings are narrated from Hasan and the fourth meaning is narrated from Rabi'.

5. "I will take you thoroughly with your spirit and your body as you are and raise you to Myself."

6. Also, some scholars accept it in a literal sense and give the following meaning: "I will cause you to die and take your soul." Therefore they narrate that before God raised Jesus to Himself, He caused him to die for three hours (and according to one narration seven hours). However, these narrations are seen as weak. The reliable narration is that neither before he was raised nor after that was his soul taken. The most relevant explanation for this is the first one [number 1]. From this narration we can understand that the view that Christianity was totally extinguished during that time for a few hours became dominant.

# Acknowledgments

My interest in writing a book discussing the role of Jesus in Islam began more than twenty years ago while I was doing research on the personification of evil in the Islam, al-Dajjal tradition. Jesus was in one sense the personification of good in the Islamic tradition. Coming to the United States and teaching at a Catholic university heightened my feeling that a book such as this one was an important and necessary contribution to the scholarly and public debate about religion here and in the world.

In the list of tasks one must undertake when preparing a book, perhaps the most enjoyable is the writing of the acknowledgments section. Not only is it the place where one is able to show his or her gratitude to the many people and groups that made the author's life bearable and the project a success, but it indicates just that: the project was a success and now it's over. With that I will now commence with my own joy and acknowledgments.

I am indebted to the many people who have given invaluable support at various stages in this work. The insightful comments of Dr. Marcia Hermansen of Loyola University Chicago on the first draft of the book made an indispensable contribution to this project. Dr. John Haught of Georgetown University also read the entire manuscript and provided me with a Christian perspective on many of the issues I address in the book. Similarly, I am thankful to Dr. Christopher Leighton, director of the Institute for Christian and Jewish Studies, for providing me with crucial sources on the messianic traditions in both Judaism and Christianity. I am also thankful to the numerous unnamed people with whom I have spoken about the subject and who have enhanced my understanding of Jesus.

As a professor with a substantial teaching load, I am especially grateful for receiving the Grauel Fellowship from John Carroll University in 2007. The fellowship allowed me to spend one semester concentrating on research and was important in getting this project off the ground.

I would like to thank the members of the Department of Theology and Religious Studies at John Carroll University for their continuing support during this project and beyond. I am also very thankful to my graduate assistants, especially Gillian Haluskar and Carson Bay, for their valuable comments. I want to thank my executive assistant, Patrick Laughlin, who provided great support and useful ideas. The students in my courses here at John Carroll who have asked me numerous questions regarding Jesus and Islam have helped me more than they might imagine.

I am appreciative of my friend and classmate Kasim Kirbiyik, who is a member of the Documentation Database staff at the library of the Center for Islamic Studies in Istanbul, for providing me with invaluable research support.

It gives me pleasure to acknowledge the editors at the University Press of Florida for their guidance and support without which this project would not have been possible. I have to emphasize that all errors and inaccuracies are mine, and I would appreciate any comments that readers have.

I would like to thank my wife, to whom I dedicate this book, and my children for their support and understanding during my work on the project. Even my youngest daughter, who often reminded me that I forgot to take her to the children's museum, has been patient and thoughtful.

Most important, I would like to thank God for giving me health and the ability to produce this work.

# Notes

## Introduction

1. In the Islamic tradition, when the name of Muhammad or the names of other prophets are mentioned, it is a sign of respect to ask God for peace and blessings to be upon them. I mention this here so that the intention will serve for the entire book without the necessity of repeating these blessings.

## Chapter 1. Jesus as God's Messenger in the Qur'an

1. Al-Jurjani, *Al-Ta'rifat*, 307.

2. Ibid., 148.

3. On Mary's place in Islam, see Smith and Haddad, "Virgin Mary in Islamic Tradition," 161–87. On debate about the prophethood of Mary, see al-Shawkani, *Fath al-Qadir*, 3:327–28.

4. It should be noted that the "holy spirit" mentioned in the Qur'an is not the same as the Holy Spirit in the Christian doctrine of Trinity. The holy spirit in this context is a strong feeling of divine presence, as if one is supported by an invisible and powerful angel.

5. The holy Qur'an frequently uses two names to refer to Jesus. "Al-Masih" is used as a title, and "'Isa" is his proper name. Muslim theologians and linguists have discussed the roots from which these two words are derived. According to some Arabic lexicons, neither of these terms is originally Arabic. The Arabic word "al-Masih" comes from the Hebrew "*māšīaḥ*" and means "anointed one." This word was also very well known before Islam among Syriac-speaking people in northern and southern Arabia. In the Islamic literature, the word is also used to refer to the opponent of Jesus, the Antichrist, or al-Dajjal. The famous early Arab philologist and lexicographer al-Farahidi (d. 791) claims, "Al-Masih is the one who has no eye or eyebrow on one side of his face. And the liar-Messiah or Antichrist has this feature; that is, he has one eye, while Jesus (the true Messiah), the son of Mary, peace and blessings be upon him, is also al-Masih." For the linguistic details of the word in Arabic lexicons, see the following: al-Farahidi, *Kitab al-'Ayn*, 3:156–57; al-Azhari, *Tahdhib al-Lugha*, 4:350; Ibn Manzur, *Lisan al-'Arab*, 13:98–102; and al-Yasu'i, *Ghara'ib al-Lugha al-'Arabiyya*, 206.

Despite the general consensus on the origin of the word "al-Masih," certain commentators on the Qur'an posited a similarity between the words "al-Masih" and "*al-mash*," which means "touching" in Arabic. In this interpretation, the word could be Arabic in origin. See al-Qurtubi, *Al-Jami' li Ahkam al-Qur'an*, 4:89; and Rida, *Tafsir al-Manar*, 1954 ed., 3:305. On the term "*al-mash*," see al-Jurjani, *Al-Ta'rifat*, 272.

One scholar records that Jesus was called al-Masih "because Gabriel touched him with a blessing, and also because Jesus touched the sick, the lepers, and the blind, and they were healed as a result of his touch." See al-Maturidi, *Ta'wilat al-Qur'an*, 4:100. So the miraculous touching of Jesus (*al-mash*) is the reason why Jesus was called al-Masih. In this case the word would mean "the one who is touched or the one who touches." In fact, the Arabic lexicons record more than one meaning for the word "*m-s-h*," or "*al-mash*." The word is used to mean "to touch with a hand," "to abolish," or "to travel." According to scholars who consider the word to be Arabic, all these meanings are applicable to Jesus. In Islamic theology, his touching was a miraculous way of healing, he abolished some laws of the Torah, and it is believed he will come back and travel to find and kill the Antichrist in the last period of his life on earth. Perhaps because of the unique aspect of the word, it was used as an adjective and only in the singular form in Arabic. As an adjective, the Arabic word "*al-masih*" is used only in the singular; it does not take a plural and can be used for opposite meanings. The word is used for "the truthful one" (Jesus) and for "the Liar" (the Antichrist). See al-Ta'i, *Ikmal al-I'lan bi Taslis al-Kalam*, 2:626; Sami, *Kamus al-A'lam*, 6:4284; and al-Yamani, *Al-Mawsu'a al-'Arabiyya*, 1:366–67.

In the Qur'an, the word "*al-masih*" is used independently and in connection to the name of Jesus (4:172, 5:70, 5:72, 5:75, 9:30–31). The term is mentioned eleven times in the Qur'an. See 3:45; 4:157, 171–72; 5:17 (twice), 5:72 (twice); 5:75; 9:30–31.

As for the word "'Isa," which is used as a proper name for Jesus, it is generally accepted that like the names of some other divine messengers mentioned in the Qur'an, such as Ibrahim for Abraham and Moosa for Moses, the word "'Isa" is also used by the Qur'an for Jesus. Some contemporary scholars, such as the Egyptian Dominican priest Georges Anawati (d. 1994), believe that the origin of this word is the word "Esau" from Hebrew. Jesus has been called 'Isa because it is believed that the spirit of Esau and the spirit of God have been transmitted into Jesus. It is interesting how Muslim linguists have elaborated on the word "'Isa," the proper name of Jesus. For instance, Ibn Manzur, a thirteenth-century Muslim philologist, indicates that "'Isa is the name of the Messiah." He also suggests that the origin of the word comes from Hebrew or Syriac. He further states that the word is derived from the name Yasu'. See Ibn Manzur, *Lisan al-'Arab*, 9:497

In his commentary on chapter 4, verse 158 of the Qur'an, Abu Mansur al-Maturidi (d. 944), one of the two great theologians of Islam, speaks of the etymology of the word "al-Masih": "Jesus was called al-Masih, because Gabriel touched him with blessing (*al-barakah*)." According to al-Maturidi, there is another possible reason for taking this name: "because he was touching the sick, the lepers, and the deaf and they would recover." Al-Maturidi, *Ta'wilat al-Qur'an*, 4:100.

Other divinely appointed prophets mentioned in the Qur'an also have two names, for example Muhammad and Ahmad, Dhulkifl and Ilyas (Elias), Isra'il and Ya'qub (Jacob), and Yunus and Dhunnun (Jonah). See al-Farahidi, *Kitab al-'Ayn*, 3:189.

6. Two concordances are especially helpful for researching words used in the Qur'an: see 'Abd al-Baqi, *Al-Mu'jam al-Mufahras*; and Flugel, *Concordance of the Koran*.

7. It is a general Qur'anic principle that even when Muhammad is the one directly being addressed, the intended audience is the entire Muslim community.

8. One interpretation of the role of Muslims in this regard can be found in Yazir, *Hak Dini Kur'an Dili*, 2:1100–1101.

10. For a good account of Jesus as he is presented in the Qur'an, see Parrender, *Jesus in the Qur'an*. See also Ess, "Islam and the Other Religions," 97–108.

11. For a discussion of the place of Jesus's miracles in early Islam, see Thomas, "The Miracles of Jesus," 221–43.

12. Al-Zamakhshari, *Al-Kashshaf 'An Haqa'iq al-Tanzil*, 1:177.

13. Abu Dawud, "Al-Adab" in *Al-Sunan*, 64.

14. Qutb, *Fi Zilal al-Qur'an*, 4:2304–2306.

15. Ibn Hanbal, *Al-Musnad*, 5:265–66.

16. For a Muslim theologian's account of Jesus, see Zwemer, "Jesus Christ in the Ihya al-Ghazzali," 144–58. For a more mystical account of Jesus in Islam, see Renard, "Jesus and Other Gospel Figures," 47–64.

17. This hadith is recorded by the two most reliable hadith scholars, Muhammad al-Bukhari (see al-Bukhari, "Al-Anbiya," in *Al-Sahih*, 49) and Muslim bin al-Hajjaj in the section "On the Merit of Jesus" (see Muslim bin al-Hajjaj, "Al-Fada'il," in *Al-Sahih*, 143).

18. For further information on this analogy, see Nursi, "Mektubat," 1:392.

19. For more analysis of this type of verse in the Qur'an, see O'Shaughnessy, *Eschatological Themes in the Qur'an*, 108–116.

20. Al-Qurtubi, *Al-Jami' li Ahkam al-Qur'an*, 16:89.

21. See Gülen, *Al-Qulub al-Dari'a*.

22. For more on this, see Lawson, "The Crucifixion of Jesus," 34. Also see Stanilaus, "Jesus' Crucifixion," 59–74.

23. For more on this, see Lawson, "The Crucifixion of Jesus"; and Lawson, *The Crucifixion and the Qur'an*. Also see Sahas, *John of Damascus on Islam*, 51–95.

24. Ibn al-Athir, *Jami' al-Usul*, 1:182. For variations of this hadith, see al-Hindi, *Kanz al-'Ummal*, 10:136.

25. For various commentaries on the phrase "but it appeared to them so," see Ayoub, "Towards an Islamic Christology," 91–121. See also Reynolds, "Muslim Jesus," 237–58.

26. For further information on Muslims' arguments about crucifixion, see Whittingham, "How Could So Many Christians Be Wrong?" 167–78.

27. Al-Maturidi, *Ta'wilat al-Qur'an*, 4:102.

28. For further information on this epistemological discourse, see al-Baqillani, *Kitab Tamhid*, 28–37.

29. The origin of the idea that Jesus's death was an illusion may lie in the fact that Muslim commentators commonly refer to ancient non-canonical texts. The Gospel of Barnabas, an apocryphal text possibly from the sixth century, describes how God's angels took Jesus before Judas and turned Judas's face into a likeness of Jesus's. Jesus then simply *appeared* to be crucified.

30. For further discussion of this, see Leirvik, *Images of Jesus Christ in Islam*, 38–39.

31. See al-Tabari, *Jami' al-Bayan fi Ta'wil*, 9:370.

32. For a Christian understanding of Qur'anic texts on crucifixion, see Moucarry, *The Prophet and the Messiah*, 127–44.

33. Hawwa, *Al-Asas fi al-Tafsir*, 2:775–76. For the source of this quote in the Gospel of Barnabas, see Ragg, *The Gospel of Barnabas*, 484–85.

## Chapter 2. A Qur'anic Perspective on the Eschatological Role of Jesus

1. Al-Tabari, *Jami' al-Bayan fi Ta'wil*, 6:420.

2. Ibn Hanbal, *Al-Musnad*, 5:262. The Qur'an relates that after leaving his wife, Hagar, and son, Ishmael, in Mecca, Abraham says the following, "Lord send forth to them a messenger of their own who shall declare to them Your revelation, and shall teach them the Book, the wisdom, and shall purify them from sin" (2:129). For comments on this, see also Ibn Kathir, *Tafsir al-Qur'an al-'Azim*, 1:323–25.

3. An important point in this particular verse is the announcement of the innocence of Mary. Also note that the Aaron mentioned here should not be confused with Aaron the brother of Moses, who is also mentioned in the Qur'an on another occasion as a supporter of Moses.

4. Al-Razi, *Mafatih al-Ghayb*, 21:178–79.

5. This would be a rational assumption for a twelfth-century Muslim theologian and Aristotelian philosopher.

6. Al-Razi, *Mafatih al-Ghayb*, 21:181–82. Similarly, al-Ghazali wrote a refutation of the divinity of Jesus; see al-Ghazali, *Al-Radd al-Jamil*.

7. The Islamic theological principle of free will is always valid and active. In Islam, even if one rejects a prophet and only believes in him at the very end of one's life, because that belief is based on free will it is valid and acceptable. The only exception to this is when one has lost his or her consciousness and therefore cannot truly believe.

8. Al-Maturidi, *Ta'wilat al-Qur'an*, 4:104.

9. For more classical interpretations of this verse, see Robinson, *Christ in Islam*, 78–89.

10. Al-Tabari, *Jami' al-Bayan fi Ta'wil*, 20:631–34.

11. Robinson, *Christ in Islam*, 90–91.

12. Parrender, *Jesus in the Qur'an*, 124.

13. Al-Qurtubi, *Al-Jami' li Ahkam al-Qur'an*, 8:105.

14. Rida, *Fatawa*, 5:2025.

15. Shaltout, *Al-Fatawa*, 74–75.

16. Ibid., 76.

17. Ibid., 77.

18. Shaltout, "The Ascension of Jesus," 192.

19. Ibid., 193.

20. Sa'id Ramadan al-Buti (d. 2013) was a noted Syrian scholar who contended, based on accounts of scholars at Al-Azhar University who were companions of Mahmud Shaltout, that Shaltout changed his theological view about the Islamic understanding of Jesus's descent and returned to the faith of the majority of Muslims after having a stroke and being housebound for a while. He reported that Shaltout burned all documents that espoused his old views on the denial of Jesus's descent and his similarly odd views. For this story and for al-Buti's view on

the subject and his responses to both Shaltout and Mirza Ghulam Ahmad, the founder of the Ahmadiyyah movement, see al-Buti, *Kubra al-Yaqiniyyat al-Kawniyya*, 304–314.

21. Al-Bukhari, "Al-Tahajjud," in *Al-Sahih*, 14.

22. Al-Maraghi, *Tafsir al-Maraghi*, 4:12–13.

23. For a good account of the role of Jesus in the dialogue among members of Abrahamic faiths, see Osman, "Jesus in Jewish-Christian-Muslim Dialogue," 353–76.

## Chapter 3. Islamic Eschatology and Jesus as a Sign of the Hour

1. On various Qur'anic descriptions of the Final Hour, see Qutb, *Mashahid al-Qiyama*.

2. The focus of this section will be on examples from Hadith, but some Qur'anic references are 7:187, 33:63, and 79:42.

3. Al-Bukhari, "Al-Riqaq," in *Al-Sahih*, 35.

4. Al-Bukhari, "Al-Adab," in ibid., 96.

5. Al-Bukhari, "Al-Riqaq," in ibid., 43.

6. Ibn Hanbal, *Al-Musnad*, 5:74–75.

7. Al-Bukhari, "Al-Iman," in *Al-Sahih* 37; Muslim bin al-Hajjaj, "Al-Iman," in *Al-Sahih*, 1.

8. For more on eschatological themes in the Qur'an, see O'Shaughnessy, *Eschatological Themes in the Qur'an*.

9. Al-Bukhari, "Al-Riqaq," in *Al-Sahih*, 39.

10. See Crone, *God's Rule*, 75. Crone refers to some authors who have claimed this. See, for example, Donner, "The Sources of Islamic Conceptions of War," 43; Cook, "Muslim Apocalyptic and Jihad," 66–104; and Arjomand, "Messianism, Millennialism, and Revolution in Early Islamic History," 106–125.

11. Murphy, *Apocalypticism in the Bible and Its World* is an excellent resource for information on Judaic and early Christian apocalyptic traditions.

12. See, for example, Ibn Hammad, *Kitab al-Fitan*.

13. For further discussion of the miracles of the Prophet and his prophecies, see Nursi, *The Letters*, 128–36.

14. Al-Bukhari, "Al-Sulh," in *Al-Sahih*, 9.

15. Al-Bukhari, "Al-Jihad," in ibid., 94.

16. Al-Bukhari, "Al-Tafsir," in ibid., 129.

17. One famous story says that a group of Meccans asked the Prophet to show them a miracle. The Prophet pointed at the moon, whereupon the moon immediately split in two and then returned to normal. They did not deny the miracle but said, "Muhammad's magic even affected the sky" (Qur'an 54:1). For commentary on this miracle of the Prophet, see Nursi, *The Letters*, 247–51.

18. Ibn Hammad, *Kitab al-Fitan*, 371–78.

19. Muslim bin al-Hajjaj, "Al-Fitan," in *Al-Sahih*, 39.

20. Timothy Weber notes in his recent book on dispensationalism that "dispensationalists' views of Bible prophecy also make them skeptical about and sometimes even opposed to efforts to bring peace to the Middle East." Weber, *On the Road to Armageddon*, 18. Overall, Weber's

book argues that dispensationalist Christians, who view the Bible more or less literally, have recently become active players in attempting to make Bible prophecy come true.

21. The following chapters of the Qur'an have titles with eschatological overtones: chapter 22, "The Hour" or "The Pilgrimage" (the chapter has two names); chapter 44, "The Smoke"; chapter 45, "The Kneeling"; chapter 56, "The Event"; chapter 59, "The Bringing Together"; chapter 69, "The Reality"; chapter 75, "The Resurrection"; chapter 78, "The News"; chapter 81, "The Darkened Sun"; chapter 82, "The Shattering of the Sky"; chapter 84, "The Sundering"; chapter 88, "The Overwhelming"; chapter 99, "The Earthquake"; and chapter 101, "The Calamity."

22. Nursi, "Sözler," 578.

23. Ibid.

24. For a medieval Islamic account of this, see al-Ghazali, *The Remembrance of Death and the Afterlife*.

25. Al-Kalabadhi, *Kitab al-Ta'arruf*, 31–32. For an English translation of this work, see Arberry, *The Doctrines of the Sufis*, 7.

26. Nursi, "Lem'alar," 585.

27. Some minor Islamic theological sects have denied the possibility of intercession of the prophets in the afterlife because of their extreme emphasis on relying on human actions. The Mu'tazilite is one such group.

28. Muslim bin al-Hajjaj, "Al-Iman," in *Al-Sahih*, 47.

29. Ibn Hanbal, *Al-Musnad*, 3:492.

## Chapter 4. The Hadith and Jesus's Eschatological Descent

1. For the section on Jesus in al-Ya'qubi, see Donaldson, "Al-Ya'qubi's Chapter about Jesus Christ," 1:74–89. See also Ibn 'Asakir, *Tarikh Madinat Dimashq*, 47:347–524; Mourad, "A Twelfth-Century Muslim Biography of Jesus," 39–45; and al-Waqidi, *Futuh al-Sham*, 215–18.

2. Ibn 'Asakir, *Tarikh Madinat Dimashq*, 47:496–97.

3. Ibn Hanbal, *Al-Musnad*, 2:298, 299, 394.

4. Al-Kashmiri, *Al-Tasrih bima Tawatar*, 91–293. For earlier references to sayings of the Prophet on the descent of Jesus, see al-Suyuti, *Nuzul 'Isa bin Maryam*. Many popular books in the same genre can be found on the streets of major cities in the Islamic world such as Cairo, Istanbul, Karachi, and Jakarta. For example, see Herras, *Fasl al-Maqal fi Nuzul*; and al-Kurdi, *'Aqidat al-Islam*. This genre is mostly composed of the sayings of the Prophet on the subject and generally contains few if any interpretations.

5. Al-Kawthari, *Nazra 'Abera*, 146.

6. Al-Ghumari, *Iqamat al-Burhan*, 25–74.

7. Ibid., 75.

8. The Prophet's companions who are mentioned as the narrators of hadith concerning the descent of Jesus are 'Imran bin Husayn, Nafi' bin 'Utba, Abu Barza, Hudhayfa bin Aseed, Abu Huraira, Kaysan, 'Uthman bin al-'As, Jabir bin 'Abdillah, Abu Umama, Ibn Mas'ud, 'Abdullah bin 'Amr, Samura bin Jundub, Nawwas bin Sam'an, 'Amr bin 'Awf, and Hudhayfa bin al-Yaman.

9. This hadith is narrated in al-Bukhari, "Buyu'," in *Al-Sahih*, 102; al-Bukhari, "Al-Mazalim,"

in *Al-Sahih*, 31; al-Tirmidhi, "Fitan," in *Al-Jami' al-Sahih*, 54; and Ibn Hanbal, *Al-Musnad*, 2:240, 272, 290, 394, 538.

10. Al-Bukhari, "Al-Anbiya'," in *Al-Sahih*, 49.

11. Ibn Majah, "Al-Fitan," in *Al-Sunan*, 33.

12. Ibid. See also al-Nisaburi, *Al-Mustadrak 'ala al-Sahihayn*, 4:536. In his famous interpretation of the Qur'an, Al-Suyuti mistakenly attributes this hadith to Abu Dawud al-Sijistani; see al-Suyuti, *Al-Durr al-Manthur*, 2:224–27.

13. Al-'Asqalani, *Tabaqat al-Mudallisin*, 29.

14. Al-'Asqalani, *Taqrib al-Tahzib*, 2:355.

15. Ibid., 1:69.

16. Al-Kashmiri, *Al-Tasrih bima Tawatar*, 152–53.

17. Bell, *The Origin of Islam*, 204.

18. Hadith sources record that 'Abd al-'Uzza bin Qatan asked the Prophet, "O Messenger of God, does such a resemblance to the Antichrist harm me?" The Prophet replied, "No, you are a Muslim person and he is a disbeliever person." See al-Hindi, *Kanz al-'Ummal*, 8:542.

19. For a full text of this hadith, see Muslim bin al-Hajjaj, "Al-Fitan," in *Al-Sahih*, 110.

20. Al-Nawawi, *Sharh Sahih Muslim*, 18:64.

21. Al-Nisaburi, *Al-Mustadrak 'ala al-Sahihayn*, 4:492.

22. Ibn Majah, "Al-Fitan," in *Al-Sunan*, 33.

23. Muslim bin al-Hajjaj, "Al-Iman," in *Al-Sahih*, 273, 275, 277; Malik bin Anas, "Sifat al-Nabi," in *Al-Muwatta'*, 2; and Ibn Hanbal, *Al-Musnad*, 2:22, 39, 144, 154.

24. Muslim bin al-Hajjaj, "Al-Iman," in *Al-Sahih*, 247; Abu Dawud, "Al-Fitan," in *Al-Sunan*, 1; and Ibn Hanbal, *Al-Musnad*, 4:93, 99, 104, 244.

## Chapter 5. Speculations about Jesus's Return

1. 'Abd al-Karim al-Khatib denies the reliability of Islamic sources on the signs of the Hour, and he believes expectations about the coming of messianic figures such as Jesus and the Mahdi are an escape from the real world. See al-Khatib, *Al-Mahdi*, 6. Also see his *Al-Masih*, 537–38. Despite this belief, he considers the coming of Jesus to be among the most important elements of this genre.

2. Ibn Hanbal, *Al-Musnad*, 2:298–99. Nur al-Din 'Ali bin Abi Bakr al-Haythami (d. 1405), a well-known fifteenth-century scholar of Hadith criticism, says that the narrators of this hadith are the narrators of the authentic hadith collections. Therefore, methodologically speaking, this hadith is authentic. See his book *Majma' al-Zawa'id wa Manba' al-Fawa'id*, 8:5. Also, for al-Haythami's view on the Mahdi, see his book *Al-Qawl al-Mukhtasar*.

3. Al-Bukhari, "Al-Fitan," in *Al-Sahih*, 11.

4. In the Muslim tradition of praying together, the imam, or leader, is about one meter in front of the community; thus, the community prays behind the imam. In other words, the community prays with the imam. This does not indicate a greater importance of the imam, and there are hadith that record that when the Prophet was sick, he asked Abu Bakr to lead the community in prayer.

5. Ibn Hanbal, *Al-Musnad*, 3:367–68.

6. Ibid., 4:104.

7. Ibn Majah, "Al-Fitan," in *Al-Sunan*, 33.

8. Ibn Khaldun, *Muqaddimah: An Introduction to History*, 2:195. For the original Arabic, see Ibn Khaldun, *Muqaddimat Ibn Khaldun*, 2:754.

9. Ibn Khaldun, *Muqaddimah: An Introduction to History*, 2:196. Here Ibn Khaldun criticizes those who blindly follow charlatans who claim they are the Islamic messianic figure. He also gives examples from his own time.

10. On the virtue of Damascus and this hadith, see Ibn Manzur, *Mukhtasar Tarikh Dimashq*, 93. For the hadith itself, see Muslim bin al-Hajjaj, "Al-Fitan," in *Al-Sahih*, 110. It is worth noting that Pope John Paul II visited the Umayyad Mosque and prayed with Muslims during his historic visit to Syria in 2000, making him the first pope to visit a mosque.

11. Al-Qari, *Mirqat al-Mafatih*, 5:197. The Umayyad Mosque is the earliest stone mosque, completed in the beginning of the eighth century CE. It sits on the site of an earlier Hellenistic temple and a subsequent Christian church. It is believed that the head of John the Baptist, which was said to be found at the church, still resides in the mosque.

12. Al-Suyuti, *Nuzul 'Isa bin Maryam*, 86.

13. Ibn Hanbal, *Al-Musnad*, 5:13.

14. Ibid., 5:91.

15. Ibn al-Athir, *Usd al-Ghaba*, 3:247.

16. Muslim bin al-Hajjaj, "Al-Fitan," in *Al-Sahih*, 116.

17. Al-Bukhari, "Ta'bir al-Ru'ya," in *Al-Sahih*," 33; and Al-Bukhari, "Al-Anbiya," in *Al-Sahih*, 48.

18. Al-Bukhari, "Al-Anbiya," in *Al-Sahih*, 50.

19. For a more practical comparison between the Shi'ite belief in the Mahdi and the Christian belief in Jesus, see Finger, "Jesus and the Shia Savior," 27–28.

20. Al-'Asqalani, *Fath al-Bari*, 13:256.

21. Al-Bukhari, "Al-Anbiya," in *Al-Sahih*, 50.

22. Al-Suyuti, *Kitab al-I'lam*, 2:338–55.

23. I will use the term "renewer" interchangeably with the term "reformer." However, since the hadith on the renewer of religion at the beginning of every century uses the word "*tajdid*," which can be translated as "renewal," I prefer to use the term renewer for the Muslim figures who are known as fulfillment of this hadith. In Islam, the Prophet Muhammad is the final prophet and there is no prophet after him. Therefore, for Islam to keep its vitality and dynamism, this prophetic role of reform and renewal is given to "renewers." They renew the message of the religion of Islam, which might have become faded through the passing of time.

24. Al-Qurtubi, *Al-Jami' li Ahkam al-Qur'an*, 16:107.

25. Al-Suyuti, *Kitab al-I'lam*, 2:156.

26. Al-Qurtubi, who narrates this consensus, dedicates a long section to the turmoil and signs of the Hour. See *Al-Tadhkira fi Ahwal*, 686–831. The trend of dedicating an entire book to the subject of turmoil and the signs of the Hour continued into the eleventh century CE. For example, Abu 'Amr al-Dani (d. 1053) puts all related hadith together in one volume, which has recently become available as six volumes. See *Al-Sunan al-Warida*. We see the same trend in the work Ibn Kathir; see his reputable book, *Al-Nihaya*.

27. Al-Qurtubi, *Al-Tadhkira fi Ahwal*, 774.

28. Al-Bukhari, "Al-I'tisam," in *Al-Sahih*, 10.

29. Ibn Hibban, *Al-Sahih*, 4:467.

30. Even though the hadith in question does not use the word "Mahdi," in his commentary Nursi employs the idea, likely for historical reasons beyond the scope of this work.

31. Nursi, "Mektubat," 347; Nursi, "Kastamonu Lahikasi," 1615; Nursi, "Emirda{gc} Lahikasi," 1704.

32. See The Republican Brothers, "The Return of Christ." For more information on Taha and his thought, see Mahmoud Mohamed Taha, *The Second Message of Islam*; and Mahmoud, *Quest for Divinity*.

## Chapter 6. The Mahdi and Jesus as Allies against al-Dajjal (the Antichrist)

1. Sunni Muslims constitute approximately 85 percent of all Muslims around the world, while Shi'ite Muslims constitute around 15 percent. Shi'ite Muslims live mostly in Iran, Iraq, and in some countries in the Persian Gulf region, with scattered populations in some other countries.

2. For an elaborate account of the Mahdi in the Twelver Shi'ite tradition, see Sachedina, *Islamic Messianism*.

3. Rida, *Fatawa*, 1:108.

4. The word *muhtadun* is mentioned in the Qur'an: 3:51–56, 3:90, 6:82, 4:175.

5. Ibn Manzur, *Lisan al-'Arab*, 15:354. Ibn Manzur says that "Mahdi" is a common given name. Thus, the person whose coming at the end of time has been given as good news by the Prophet is named Mahdi.

6. Muslim bin al-Hajjaj, "Al-Jana'iz," in *Al-Sahih*, 7; Abu Dawud, "Al-Jana'iz," in *Al-Sunan*, 17; Ibn Hanbal, *Al-Musnad*, 6:297.

7. Al-Tirmidhi, "Al-'Ilm," in *Al-Jami' al-Sahih*, 16.

8. Al-Taftazani, *Sharh al-Maqasid*, 5:314.

9. For further details, see Crone, *God's Rule*, 75, and sources cited therein.

10. Abu Dawud, "Al-Malahim," in *Al-Sunan*, 1.

11. Al-Sallabi, *'Umar bin 'Abd al-'Aziz*, 36–94. Similarly, Hasan al-Basri (d. 728), an earlier theologian and Sufi who thought of Jesus as the Mahdi, opposed the belief in the coming of the Mahdi but contended that if there were one, it would be 'Umar bin 'Abd al-'Aziz. See Madelung, "Al-Mahdi," 1234.

12. For more information on this, see Bacharach, "Laqab for a Future Caliph," 271–74.

13. For further information on the Mahdi, see Blichfeldt, *Early Mahdism*; Goldziher, *Introduction to Islamic Theology and Law*, 197–98; and Madelung, "Abd Allah b. al-Zubair," 291–305. Also see Voll, "Mahdis, Walis, and New Men," 367–84.

14. In the very early period of the history of Islam, a small group of Muslim scholars, especially Hanafi scholars, denied the emergence of the Mahdi and suggested that only Jesus would come. Perhaps this is because the Mahdi and Jesus share similar roles in Islamic eschatology. It is said that the Prophet of Islam said, "There is no Mahdi except Jesus" (Ibn Majah, "Al-Fitan," in *Al-Sunan*, 34). Abu Hanifa (d. 767), did not mention the coming of the Mahdi in his brief

book on the Islamic creed, *Al-Fiqh al-Akbar*, when he listed the subjects of the Sunni creed. Commenting on the absence of the Mahdi in Abu Hanifa's book, A. J. Wensinck says, "It must be observed that in the present article no mention is made of the Mahdi, who in later Muslim eschatology becomes more conspicuous than Jesus. It is said that right up to the present day the Hanafites cling to the old view of Jesus as the vicegerent of God on earth in the last days, to the exclusion of the Mahdi, whom they do not expect. The fact that the Mahdi is not mentioned in *Al-Fiqh al-Akbar* may be due to the Hanafi origin of this creed." See Wensinck, *The Muslim Creed*, 244.

15. Al-Taftazani, *Sharh al-Maqasid*, 5:314.

16. See, for instance, the collections of Ahmad bin Hanbal (d. 857), Ibn Majah (d. 886), al-Tirmidhi (d. 888), Ahmad al-Bazar (d. 904), Abu Ya'la al-Mawsili (d. 919), al-Tabarani (d. 971), and al-Hakim al-Nisaburi (d. 1040).

17. Ibn Khaldun, *Muqaddimah: An Introduction to History*, 2:156. For the original Arabic see Ibn Khaldun, *Muqaddimat Ibn Khaldun*, 2:725–26.

18. Abu Dawud, "Al-Mahdi," in *Al-Sunan*, 1.

19. Ibn Khaldun, *Muqaddimah: An Introduction to History*, 2:156–57. The English translator, Franz Rosenthal has given an erroneous translation of this passage, perhaps confusing the word *khalqan*, which means "physically," with *khuluqan*, which means "morally and spiritually." See *Muqaddima Ibn Khaldun*, 2:900; and Ibn Khaldun, *Muqaddimah: An Introduction to History*, 2:163–64.

20. Muslim bin al-Hajjaj, "Al-Fitan," in *Al-Sahih*, 67–69. See also Ibn Majah, "Al-Fitan," in *Al-Sunan*, 34; Ibn Hanbal, *Al-Musnad*, 3:22.

21. Patricia Crone and Martin Hinds have a good account of sources on this. See Crone and Hinds, *God's Caliph*, 114.

22. For details on the use of the term *khalifat Allah*, see ibid., 4–23.

23. Muslim bin al-Hajjaj, "Al-Iman," in *Al-Sahih*, 247.

24. Ibn Khaldun dedicates a chapter to the emergence of the Mahdi, whom he calls the Fatimi, in reference to the daughter of the Prophet, Fatima. Ibn Khaldun believes that mystics who spoke of the Mahdi generally relied upon their own findings during their spiritual journeys rather than the sayings of the Prophet. He mentions a dozen sayings of the Prophet and occasionally refers to problems with their authenticity. He speaks of Ibn al-'Arabi's understanding of the Mahdi and describes Ibn al-'Arabi as the one who spoke the most about the Mahdi. According to Ibn Khaldun, most of Ibn al-'Arabi's statements were allegorical riddles. In Ibn al-'Arabi's view, the Mahdi is the "Seal of the Saints" (Khatam al-Awliya'), just as the Prophet Muhammad had been the "Seal of the Prophets" (Khatam al-Anbiya').

While criticizing those who give a specific date for the emergence of the Mahdi, Ibn Khaldun narrates that according to Ibn al-'Arabi, the time of the emergence of the Mahdi is the year 683 of the Islamic calendar, which corresponds to 1284 CE. For further discussion by Ibn Khaldun of the Mahdi according to Ibn al-'Arabi in particular and in the Sufi tradition of Islam in general, see Ibn Khaldun, *Muqaddimah: An Introduction to History*, 2:186–200, 298.

25. Abu Dawud, "Al-Malahim," in *Al-Sunan*, 1.

26. See Algar, "The Centennial Renewer," 291–311.

27. For a useful comparison of Mary and Fatima, see Thurlkill, *Chosen Among Women*.

28. Ibn Babawayh, *Risala al-I'tiqadat al-Imamiyya*, 69.

29. Al-Tabarsi, *Majma' al-Bayan*, 2:758–59; 9:81–83.

30. Fayd-i Kashani, *'Ilm al-Yaqin fi Usul al-Din*, 1:421–25.

31. Al-Tabataba'i, *Al-Mizan fi Tafsir al-Qur'an*, 3:307–308.

32. Ibn Khaldun, *Muqaddimah: An Introduction to History*, 1:406.

33. Ibid., 2:195.

34. The Kharijites were an offshoot of the Shi'ites, who after originally supporting 'Ali's rule later turned against him.

35. Al-Ash'ari, *Al-Maqalat al-Islamiyyin*, 9; Hodgson, "'Abdulla bin Saba,'" 51.

36. Nicholson, *A Literary History of the Arabs*, 215.

37. On the idea of the expected Messiah in Islam, see al-Saqqa, *Al-Masia al-Muntazar*.

38. See Qur'anic verses 2:56–57, 4:51, 60:76, 5:36, 16:36, and 39:17.

39. Ahmad bin 'Ali bin Hajar al-'Asqalani tells a story in which al-'As bin Wa'il, a forceful opponent of the Prophet, referred to Muhammad as *abtar*, a pejorative term used in the Arabian culture of the time for those who have no surviving male children. This occurred on the occasion of the death of his first son, al-Qasim, and again after the death of his second son, 'Abdullah. Al-'As bin Wa'il used the term to suggest that Muhammad was without heirs. Allah comforted the Prophet with the revelation through the angel Gabriel. Muhammad was promised that he will be given *kauthar*, or abundance, while his enemy is actually the one who is cut off, or *abtar*. See al-'Asqalani, *Al-Isaba fi Tamyiz al-Sahaba*, 5:515. Also see McGinn, *Antichrist*, 111.

40. Al-Bukhari, "al-Fitan," in al-Sahih, 26; McGinn, *Antichrist*, 315n165.

41. Muslim bin al-Hajjaj, "Al-Fitan," in *Al-Sahih*, 110.

42. Nursi, "Şualar," in *Risale-i Nur Külliyati*, 1:887; Nursi, "Sözler," in *Risale-i Nur Külliyati*, 1:319.

43. Al-Bukhari, "Al-Janai'z," in *Al-Sahih*, 86.

44. For further details on the Antichrist, see Saritoprak, "The Legend of al-Dajjal," 290–306.

45. Al-Tayalisi, *Al-Musnad*, 327.

46. For a good source on hadith on the subject, see al-'Adawi, *Al-Sahih*, especially pages 500–562, which are dedicated to narratives on and commentaries about Jesus and the Antichrist.

47. Al-Bukhari, "Al-Zakat," in *Al-Sahih*, 11; and Muslim bin al-Hajjaj, "Al-Fada'il," in *Al-Sahih*, 101.

48. Mittleman, "Messianic Hope," 222–43.

## Chapter 7. Literalist Approaches to Jesus's Eschatological Role in Islamic Theology

1. Al-Barzanji, *Al-Isha'a li Ashrat al-Sa'a*.

2. Abu Hanifa, *Al-Fiqh al-Akbar*, 166–68. This treatise is quite small, roughly twenty pages, but it is considered to be highly significant. Some scholars question whether Abu Hanifa actually wrote the treatise and believe that it was written by his students and then attributed to him. Whatever the case may be, it does not limit the importance of the treatise for our discussion.

3. Al-Lalekai', *Sharh Usul I'tiqad Ahl*, 1:166.

4. Ibn Abi al-'Izz, *Sharh al-'Aqida al-Tahawiyya*, 2:754–57.

5. Al-Ash'ari, *Al-Maqalat al-Islamiyyin*, 295.

6. Al-Maturidi, *Ta'wilat al-Qur'an*, 4:104.

7. Ibid., 104–105.

8. Al-Ajurri, *Kitab al-Shar'ia*, 311–12.

9. Ibn Hazm, *'Ilm al-Kalam*, 30; and Ibn Hazm, *Al-Usul wa al-Furu'*, 1:48.

10. Ibn Taymiyya, *Majmu'at al-Fatawa*, 4:316.

11. Ibid., 4:316, 322–23, 328–29.

12. Al-Hijazi, "Sawa' al-Sirat." To my knowledge, this is still an unpublished manuscript in the special collections of the Egyptian National Library.

13. An early example of this is 'Ali bin Muhammad al-Mili (d. 1833), *Ashrat al-Sa'a wa Khuruj al-Mahdi* [The Signs of the Hour and the Emergence of the Mahdi], which was likely written in response to the Napoleonic invasion of Egypt.

14. For example, see 'Ata, *Al-Masih 'Isa*; and Ata ur-Rahim, *Jesus*.

15. Al-Ghazali, *'Aqidat al-Muslim*, 261.

16. Al-Jaza'iri, *'Aqidat al-Mu'min*, 261. For the verse in question, see the Qur'an 43:61.

17. Khan, *Al-Idha'ah Lima Kan*, 197–202.

18. Harputi, *Tankih al-Kalam*, 353–55.

## Chapter 8. Symbolic, Allegorical, and Other Interpretive Approaches to Jesus's Eschatological Role

1. Methodologically speaking, any dogma (especially among the sayings of the Prophet) that does not have a strong chain of narration or a recurrently transmitted chain cannot be considered a textual proof in the matter of creeds. This does not mean that the hadith is wrong or fabricated; it means that the statement might belong to the Prophet but since we do not have a sound chain of narration, we cannot accept it as a valid reference to establish an object of faith in Islamic theology. Such a dogma may suggest certain religious views but cannot be a binding principle of the Islamic creed, the denial of which would result in a punishment in the afterlife.

2. Al-Shatibi, *Al-Muwafaqat fi Usul al-Shari'a*, 20–24.

3. Al-Halimi, *Kitab al-Minhaj*, 1:425.

4. Other theologians shared similar ideas, especially theologians from the Mu'tazili school of thought. Here I will limit my survey to a few Muslim theologians.

5. Al-Taftazani, *Sharh al-Maqasid*, 3:312.

6. Ibid., 5:314.

7. Ibid., 5:317.

8. We should remember that humanity was rapidly approaching one of the most catastrophic events of its history, the First World War, when Abduh was writing this.

9. Rida, *Tafsir al-Manar*, 1954 ed., 3:261.

10. Ibid.

11. Ibid., 3:317.

12. Al-Juwayni, *Kitab al-Irshad*, 25.

13. Ibid., 31.

14. Rida, *Fatawa*, 5:2022.

15. Jawhari, *Al-Jawahir*, 3:125–26.

16. Ibid., 3:127.

17. For the text of this sermon, see Nursi, *The Damascus Sermon*.

18. Nursi, *The Letters*, 22; see also Nursi, "Kastamonu Lahikasi," in *Risale-i Nur Kulliyati*, 2:1601, 2:1614.

19. Al-Ghazali, *The Niche of Lights*, 33.

20. Ibid.

21. See Rahner, *Theological Investigations*, 14:283.

22. Nursi, "Mektubat," 1:413.

23. For a detailed account of this cooperation and understanding, see Menocal, *The Ornament of the World*.

24. See Bulliet, *The Case for Islamo-Christian Civilization*.

25. For examples of such practices, see Kelly, *Origins of Christmas*, 111–28.

26. Nursi, "Mektubat," 1:371–72.

27. Ibn al-'Arabi, *Al-Futuhat al-Makkiya*, 13:136–37.

28. Ibid., 2:252.

29. Ibid., 12:119–20, 126–27.

30. Ibid., 11:289–90.

31. See Ibn al-'Arabi, *Fusus al-Hikam*, 378–79.

32. For more details on Isaiah's vision of God's reign, see Isaiah chapter 11 in the New American Standard Bible.

33. Ibn al-'Arabi, *Fusus al-Hikam*, 381.

34. Rumi, *The Mathnawi*, 5:2503.

35. Ibid., 6:4364–71.

36. The chapter is composed of five verses: "Have you not seen how your Lord punished the friends of the elephant [Abraha]? Did not He bring failure to their stratagem? And sent against them flocks of birds? [They] pelted them with stones of baked clay. Then [He] made them like withered stalks of plants devoured by cattle." (Qur'an 105:1–5).

37. Rumi, *The Mathnawi*, 6:4375–85.

38. Ibid., 3:298–309.

39. Ibid., 2570–98.

40. Ibid., 3504–3505.

41. Ibid., 4258.

42. Ibid., 4:2673.

43. Gölpinarli, *Mesnevi Tercemesi ve Şerhi*, 1:202. For the Khidr, see the Qur'an 18:60–82.

44. Rumi, *The Mathnawi*, 6:4039–40.

45. Rumi, *The Mathnawi*, 1:500–501. Gölpinarli refers to a similar story. He recounts a story from Şeyh Zade, a sixteenth-century Ottoman commentator on the Qur'an, that Jesus's mother sent the child Jesus to a dyer as a novice. One day, the master instructed Jesus that each of the cloths had a separate sign indicating which color is proper and thus each should be dyed sepa-

rately. Jesus put all the cloths into one jar. When the master came he realized that all the cloths were in one jar and he became very worried and did not know how to respond. Jesus said to him, "Do not worry," and took out each cloth one by one, and each cloth was dyed without being mixed with the others. The people who witnessed this were perplexed. Gölpinarli, *Mesnevi Tercemesi ve Şerhi*, 1:98.

46. Al-Sha'rani, *Kitab al-Yawaqit*, 2:164.

47. Ibid.

48. Bursevi, *Ruhul Beyan*, 2:40–41.

49. *Murad Nameh* is a Mathnawi-style book of poetry presented to Murad II (r. 1421–51). See Ceyhan, *Bedr-i Dilşad ve Murad-namesi*.

## Chapter 9. Jesus's Descent and Theologies of Muslim-Christian Cooperation

1. For examples, see 'Abd al-Baqi, *Al-Mu'jam al-Mufahras*, 93–94.

2. In Western scholarship the date for the revelation is usually given as 610. However, according to my research, 609 is a more accurate date.

3. Muhammad responded with force only when the polytheists of Mecca formed an army and traveled all the way from Mecca to Medina, about 280 miles, to attack him and his followers. He had no choice but to defend his followers or be killed. The Prophet defeated the polytheists' well-equipped army of 1,000 with his force of 300. The Prophet hoped that this would be the end of the conflict, but the Meccan leaders looked for revenge. For further information on the life of the Prophet, see Lings, *Muhammad*.

4. Al-Bayhaqi, *Shu'ab al-Iman*, 7:55. See also al-Suyuti, *Al-Durr al-Manthur*, 7:112.

5. For the details of these laws, see Doi, *Non-Muslims under Shari'a*, 22–40. See also Saritoprak, "Said Nursi's Teachings on the People of the Book," 319–32.

6. This address should be taken literally because the Abbasid caliphs came from the offspring of 'Abbas, the uncle of the Prophet.

7. Abu Yusuf, *Kitab al-Kharaj*, 134–35.

8. Ibid.

9. Al-Bukhari, "Al-Khusumat," in *Al-Sahih*, 1.

10. Al-Bukhari, "Al-Anbiya'," in *Al-Sahih*, 34.

11. Al-Bukhari, *Al-Adab al-Mufrad*, 66.

12. Al-'Asqalani, *Itraf al-Musnid*, 7:425.

13. For details on common ground between Christians and Muslims, see Zahniser, *The Mission and Death of Jesus*, 1–8 and 245–58.

14. Prophethood is also a common theme among Muslims and Jews. The focus of this study is Muslim-Christian relationships; thus, I will not focus on Muslim-Jewish relationships, a topic which would require a lengthy study to cover adequately.

15. hooks, *Teaching to Transgress*, 42.

16. Abu Dawud, "Al-Adab," in *Al-Sunan*, 152. The hadith goes as follows: "Abu Umama narrates that the Prophet came to us leaning on his staff. We stood up before him as respect for his presence and he said 'Do not stand up like some al-A'ajim [non-Arab nations, or Persians] exalting each other by standing up.'"

17. Ayoub, "Christian-Muslim Dialogue," 313–20.

18. For details, see Ibn Kathir, *Al-Sirq*, 2:15–22; also see Saritoprak, "Said Nursi on Muslim-Christian Relations," 25–37.

19. Part of this story is depicted in the 1977 film *The Message*, dir. Moustapha Akkad.

20. Al-Bukhar, "Al-Jana'iz" in Al-Sahih, 54.

21. The legacy of al-Najashi endures today. Some Turkish businessmen, inspired by the teachings of Fethullah Gülen, have established schools in Ethiopia named Nejashi Ethio-Turkish International Schools. These schools were established in the capital city, Addis Ababa, in 2003. Christians and Muslims are educated together in a peaceful environment in these schools.

22. For example, see Qur'an 2:109, 3:72–75, 3:113, 3:69.

23. On these mystics and other Sufi masters of the time, see Schimmel, *The Triumphal Sun*, 10.

24. "Pope Innocent III (A.D. 1213) designated Mohammed as Antichrist; and as the number of the beast, 666, was held to indicate the period of his dominion, it was supposed that the Mohammedan power was soon to fall." McClintock and Strong, *Cyclopedia of Biblical, Theological, and Ecclesiastical Literature*, 1:258.

25. Abbott, *Documents of Vatican II*, 663.

26. Vatican Radio, "Pope to Muslims for End of Ramadan: Promoting Mutual Respect through Education."

27. See Gaudeul, *Encounters and Clashes*, 2:242.

28. See Esposito and Voll, "Islam and the West," 613–39.

29. Saritoprak and Griffith, "Fethullah Gülen," 329–40.

30. Huntington, *Clash of Civilizations*.

31. Saritoprak, "Fethullah Gülen: A Sufi in His Own Way," 156–69.

32. Saritoprak and Griffith, "Fethullah Gülen," 329–40.

33. Nuriye Akman, "Fethullah Gülen ile Roportaj," *Zaman Gazetesi*, March 31, 2004. This is an interview with Gülen.

34. Personal notes of Ahmet Özer, taken during his conversation with Gülen on June 25, 2002.

35. Ibid.

36. Ibid., June 12, 2002.

37. Huntington, *Clash of Civilizations*.

38. Gülen, *Towards the Lost Paradise*, 40–42; see also Gülen, *Fatiha Üzerine Mulahazalar*, 90–95.

39. Gülen, *Hoşgörü ve Diyalog Iklimi*, 23–26.

40. Ibn Hanbal, *Al-Musnad*, 5:441.

41. See Saritoprak, "Said Nursi's Teachings on the People of the Book," 319–32.

42. I have detailed these commentators' views on the verse in question in my article, "How Commentators of the Qur'an Define 'Common Word,'" 34–45.

43. The Common Word initiative has established a Web site that includes a version of the original letter and responses to it and other relevant information on the project and interfaith dialogue in general. See http://www.acommonword.com.

44. For example, Muhammad bin 'Ali al-Shawkani (d. 1834) suggests that the phrase in the

verse "We take no one as Lord except God" (3:64) implies a "reproach for those who believe in the divinity of Jesus and 'Uzair [Ezra], and it is pointing out that these are human beings." Al-Shawkani is referring to the Qur'anic verse "The Jews say, 'Ezra is the son of God'; the Christians say, 'The Messiah is the son of God.' That is what they say with their mouths. They imitate the sayings of the disbelievers of old. . . . and they were not commanded to serve but One God, there is no deity save Him; God is above their claims that idols are partner to Him" (9:30–31). See al-Shawkani, *Fath al-Qadir*, 1:348.

45. Al-Tabari, *Jami' al-Bayan*, 3:301–303.

46. Ibid., 303.

47. Nursi, "Işaratü'l-I'caz," in *Risale-i Nur Kulliyati*, 2:1175. See also Saritoprak, "Said Nursi on Muslim-Christian Relations."

48. See United States Conference of Catholic Bishops, "Midwest Muslim-Catholic Dialogue Completes Latest Round."

49. Al-Tabari, *Tahdhib al-Athar*, 18.

## Conclusion

1. Al-Qurtubi, *Al-Tadhkira fi Ahwal*, 774.

## Appendixes

1. Gülen's quotations from the Bible appear to be based on the Good News Translation.

2. The Muslim residents of Medina who were residing there when the Prophet and his followers emigrated to the city. In Islam they are known as *ansar*, or helpers.

3. Yazir seems to have misunderstood the Christian understandings of heaven and God. Generally, there is a consensus that Christians do not equate "heaven" with God. The confusion might have come from the word heavenly, which generally is understood as "divine," as in the idea of heavenly revelation, or a revelation that comes from God.

4. The Qur'an does not obviously refer to the Israelites per se; instead, it uses only the pronoun "they" for those who plotted against and attempted to kill Jesus. Yazir follows many Qur'an commentators who have interpreted the pronoun "they" as a reference to some Israelites at the time of Jesus. Grammatically, this is possible since an earlier verse says that Jesus was sent as a messenger of God to the "Children of Israel." As a principle, the Qur'an avoids generalization. Theologically speaking, the Qur'an and the prophetic traditions do not target any specific ethnic or religious group. It would be against Islamic teaching to vilify or slander Jewish people because of their Jewishness. The Qur'an speaks against bad characters, which can be found in any religious group or ethnicity. These individuals are who are blamed in the Qur'an, not ethnic groups.

In fact, Yazir himself, in his commentary on a later verse (p. 1115) says that Qur'anic criticism of Jews is not because of their Jewishness but because of the attribute of disbelief that some of them had. It is evident that bad attributes can be found in any ethnic or religious group. Historical events should be considered within their historical context, and it is wrong to bring them into our time and treat them as if they happened today. Therefore, no matter who *tried* to kill Jesus, it would be wrong to see this as a condemnation of any living people, be they Jews or Italians, as the Qur'an explicitly forbids the blaming of children for the misdeeds of their parents or ancestors. Furthermore, any generalization in this context would go against the larger Qur'anic prohibition against "going too far." It should also be remembered that the Qur'an praises those who helped Jesus, who were themselves Jews. Also, it praises the followers of Moses.

5. This sentence indicates that Muhammad's raising of the dead is something that encompasses the miracles of all other prophets. So for him it is a part of his lived reality and not an occasional event.

# Bibliography

Abbott, Walter M., ed. *The Documents of Vatican II*. New York: Herder and Herder, 1966.

'Abd al-Baqi, Muhammad Fu'ad. *Al-Mu'jam al-Mufahras li Alfaz al-Qur'an al-Karim* [Concordance of the Qur'an]. Istanbul: al-Maktaba al-Islamiyya, 1982.

Abu Dawud, Sulaiman bin al-Ash'ath al-Azdi al-Sijistani. *Al-Sunan*. Edited by Muhammad 'Awwama. 4 vols. Beirut: Mu'assasat al-Rayyan, 1998.

——. *Sunan*. Istanbul: Şamil Yayincilik, 2003.

Abu Hanifa, Nu'man bin Thabit. *Al-Fiqh al-Akbar* [The Great Understanding]. In 'Ali al-Qari, *Sharh Kitab al-Fiqh al-Akbar* [*Commentary on the Book of Great Understanding*]. Beirut: Dar al-Kutub al-'Ilmiyya, 1984.

Abu Yusuf, Ya'qub bin Ibrahim al-Ansari. *Kitab al-Kharaj* [The Book on Taxation]. Cairo: al-Matba'a al-Salafiyya, 1976.

'Adawi, Abu 'Abdillah Mustafa bin, Al-. *Al-Sahih al-Musnad min Ahadith al-Fitan wa al-Malahim* [The Sound Narrations of the Hadith on Trials and End-Time Turmoils]. Riyadh: Dar Balansiyya, 2002.

Algar, Hamid. "The Centennial Renewer: Bediüzzaman Said Nursi and the Tradition of Tajdid." *Journal of Islamic Studies* 12, no. 3 (2001): 291–311.

Ajurri, Abu Bakr Muhammad, Al-. *Kitab al-Shari'a* [The Book of Shari'a]. Edited by Muhammad bin al-Hasan Isma'il. Beirut: Dar al-Kutub al-'Ilmiyya, 1995.

Amin, Ahmad. *Al-Mahdi wa al-Mahdawiyya* [The Mahdi and Mahdism]. Cairo: Dar al-Ma'arif, 1951.

Arberry, A. J. *The Koran Interpreted: A Translation*. New York: Macmillan, 1955.

Arjomand, Said Amir. "Messianism, Millennialism, and Revolution in Early Islamic History." In *Imagining the End: Visions of Apocalypse from the Ancient Middle East to Modern America*, edited by Abbas Amanat and Magnus Bernhardsson, 106–125. New York and London: I. B. Tauris, 2002.

Ash'ari, Abu al-Hasan 'Ali bin Isma'il, Al-. *Al-Maqalat al-Islamiyyin wa Ikhtilaf al-Musallin* [The Sects of Muslims and the Division of Worshippers]. Edited by Helmutt Ritter. Wiesbaden: Franz Steiner Verlag, 1963.

'Asqalani, Ahmad bin 'Ali bin Hajar, Al-. *Fath al-Bari' bi Sharh Sahih al-Bukhari* [The Victory of the Creator: A Commentary on al-Bukhari's *Sahih*]. Edited by Taha 'Abd al-Ra'uf Sa'd and

Mustafa Muhammad al-Hawari, and al-Sayyid Muhammad 'Abd al-Mu'ti. 28 vols. Cairo: Maktabat al-Kulliyat al-Azhariyya, 1978.

———. *Al-Isaba fi Tamyiz al-Sahaba* [The Right Criteria in Distinguishing the Companions of the Prophet]. Beirut: Dar al-Kutub al-'Ilmiyya, 1995.

———. *Itraf al-Musnid al-Mu'tali bi Atraf al-Musnad al-Hanbali* [A Commentary on Various Aspects of Ahmad bin Hanbal's *al-Musnad*]. Beirut: Dar Ibn Kathir, 1993.

———. *Tabaqat al-Mudallisin* [The Different Level of Those Who Mix Hadith with Other Words]. Edited by 'Asim bin 'Abdillah Qaryuti. Cairo: Matba'at al-Manar, 1983.

———. *Taqrib al-Tahzib* [On the Evaluation of Narrators]. Edited by 'Abd al-Wahhab 'Abd al-Latif. 2 vols. Beirut: Dar al-Ma'rifa, 1975.

'Ata, 'Abd al-Qadir. *Al-Masih 'Isa wa Nuzuluh Akhir al-Zaman wa Qitaluh li al-Dajjal* [Jesus the Messiah and His Descent at the End of Time and His Fight against the Antichrist]. Cairo: Maktabat al-Turath al-Islami, 1989.

'Ata ur-Rahim, Muhammad. *Jesus: A Prophet of Islam.* London: MWH London Publishers, 1979.

Ayoub, Mahmoud. "Christian-Muslim Dialogue: Goals and Obstacles." *Muslim World* 94, no. 3 (July 2004): 313–19.

———. "Towards an Islamic Christology, II: The Death of Jesus, Reality or Delusion: A Study of the Death of Jesus in Tafsir Literature." *Muslim World* 70, no. 2 (April 1980): 91–121.

Azhari, Abu Mansur Muhammad, Al-. *Tahdhib al-Lugha* [Decoration of the Language]. Cairo: al-Hay'a al-Misriyya al-'Amma li al-Kitab, 1975.

Bacharach, Jere L. "Laqab for a Future Caliph: The Case of the Abbasid al-Mahdi." *Journal of the American Oriental Society* 113, no. 2 (April–June 1993): 271–74.

Baqillani, al-Qadi Abu Bakr Muhammad, Al-. *Kitab Tamhid al-Awa'il wa Talkhis al-Dala'il* [The Book of Preparation of the First Principles and Summarizing the Proofs]. Beirut: Mua'ssasat al-Kutub al-Thaqafiyya, 1978.

Barzanji, Muhammad bin 'Abd al-Rasul al-Husainy, Al-. *Al-Isha'a li Ashrat al-Sa'a* [Unveiling the Portents of the Hour]. Jeddah: Dar al-Minhaj, 1997.

Bayhaqi, Abu Bakr Ahmad bin al-Husain bin 'Ali, Al-. *Shu'ab al-Iman* [Branches of Fatih]. Edited by Abu Hajar Muhammad Zaghlul. 7 vols. Beirut: Dar al-Kutub al-'Ilmiyya, 1990.

Bell, Richard. *The Origin of Islam and Its Christian Environment.* London: Frank Cass and Co., 1968.

Bilmen, Omer Nasuhi. *Muvazzah Ilm-i Kelam* [Detailed Explained Science of Kalam]. Istanbul: Ergin Kitabevi, 1955.

Blair, Sheila S., and Jonathan M. Bloom. *Images of Paradise in Islamic Art.* Hanover, NH: Hood Museum of Art, 1990.

Blichfeldt, Jan-Olaf. *Early Mahdism: Politics and Religion in the Formative Period of Islam.* Leiden: E. J. Brill, 1985.

Borelli, John, ed. *A Common Word and the Future of Christian-Muslim Relations.* Prince Al-waleed Bin Tallal Center for Muslim Christian Understanding Occasional Papers. Washington, D.C.: Georgetown University, 2009.

Bukhari, Abu 'Abdillah Muhammad bin Isma'il, Al-. *Al-Sahih.* Edited by Mustafa Dayb al-Bugha. Damascus: Dar Ibn Kathir, 1990.

――. *Al-Adab al-Mufrad* [The Unique Etiquette]. Edited by Muhammad Nasir al-Din al-Albani. Riyadh: Maktabat al-Dalil, 1997.

Bulliet, Richard. *The Case for Islamo-Christian Civilization*. New York: Columbia University Press, 2006.

Bursevi, Ismail Hakki. *Ruhul Beyan* [The Spirit of the Qur'an]. Istanbul: Eser Kitabevi, 1969.

Buti, Sa'id Ramadan, Al-. *Kubra al-Yaqiniyyat al-Kawniyya* [The Greatest Certain Universal Realities]. Damascus: Dar al-Fikr, 1969.

Ceyhan, Adem. *Bedr-i Dilşad ve Murad-namesi* [Badr-i Dilshad and His Murad-Name Treatise]. Ankara: Milli Eğitim Bakanliği Yayinlari, 1997.

Collins, John J. *Introduction to the Hebrew Bible*. Minneapolis: Fortress, 2004.

Cook, David. "Muslim Apocalyptic and Jihad." *Jerusalem Studies in Arabic and Islam* 20 (1996): 66–104.

Crone, Patricia. *God's Rule: Government and Islam*. New York: Columbia University Press, 2004.

Crone, Patricia, and Martin Hinds. *God's Caliph: Religious Authority in the First Century of Islam*. Cambridge: Cambridge University Press, 1986.

Dani, Abu 'Amr, Al-. *Al-Sunan al-Warida fi al-Fitan* [The Hadith Narrated on Trials]. Riyadh: Dar al-'Asima, 1995.

Doi, 'Abdur Rahman I. *Non-Muslims under Shari'a (Islamic Law)*. Lahore: Kazi Publications, 1995.

Donaldson, Dwight M. "Al-Ya'qubi's Chapter about Jesus Christ." In *The Macdonald Presentation Volume*, edited by W. G. Shellabear, E. E. Calverley, et al., 89–195. Princeton, NJ: Princeton University Press, 1933.

Donner, F. M. "The Sources of Islamic Conceptions of War." In *Just War and Jihad: Historical and Theoretical Perspectives on War and Peace in Western and Islamic Traditions*, edited by John Kelsay and James Turner Johnson, 31–70. New York: Greenwood Press, 1991.

Esposito, John, and John Voll. "Islam and the West: Muslim Voices of Dialogue." *Millennium: Journal of International Studies* 29, no. 3 (December, 2000): 613–39.

Ess, Josef Van. "Islam and the Other Religions: Jesus in the Qur'an: Islamic Perspectives." In *Christianity and World Religions: Paths of Dialogue with Islam, Hinduism, and Buddhism*, edited by Hans Küng, Josef van Ess, Heinrich von Stietencron, and Heinz Bechert, 97–108. London: SCM Press, 1993.

Farahidi, Khalil bin Ahmad, Al-. *Kitab al-'Ayn* [The Book of 'Ayn]. Edited by Mahdi al-Makhzumi and Ibrahim al-Samara'i. Baghdad: Dar al-Shu'un al-Thaqafa, 1967.

Fayd-i Kashani, Muhsin Muhammad bin al-Murtadha. *'Ilm al-Yaqin fi Usul al-Din* [The Knowledge of Certainty in Islamic Theology]. Qum: Intisharat-i Bidar, 1979.

Finger, Thomas. "Jesus and the Shi'a Savior: Waiting for the Mahdi." *Christian Century*, June 17, 2008, 27–28.

Flugel, Gustav. *Concordance of the Koran*. New Delhi: Kitab Bhavan, 1992.

Galloway, Dalton. "The Resurrection and Judgment in the Kor'an." *Moslem World* 12 (1922): 348–72.

Gaudeul, Jean-Marie. *Encounters and Clashes: Islam and Christianity in History*. 2 vols. Rome: Pontificio istituto di studi arabi e d'islamistica, 1990.

Ghazali, Abu Hamid Muhammad bin Muhammad, Al-. *Ihya' 'Ulum al-Din* [The Revival of Religious Sciences]. Dersaadet, Istanbul: Arif Efendi Matbaasi, 1906.

———. *Ihya' 'Ulum al-Din* [The Revival of Religious Sciences]. Beirut: Dar al-Ma'rifa, 1980.

———. *Al-Munqidh min al-Dalal* [The Deliverance from Error]. Damascus: Matba'at al-Taraqqi, 1939.

———. *The Niche of Lights*. Translated by David Buchman. Provo: Brigham Young University Press, 1998.

———. *Al-Radd al-Jamil li Ilahiyat 'Isa bi Sarih al-Injil* [The Beautiful Response with Clear Text of the Gospel against the Divinity of Jesus]. Edited by Muhammad 'Abdullah al-Sharqawi. Riyadh: Dar Aya, 1983.

———. *The Remembrance of Death and the Afterlife*. Book 40 of *The Revival of the Religious Sciences*. Translated by T. J. Winter. Cambridge: The Islamic Texts Society, 1999.

Ghazali, Muhammad, Al-. *'Aqidat al-Muslim* [The Creed of the Muslim]. Edited by 'Abdullah bin Ibrahim al-Ansari. Doha: Idara Ihya al-Turath al-Islami, 1983.

Ghumari, 'Abdullah bin Muhammad bin al-Siddiq, Al-. *Iqamat al-Burhan 'ala Nuzul-i 'Isa fi Akhir al-Zaman* [Establishing Proof for the Descent of Jesus at the End of Time]. Beirut: 'Alam al-Kutub, 1990.

Goldziher, Ignaz. *Introduction to Islamic Theology and Law*. Translated by Andras and Ruth Hamory. Princeton, NJ: Princeton University Press, 1981.

Gölpinarli, Abdulbaki. *Mesnevi Tercemesi ve Şerhi* [The Translation and Commentary of the Mathnawi]. 6 vols. Istanbul: Inkilap Kitabevi, 2003.

Guillaume, Alfred, ed. *The Summa Philosophiae of al-Shahrastani Kitab Nihayat al-Iqdam fi 'Ilmi al-Kalam*. London: Oxford University Press, 1934.

Gülen, M. Fethullah. *Fatiha Üzerine Mulahazalar* [Some Thoughts on the Opening Chapter of the Qur'an]. Izmir: Nil Yayinlari, 1997.

———. *Hoşgörü ve Diyalog Iklimi* [The Climate of Tolerance and Dialogue]. Edited by Selcuk Camci and Kudret Ünal. Izmir: Merkur Yayinlari, 1998.

———. *Towards the Lost Paradise*. London: Trustar, 1996.

———, ed. *Al-Qulub al-Dari'a* [The Supplicating Hearts]. Istanbul: Dar al-Nil, 2007.

Hajjaj, 'Abdullah. *'Alamat al-Qiyama al-Kubra min Bi'that al-Nabi Hatta Nuzul 'Isa* [The Major Signs of the Day of Resurrection from the Beginning of the Prophethood of the Prophet until the Descent of Jesus]. Beirut: Dar al-Jil, 1987.

Halimi, Abu 'Abdillah al-Husain bin al-Hasan, Al-. *Kitab al-Minhaj* [The Book of the Path]. Edited by Hilmi Muhammad Fudah. 3 vols. Beirut: Dar al-Fikr, 1979.

Hamsh, Adab Mahmud, Al-. *Al-Mahdi al-Muntazar fi Riwayat Ahl al-Sunnah wa al-Shi'a al-Imamiyya* [The Expected Mahdi in the Narrations of Sunnites and Imamiyya Shi'ites]. Amman: Dar al-Fath li al-Nashr wa al-Tawzi', 2001.

Harputi, 'Abdullatif. *Tankih al-Kalam fi 'Aka'id Ahl al-Islam* [The Revision of Kalam in the Creeds of the People of Islam]. Dersaadet: Necm-i Istikbal Matbaasi, 1911.

Hawwa', Sa'id. *Al-Asas fi al-Tafsir* [The Essence in Commentary on the Qur'an]. 11 vols. Cairo: Dar al-Salam li al-Tiba'a wa al-Nashr, 1989.

Haythami, Nur al-Din 'Ali bin Abi Bakr, Al-. *Majma' al-Zawa'id wa Manba' al-Fawa'id* [The

Gathering Place of Additional Sound Hadith and The Source of Benefits]. 5 vols. Beirut: Dar al-Kitab al-'Arabi, 1967.

———. *Al-Qawl al-Mukhtasar fi 'Alamat al-Mahdi al-Muntazar* [The Short Statement on the Signs of the Expected Mahdi]. Edited by Mustafa 'Ashur. Cairo: Maktabat al-Qur'an, 1987.

Herras, Muhammad Khalil. *Fasl al-Maqal fi Nuzul 'Isa wa Qatlih al-Dajjal* [The Explanation of the Discussion on Jesus's Descent and His Killing of the Antichrist]. Cairo: Maktabat al-Sunna, 1993.

Hijazi, Muhammad bin 'Abdillah al-Wa'iz, Al-. "Sawa' al-Sirat fi Dhikr al-Sa'a wa al-Ashrat" ["The Right Path on Mentioning the Hour and Its Portents"]. Unpublished manuscript in the Egyptian National Library, Ghaybiyat Taymur section, no. 26.

Hindi, 'Ala al-Din 'Ali bin Husam al-Din al-Muttaqi, Al-. *Kanz al-'Ummal fi Sunan al-Aqwal wa al-Af'al* [The Treasure of Workers on the Sayings and Actions of the Prophet]. Edited by Bakri Hayyani and Safwa al-Saqqa. 8 vols. Beirut: Mu'assasat al-Risala, 1981.

Hodgson, M. G. S. "'Abdulla bin Saba.'" In *Encyclopedia of Islam*, vol. 1, *A–B*. 2nd ed. Leiden: Brill, 1960.

hooks, bell. *Teaching to Transgress: Education as the Practice of Freedom*. New York: Routledge, 1994.

Huntington, Samuel P. *Clash of Civilizations and the Remaking of World Order*. New York: Touchstone, 1997.

Ibn Abi al-'Izz, 'Ali bin 'Ali bin Muhammad. *Sharh al-'Aqida al-Tahawiyya* [A Commentary on the Creed by al-Tahawi]. Edited by 'Abdullah bin 'Abd al-Muhsin al-Turki and Shu'ayb al-Arnauot. 2 vols. Beirut: Mu'assasat al-Risala, 1987.

Ibn al-'Arabi, Muhyi al-Din. *Fusus al-Hikam* [The Pearls of Wisdom]. Translation and commentary by Ahmed Avni Konuk. Edited by Mustafa Tahrali and Selçuk Eraydin. Istanbul: Ilahiyat Fakültesi Vakfi Yayinlari, 1990.

———. *Al-Futuhat al-Makkiya* [The Conquests of Mecca]. 14 vols. Edited by 'Uthman Yahya and Ibrahim Madkur. Cairo: al-Hay'ah al-Misriyya al-'Amma li al-Kitab, 1990–92.

Ibn 'Asakir, Abu al-Qasim 'Ali bin Hasan. *Tarikh Madinat Dimashq* [The History of the City of Damascus]. Edited by Muhibb al-Din Abu Sa'id 'Umar bin Gharama. 80 vols. Beirut: Dar al-Fikr, 1997.

Ibn al-Athir, Abu al-Hasan 'Ali bin Muhammad al-Jazari. *Usd al-Ghaba fi Ma'rifat al-Sahaba* [The Lions of Wilderness: On the Knowledge of the Companions of the Prophet]. 7 vols. Beirut: Dar al-Ma'rifa, 1997.

Ibn al-Athir, Majd al-Din Ibn Muhammad al-Jazari. *Jami' al-Usul fi Ahadith al-Rasul* [Collection of the Methodology on the Sayings of the Messenger]. Edited by 'Abd al-Qadir al-Arnaout. 15 vols. Cairo: Maktabat al-Halawani, 1969–72.

Ibn Babawayh, Muhammad bin Ali bin. *Risala al-I'tiqadat al-Imamiyya* [A Treatise on the Creeds of the Imammiya Sect]. Ankara: Ankara Universitesi Ilahiyat Fakultesi, 1978.

Ibn Hammad, Nu'aym. *Kitab al-Fitan* [The Book of Trials]. Edited by Suhail Zakkar. Beirut: Dar al-Fikr, 1993.

Ibn Hanbal, Ahmad. *Al-Musnad*. 6 vols. Cairo: Mataba'a al-Maymaniyya, 1895.

Ibn Hazm, 'Ali bin Ahmad. *'Ilm al-Kalam 'ala Mazhab Ahl al-Sunna wa al-Jama'a* [The Science of Kalam on the Way of the People of the Sunni Tradition]. Edited by Ahmad Hijazi al-Saqqa. Cairo: al-Maktaba al-Thaqafiyya, 1979.

———. *Al-Usul wa al-Furu'* [The Foundations and Branches]. 2 vols. Beirut: Dar al-Kutub al-'Ilmiyya, 1984.

Ibn Hibban, Abu Hatim Muhammad. *Al-Sahih*. Edited by Shu'ayb al-Arnaout and Husain Asad. Beirut: Mua'ssasat al-Risala, 1984.

Ibn Kathir, Abu al-Fida' Isma'il. *Al-Nihaya fi al-Fitan wa al-Malahim* [The Finality on Trials and End-Time Conflicts]. 2 vols. Beirut: Dar al-Kutub al-'Ilmiyya, 1988.

———. *Al-Sira al-Nabawiyya* [The Life of the Prophet]. Edited by Mustafa Abd al-Wahid. 4 vols. Beirut: Dar al-Marifa, 1976.

———. *Tafsir al-Qur'an al-'Azim* [Commentary on the Glorious Qur'an]. 7 vols. Beirut: Dar al-Andalus, 1966.

———. *Tafsir al-Qur'an al-'Azim*. Cairo: Dar al-Tiba, 1999.

Ibn Khaldun, 'Abd al-Rahman. *Al-Muqaddima* [The Introduction]. Edited by 'Abd al-Wahid al-Wafi. 2 vols. Cairo: Lajnat al-Bayan al-'Arabi, 1965.

———. *Al-Muqaddima*. 2 vols. Algeria: al-Dar al-Tunusiyya li al-Nashr, 1984.

———. *The Muqaddimah: An Introduction to History*. 3 vols. Translated by Franz Rosenthal. New York: Pantheon Books, 1958.

———. *Muqaddimat Ibn Khaldun*. Edited by 'Ali 'Abd al-Wahid Wafi. 3 vols. Cairo: Lajnat al-Bayan al-'Arabi, 1958.

Ibn Majah, Abu 'Abdillah Muhammad bin Yazid al-Qazwini. *Al-Sunan*. Edited by Muhammad Fu'ad 'Abd al-Baqi. Beirut: Dar Ihya' al-Turath al-'Arabi, 1975.

Ibn Manzur, Abu al-Fadl Muhammad bin Mukarram al-Ifriqi. *Lisan al-'Arab* [The Language of the Arab]. 20 vols. Beirut: Dar Ihya' al-Turath al-'Arabi, 1997.

———. *Lisan al-'Arab*. 6 vols. Cairo: J. M. 'A., 1981.

———. *Mukhtasar Tarikh Dimashq li Ibn 'Asakir* [A Compendium of Ibn 'Asakir's History of Damascus]. Edited by Reyad 'Abd al-Hamid. Damascus: Dar al-Fikr, 1990.

Ibn Sa'd, Abu 'Abdillah Muhammad. 7 vols. *Al-Tabaqat al-Kubra*. Beirut: Dar Sadr, 1968.

Ibn Sina, Abu 'Ali. *Kitab al-Najat* [The Book of Salvation]. Beirut: Dar al-Afaq al-Jadida, 1982.

Ibn Taymiyya, Taqiyyuddin Ahmad bin 'Abd al-Halim. *Majmu'at al-Fatawa* [The Collection of Religious Decrees]. 36 vols. Riyadh: Maktabat al-'Ubayqan, 1997.

Jaza'iri, Abu Bakr Jabir, Al-. *'Aqidat al-Mu'min* [The Creed of the Believer]. Cairo: Dar al-Kutub al-Salafiyya, n.d.

Jurjani, 'Ali bin Muhammad al-Sayyid al-Sharif, Al-. *Al-Ta'rifat* [The Dictionary of Terminology]. Beirut: Dar al-Kitab al-'Arabi, 1984.

Juwayni, Imam al-Haramayn Abu al-Ma'ali 'Abd al-Malik, Al-. *Kitab al-Irshad ila Qawati' al-Adilla fi Usul al-I'tiqad* [The Book of Guidance to the Firm Proofs on the Foundations of Faith]. Edited by As'ad Tamim. Beirut: Mu'assasat al-Kutub al-Thaqafiyya, 1985.

Kalabadhi, Abu Bakr Muhammad, Al-. *The Doctrines of the Sufis*. Trans. A. J. Arberry. Cambride: Cambridge University Press, 1935.

———. *Kitab al-Ta'arruf* [The Doctrine of the Sufis]. Cairo: Maktabat al-Kulliyat al-Azhariyya, 1980.

Kashmiri, Muhammad Anwar Shah, Al-. *Al-Tasrih bima Tawatar fi Nuzul al-Masih* [Proclamation on What Is Recurrently Transmitted on the Descent of the Messiah]. Edited by 'Abd al-Fattah Abu Ghudda. Aleppo: Dar al-Salam, 1965.

———. *Al-Tasrih bima Tawatar fi Nuzul al-Masih*. Aleppo: Dar al-Salam, 1982.

Kawthari, Muhammad Zahid, Al-. *Nazra 'Abera fi Maza'im Man Yunkir Nuzul 'Isa Qabl al-Akhira* [A Quick Look at the Claims of Those Who Deny the Descent of Jesus before the Final Day]. Cairo: Dar al-Jil li al-Tiba'a, 1987.

Kelly, Joseph. *The Origins of Christmas*. Collegeville, Minn.: Liturgical Press, 2004.

Khan, Siddiq Hasan. *Al-Idha'a Lima Kan wa ma Yakun Bayn al-Yaday al-Sa'a* [The Announcement of What Happened and What Will Happen before the Hour]. Beirut: Dar Ibn Hazm, 2000.

Khatib, 'Abd al-Karim, Al-. *Al-Mahdi al-Muntazar wa Man Yantazirunah* [The Expected Mahdi and Those Who Wait for Him]. Cairo: Dar al-Fikr al-'Arabi, 1980.

———. *Al-Masih fi al-Qur'an Wa al-Tawra Wa al-Injil* [The Messiah in the Qur'an, the Torah, and the Gospel]. Cairo: Dar al-Fikr al-'Arabi, 1965.

Kurdi, Muhammad Ziya al-Din, Al-. *'Aqidat al-Islam fi Raf 'i Sayyidina 'Isa wa Nuzulih 'Alayh al-Salam fi Akhir al-Zaman wa ba'd Ashrat al-Sa'a al-'Izam* [The Creed of Islam about the Ascension of Jesus our Master, Peace Be upon Him, and His Return at the End of Time and Some Major Signs of the Hour]. Cairo: Matba'at al-Sa'ada, 1982.

Kurt, Saban, ed. *A Modern Concordance of the Holy Qur'an*. Istanbul: Çağri Yayinlari, 2009.

Lalekai', Abu al-Qasim Hibat Allah bin al-Hasan, Al-. *Sharh Usul I'tiqad Ahl al-Sunna wa al-Jama'a* [A Commentary on the Foundations of the Creed of the People of the Sunni Tradition]. 2 vols. Riyadh: Dar Tayba, n.d.

Lawson, Benjamin Todd. *The Crucifixion and the Qur'an: A Study in the History of Muslim Thought*. Oxford: Oneworld Publications, 2009.

———. "The Crucifixion of Jesus in the Qur'an and Qur'anic Commentary: A Historical Survey, Part 1." *Bulletin of Henry Martin Institute of Islamic Studies* (Hyderabad, India) 10, no. 2 (1991): 34–62.

Leirvik, Oddbjørn. *Images of Jesus Christ in Islam*. Uppsala: Swedish Institute of Missionary Research, 1998.

Lings, Martin. *Muhammad: His Life Based on the Earliest Sources*. 2nd ed. Rochester, VT: Inner Traditions, 2006.

Madelung, Wilfred. "Abd Allah b. al-Zubair and the Mahdi." *Journal of Near Eastern Studies* 40, no. 10 (1981): 291–305.

———. "Al-Mahdi." *Encyclopedia of Islam*. Vol. 5, *Khe-Mahi*. 2nd ed. Leiden: Brill, 1986.

Mahmoud, Mohamed. *Quest for Divinity: A Critical Examination of the Thought of Mahmud Muhammad Taha*. Syracuse, NY: Syracuse University Press, 2007.

Malik bin Anas, Abu 'Abdillah al-Asbahi al-Himyari. *Al-Muwatta'* [The Beaten Path]. 2 vols. Rabat: Dar al-Aafaq al-Jadida, 1992.

Maraghi, Ahmad Mustafa, Al-. *Tafsir al-Maraghi*. 10 vols. Cairo: Mustafa Babi al-Halabi, 1953.

Jawhari, Tantawi al-Misri. *Al-Jawahir fi Tafsir al-Qur'an al-Karim* [Jewels on the Commentary of the Glorious Qur'an]. Vol. 3. Edited by Muhammad 'Abd al-Salam Shaheen. Beirut: Dar al-Kutub al-'Ilmiyya, 1984.

Maturidi, Abu Mansur, Al-. *Ta'wilat al-Qur'an* [Interpretations of the Qur'an]. 7 vols. Edited by Mehmet Boynukalin and Bekir Topaloğlu. Istanbul: Mizan Yayinevi, 2005.

McClintock, John, and James Strong. *Cyclopedia of Biblical, Theological, and Ecclesiastical Literature.* Vol. 1. New York: Harper, 1880.

McGinn, Bernard. *Antichrist: Two Thousand Years of the Human Fascination with Evil.* New York: Columbia University Press, 2000.

Menocal, Maria Rosa. *The Ornament of the World: How Muslims, Jews and Christians Created a Culture of Tolerance in Medieval Spain.* Boston: Back Bay Books, 2002.

Mittleman, Alan. "Messianic Hope." In *Covenant and Hope: Christian and Jewish Reflections,* edited by Robert W. Jenson and Eugene B. Korn, 222–43. Grand Rapids, Mich.: Eerdmans, 2012.

Moucarry, Chawkat. *The Prophet and the Messiah: An Arab Christian's Perspective on Islam and Christianity.* Downers Grove, IL: InterVarsity Press, 2001.

Mourad, Sulaiman A. "A Twelfth-Century Muslim Biography of Jesus." *Islam and Christian Muslim Relations* 7, no. 1 (1996): 39–45.

Muqaddasi, Mar'i bin Yusuf bin Abu Bakr bin Ahmad al-Karami, Al-. "Irshad Dhu al-Afham li Nuzul 'Isa 'Alayh al-Salam" [A Guidance to the Descent of Jesus, Peace Be upon Him, for Those with Comprehension]. Unpublished manuscript, Istanbul Suleymaniye Library, Esat Efendi section, no. 1446/8.

Murphy, Frederick J. *Apocalypticism in the Bible and Its World: A Comprehensive Introduction.* Grand Rapids, MI: Baker Academic, 2012.

Muslim bin al-Hajjaj, Abu al-Husain al-Qushayri al-Nisaburi. *Al-Sahih.* Edited by Muhammad Fu'ad 'Abd al-Baqi. Istanbul: al-Maktabat al-Islamiyya, n.d.

———. *Sahih Muslim.* Riyadh: Dar Tayba, 2006.

Nawawi, Yahya bin Sharaf, Al-. *Sharh Sahih Muslim* [Commentary on Muslim bin al-Hajjaj's *al-Sahih*]. Edited by Hasan 'Abbas Qutb. 18 vols. Riyadh: Dar 'Alam al-Kitab, 2003.

Nicholson, Reynold A. *A Literary History of the Arabs.* Cambridge: Cambridge University Press, 1953.

Nisaburi, Abu 'Abdillah Muhammad al-Hakim, Al-. *Al-Mustadrak 'ala al-Sahihayn*[The Additions to the Two Sound Hadith Sources]. 4 vols. Hyderabad: Matba'at Majlis Da'irat al-Ma'arif al-Nizamiya, 1915–23.

Nursi, Bediüzzaman Said. *The Damascus Sermon.* Translated by Şukran Vahide. Istanbul: Sözler Publications, 1989.

———. "Emirdağ Lahikasi" [The Appendix of Emirdağ]. In *Risale-i Nur Külliyati.* Istanbul: Nesil Yayinlari, 1996.

———. "Işaratü'l-I'caz" [Isharat al-I'jaz fi Mazann al-Ijaz; The Signs of Miraculousness in the Brievity of the Qur'an]. In *Risale-i Nur Külliyati.* Istanbul: Nesil Yayinlari, 2002.

———. "Kastamonu Lahikasi" [The Appendix of Kastamonu]. In *Risale-i Nur Kulliyati.* Istanbul: Nesil Yayinlari, 1996.

———. "Lem'alar" [The Flashes]. In *Risale-i Nur Kulliyati.* Istanbul: Nesil Yayinlari, 1996.

———. *The Letters.* Translated by Sukran Vahide. Istanbul: Sözler Neşriyat, 1997.

———. "Mektubat" [The Letters]. In *Risale-i Nur Kulliyati.* Istanbul: Nesil Yayinlari, 1996.

———. *Risale-i Nur Kulliyati* [The Collections of the Treatises of Light]. 2 vols. Istanbul: Nesil Yayinlari, 1996.

——. "Sözler" [The Words]. In *Risale-i Nur Kulliyati*. Istanbul: Nesil Yayinlari, 1996.

——. *Sözler*. Istanbul: Şahdamar, 2007.

——. "Şualar" [The Rays]. In *Risale-i Nur Kulliyati*. Istanbul: Nesil Yayinlari, 1996.

O'Shaughnessy, Thomas J. *Eschatological Themes in the Qur'an*. Manila: Cardinal Bea Institute, Ateneo de Manila University, 1986.

Osman, Fathi. "Jesus in Jewish-Christian-Muslim Dialogue." In *Muslims in Dialogue: The Evolution of a Dialogue*, edited by Leonard Swidler, 353–76. Lewiston, NY: Edwin Mellen Press, 1992.

Parrender, E. Geoffrey. *Jesus in the Qur'an*. Oxford: One World, 1995.

Pickthall, Mohammad Marmaduke, trans. *The Glorious Qur'an*. Chicago: Library of Islam, 1994.

Qari, 'Ali bin Sultan Muhammad, Al-. *Mirqat al-Mafatih* [A Ladder to the Keys]. 5 vols. Cairo: Dar Ihya al-Turath, 1892.

Qurtubi, Abu 'Abdillah Muhammad, Al-. *Al-Jami' li Ahkam al-Qur'an*. [The Compendium of the Laws of the Qur'an]. 20 vols. Beirut: Dar al-Kitab al-'Arabi, 1967.

——. *Al-Jami' li Ahkam al-Qur'an*. Edited by Hisham Samir al-Bukhari. 20 vols. Riyadh: Dar 'Alam al-Kutub, 2003.

——. *Al-Tadhkira fi Ahwal al-Mawta wa al-Akhira* [The Reminder of the Situations of the Dead and the Afterlife]. 2 vols. Beirut: Dar al-Kutub al-'Ilmiyya, 1985.

Qutb, Sayyid. *Fi Zilal al-Qur'an* [In the Shadow of the Qur'an]. 30 vols. Beirut and Cairo: Dar al-Shrooq, 1985.

——. *Mashahid al-Qiyama fi al-Qur'an* [Scenes of the Day of Resurrection in the Qur'an]. Cairo: Dar al-Ma'arif, 1961.

Ragg, Londsdale, and Laura Ragg, eds. *The Gospel of Barnabas*. Oxford: Clarendon Press, 1907.

Rahner, Karl. *Theological Investigations*. Vol. 14. Translated by David Bourke. London: Darton, Longman & Todd, 1976.

Razi, Fakhr al-Din bin 'Umar, Al-. *Mafatih al-Ghayb* [The Keys of the Unseen]. 16 vols. Beirut: Dar al-Kutub al-'Ilmiyya, 1990.

Renard, John. "Jesus and Other Gospel Figures in the Writings of Jalal al-Din Rumi." *Hamdan Islamicus* 10, no. 2 (Summer 1987): 47–64.

The Republican Brothers. "The Return of Christ." http://www.alfikra.org/book_view_e.php?book_id=219. Accessed August 21, 2013.

Reynolds, Gabriel Said. "Muslim Jesus: Dead or Alive?" *Bulletin of the School of Oriental and African Studies* (London) 72, no. 2 (2009): 237–58.

Rida, Rashid. *Fatawa* [Religious Decrees]. 6 vols. Beirut: Dar al-Kitab al-Jadid, 1970.

——. *Tafsir al-Manar*. 12 vols. Cairo: Dar al-Manar, 1954.

——. *Tafsir al-Manar*. 12 vols. Cairo: al-Hay'a al-Misriyya al-'Amma li al-Kitab, 1990.

Robinson, Neal. *Christ in Islam and Christianity*. Albany: State University of New York Press, 1991.

Rumi, Jalal al-Din. *The Mathnawí of Jaláluddín Rúmí*. 7 vols. Translated by Reynold A. Nicholson. London: Trustees of the E. J. W. Gibb Memorial, 1926.

Sabri, Musafa. *Mawqif al-'Aql wa al-'Ilm wa al-'Alam min Rabb al-'Alamin wa' 'Ibadat al-Mursalin* [*The Position of Reason, Science, and the Universe in Respect to the Creator of the Worlds and the Worship of the Messengers*]. 4 vols. Cairo: Maktabat 'Isa al-Babi al-Halabi, 1950.

Sachedina, Abdulaziz Abdulhussein. *Islamic Messianism: The Idea of the Mahdi in Twelver Shi'ism*. Albany: State University of New York Press, 1981.

Sahas, Daniel J. *John of Damascus on Islam*. Leiden: E. J. Brill, 1972.

Sallabi, 'Ali Muhammad, Al-. *'Umar bin 'Abd al-'Aziz: Ma'alim al-Tajdid wa al-Islah al-Rashidi 'ala Minhaj al-Nubuwwa* [Marks of Rightly Guided Renewal and Reform on the Prophetic Path: 'Umar bin 'Abd-'Aziz]. Cairo: Dar al-Tawzi' wa al-Nashr al-Islami, 2006.

Sami, Şemseddin. *Kamus al-A'lam* [Encyclopedia of Proper Names]. 6 vols. Istanbul: Mihran Matbaasi, 1898.

Saqqa, Ahmad Hijazi, Al-. *Al-Masiya al-Muntazar: Nabi al-Islam* [The Expected Messiah: the Prophet of Islam]. Cairo: Maktabat al-Thaqafa al-Diniyya, 1977.

Saritoprak, Zeki. "How Commentators of the Qur'an Define 'Common Word.'" In *A Common Word and the Future of Christian-Muslim Relations*, edited by John Borelli, 34–45. Prince Alwaleed Bin Tallal Center for Muslim Christian Understanding Occasional Papers. Washington, D.C.: Georgetown University, 2009.

———. "Fethullah Gülen: A Sufi in His Own Way." In *Turkish Islam and the Secular State: The Gülen Movement*, edited by M. Hakan Yavuz and John L. Esposito, 156–69. Syracuse, NY: Syracuse University Press, 2003.

———."The Legend of al-Dajjal (Antichrist): The Personification of Evil in the Islamic Tradition." *Muslim World* 93, no. 2 (April 2003): 290–306.

———. "Said Nursi on Muslim-Christian Relations Leading to World Peace." *Islam and Christian-Muslim Relations* 19, no. 1 (January 2008): 25–37.

———. "Said Nursi's Teachings on the People of the Book: A Case Study of Islamic Social Policy in the Early Twentieth Century." *Islam and Christian-Muslim Relations* 11, no. 3 (2000): 319–32.

Saritoprak, Zeki, and Sydney Griffith. "Fethullah Gülen and the 'People of the Book': A Voice from Turkey for Interfaith Dialogue." *Muslim World* 95, no. 3 (July 2005): 329–40.

Shatibi, Abu Ishaq Ibrahim bin Musa, Al-. *Al-Muwafaqat fi Usul al-Shari'a* [Conformations or Reconciliation in the Methodology of Islamic Law]. 4 vols. Edited by 'Abdullah Darrazi. Cairo: Dar al-Ma'rifa, 2006.

Sha'rani, 'Abd al-Wahhab, Al-. *Kitab al-Yawaqit wa al-Jawahir fi Bayan 'Aqa'id al-Akabir* [The Book of Diamonds and Jewels on the Explanation of the Creed of Famous Personalities]. 2 vols. Cairo: Matba'at al-Azhariyya, 1889–90.

Shaltout, Mahmud. "The Ascension of Jesus." *Al-Azhar Magazine* 31, no. 6 (1960): 189–93.

———. *Al-Fatawa* [Religious Decrees]. Cairo: Dar al-Shuruq, 1983.

Shawkani, Muhammad bin 'Ali, Al-. *Fath al-Qadir* [The Victory of the Most Powerful] 5 vols. Beirut: Dar al-Fikr, 1983.

Schimmel, Annemarie. *The Triumphal Sun: A Study of the Works of Jalaloddinn Rumi*. Albany: State University of New York Press, 1993.

Smith, Jane. "Reflections on Aspects of Immortality in Islam." *Harvard Theological Review* 70, nos. 1 and 2 (January–April 1977): 85–98.

Smith, Jane, and Yvonne Y. Haddad. "Virgin Mary in Islamic Tradition and Commentary." *Muslim World* 79, nos. 3 and 4 (July–October 1989): 161–87.

Stanilaus, L. "Jesus' Crucifixion, Death and Elevation in Islam: An Effort at Comprehension." *Bulletin of Henry Martin Institute of Islamic Studies* (Hyderabad, India) 17, no. 2 (July–December 1998): 59–74.

Sullami, Yusuf bin Yahya bin ʿAli, Al-. *ʿIqd al-Durar fi Akhbar al-Muntazar* [Compact of Jewels on the Narrations of the Expected]. Edited by ʿAbd al-Fattah Muhammad al-Huluw. Beirut: Dar al-Kutub al-ʿIlmiyya, 1983.

Suyuti, Jalal al-Din ʿAbd al-Rahman, Al-. *Al-Durr al-Manthur fi al-Tafsir bi al-Maʾthur* [The Scattered Jewels: Commentary with the Narrated Hadith]. 8 vols. Beirut: Dar al-Fikr, 1983.

———. *Kitab al-Iʿlam bi Hukmi ʿIsa ʿAlayh al-Salam* [The Book of Informing about the Ruling of Jesus, Peace Be Upon Him]. In al-Suyuti, *Al-Hawi li al-Fatawa* [The Compendium of Religious Decrees]. 2 vols. Beirut: Dar al-Kitab al-ʿArabi, n.d.

———. *Nuzul ʿIsa bin Maryam Akhir al-Zaman* [The Descent of Jesus, Son of Mary, at the End of Time]. Edited by Muhammad ʿAbd al-Qadir ʿAta. Beirut: Dar al-Kutub al-ʿIlmiyya, 1985.

Tabari, Abu Jaʿfar Muhammad bin Jarir, Al-. *Jamiʿ al-Bayan fi Taʾwil Ay al-Qurʾan* [Compendium of Interpretations of the Qurʾanic Verses]. 30 vols. Beirut: Dar al-Fikr, 1978.

———. *Jamiʿ al-Bayan ʿan Taʾwil Ay al-Qurʾan.* 30 vols. Edited by ʿAbdullah bin ʿAbd al-Muhsin al-Turki. Riyadh: ʿAlam al-Kutub, 2003.

———. *Jamiʿ al-Bayan fi Tafsir Ay al-Qurʾan.* 30 vols. Beirut: Muʾassasa t al-Risala, 2000.

———. *Jamiʿ al-Bayan fi Taʾwil al-Qurʾan.* 30 vols. Edited by Salah ʿAbd al-Fattah al-Khalidi. Beirut and Damascus: Dar al-Qalam and Dar al-Shamiyya, 1997.

———. *Tahdhib al-Athar* [The Beautification of the Hadith]. 5 vols. Edited by ʿAli Rida bin ʿAbdillah. Damascus: Dar al-Maʾmun li al-Turath, 1995.

Tabarsi, Abu ʿAli Amin al-Din Fadl bin al-Hasan, Al-. *Majmaʿ al-Bayan fi Tafsir al-Qurʾan* [The Junction of Exposition of the Exegesis of the Qurʾan]. Edited by al-Sayyed Hashim al-Rasuli al-Mahallati and al-Sayyed Fadl Allah al-Yazdi al-Tabarsi. 10 vols. Beirut: Dar al-Maʿrifa, 1986.

Tabatabaʾi, Muhammad al-Husain, Al-. *Al-Mizan fi Tafsir al-Qurʾan* [The Balance in the Commentary on the Qurʾan]. 21 vols. Beirut: Muʾassasat al-ʿAlam al-Matbuʿat, 1973–1985.

Taha, Mahmoud Mohamed. *The Second Message of Islam.* Translated by Abdullahi Ahmed An-Naʾim. Syracuse, NY: Syracuse University Press, 1987.

Taftazani, Masʿud bin ʿUmar bin ʿAbdillah Saʿd al-Din, Al-. *Sharh al-Maqasid* [Commentary on the Aims]. 5 vols. Beirut: ʿAlam al-Kutub, 1989.

Tahawi, Abu Jaʿfar Ahmad bin Muhammad, Al-. *The Creed of Imam al-Tahawi.* Translated by Hamza Yusuf. Berkeley, CA: Zaytuna Institute, 2007.

Taʾi, Muhammad bin ʿAbdillah al-Jayani, Al-. *Ikmal al-Iʿlan bi Taslis al-Kalam* [A Completion of Announcement on the Flawlessness of the Word]. 2 vols. Edited by Saʿd bin Hamdan Ghamdi. Jeddah: Jamiʿat Umm al-Qura, 1984.

Tayalisi, Sulaiman bin Abi Dawud, Al-. *Al-Musnad.* Beirut: Dar al-Maʿrifa, n.d.

Taylor, Charles. *A Secular Age.* Cambridge, MA: Harvard University Press, 2007.

Tirmidhi, Abu ʿIsa Muhammad bin ʿIsa, Al-. *Al-Jamiʿ al-Sahih* [The Compendium of the Sahih]. Edited by Ibrahim ʿAtwa ʿAwad. Cairo: Maktabat Mustafa al-Babi al-Halabi, 1975.

Thomas, David. "The Miracles of Jesus in Early Islamic Polemics." *Journal of Semitic Studies* 39, no. 2 (1994): 221–43.

Thurlkill, Mary F. *Chosen among Women: Mary and Fatima in Medieval Christianity and Shi'ite Islam*. Notre Dame, IN.: University of Notre Dame Press, 2007.

Tuwayjary, Hamud bin 'Abdillah, Al-. "Iqama al-Burhan fi al-Radd 'ala man Ankar Khuruj al-Mahdi wa Nuzul al-Masih fi Akhir al-Zaman." [The Establishment of Proof Against Those Who Deny the Emergence of the Mahdi and the Descent of Jesus at the End of Time]. *Majallat al-Buhooth al-Islamiyya* (Riyadh) 13 (1982): 101–13.

United States Conference of Catholic Bishops. "Midwest Muslim-Catholic Dialogue Completes Latest Round, Muslims and Catholics in the Public Sphere, and Looks Ahead into 2012 National Plenary." United States Conference of Catholic Bishops Web site, November 1, 2011. http://usccb.org/news/2011/11-209.cfm. Accessed July 14, 2013.

Vatican Radio. "Pope to Muslims for End of Ramadan: Promoting Mutual Respect through Education." http://en.radiovaticana.va/news/2013/08/02/pope_to_muslims_for_end_of_ramadan:_promoting_mutual_respect_through/en1-716319. Accessed August 20, 2013.

Voll, John O. "Mahdis, Walis, and New Men." In *Scholars, Saints and Sufis: Muslim Religious Institutions in the Middle East Since 1500*, edited by Nikki R. Keddie, 367–84. Berkeley: University of California Press, 1978.

Watt, Montgomery. *The Faith and Practice of al-Ghazali*. London: Allen and Unwin, 1967.

———. *Muhammad: Prophet and Statesman*. London: Oxford University Press 1961.

Waqidi, Abu 'Abdillah 'Umar, Al-. *Futuh al-Sham* [The Conquests of Greater Syria]. 2 vols. Beirut: Dar al-Jil, n.d.

Weber, Timothy P. *The Road to Armageddon: How Evangelicals Became Israel's Best Friend*. Grand Rapids, MI: Baker Academic, 2004.

Wensinck, A. J. *Concordance et Indices de la Tradition Musulmane*. Leiden: E. J. Brill, 1936.

———. *The Muslim Creed*. Cambridge: Cambridge University Press, 1932.

Whittingham, Martin. "How Could So Many Christians Be Wrong? The Role of *Tawatur* (Recurrent Transmission of Reports) in Understanding Muslim Views of the Crucifixion." *Islam and Christian-Muslim Relations* 19, no. 2 (April 2008): 167–78.

Yamani, Muhammad bin Muhammad, Al-. *Al-Mawsu'a al-'Arabiyya fi al-Alfaz al-Diddiyya wa al-Shudhudhat al-Lughawiyya* [The Arabic Encyclopedia on Opposite Words and Linguistic Anomalies]. 9 vols. Beirut: Dar al-Adab, 1989.

Yasu'i, Rufa'il Nakhla, Al-. *Ghara'ib al-Lugha al-'Arabiyya* [Oddities of the Arabic Language]. Beirut: Dar Lubnan, 1986.

Yazir, Muhammed Hamdi. *Hak Dini Kur'an Dili* [The True Religion and The Qur'an's Language]. 10 vols. 1936; repr., Istanbul: Matbaa-i Abüzziya, 1979.

Zabidi, Murtada Muhammad bin Muhammad, Al-. *Ithaf al-Sada al-Muttaqin bi Sharh Asrar Ihya 'Ulum al-Din* [A Lavish Gift of the Pious Masters on the Explanation of the Secrets of *The Revival of Religious Sciences*]. 10 vols. Beirut: Dar al-Kutub al-'Ilmiyya, 2002.

Zahniser, A. H. Mathias. *The Mission and Death of Jesus in Islam and Christianity*. New York: Orbis, 2008.

Zamakhshari, Mahmud bin 'Umar, Al-. *Al-Kashshaf 'an Haqa'iq al-Tanzil* [The Revealer of the Truths of the Revelation]. 2 vols. Cairo: Dar al-Mushaf, 1977.

Zwemer, S. M. "Jesus Christ in the Ihya al-Ghazzali." *Moslem World* 7, no. 2 (1917): 144–58.

# Index

Zeki Saritoprak is Nursi Chair in Islamic Studies at John Carroll University. He is the author of *Al-Dajjal in Islamic Theology* and editor of *Fundamentals of Rumi's Thought: A Mevlevi Sufi Perspective.*